# A Leader's Guide to

## ThriveAbility

## A Multi-Capital Operating System for a Regenerative Inclusive Economy

A Guide for Executives, Investors, Change Agents,
Policymakers and Future Generations

———— by ————

## ROBIN LINCOLN WOOD

authorHOUSE®

D0124137

*AuthorHouse™ UK*
*1663 Liberty Drive*
*Bloomington, IN 47403 USA*
*www.authorhouse.co.uk*
*Phone: 0800.197.4150*

*Interior Graphics/Art Credit: Paul van Schaik*

*Published by AuthorHouse  06/12/2015*

*ISBN: 978-1-5049-3950-8 (sc)*
*ISBN: 978-1-5049-3952-2 (e)*

*Print information available on the last page.*

*This book is printed on acid-free paper.*

A Leader's Guide to ThriveAbility is a field manual for Executives, Investors, Change Agents, Policymakers and future generations. The research and fieldwork we've conducted with leaders across every industry sector and civil society has led us to the inescapable conclusion that if we wish to reinvent capitalism, *we need to reinvent capital and the organizations that generate and apply that capital.*

ThriveAbility offers us the possibility of transitioning from the current degenerative, exclusive form of capitalism we are living in, to a regenerative, inclusive kind of of capitalism, where instead of the perverse incentives which arise when we optimise financial capital alone, we rebalance human, social, natural, manufactured, financial and intellectual capitals for a viable future.

In this book you will discover how the ThriveAbility Operating System enables every leader, investor and change agent on the planet to help organisations and markets upgrade their own operating systems through a series of five stages known as the "ThriveAbility Journey".

How can you, as a leader, use ThriveAbility to build a vibrant future for your organization or business as part of a ThriveAble world? Some of the key questions that you will need to grapple with include:

1. What are the unique capabilities needed to maximise the thriving of my organization and its stakeholders for the smallest footprint?

2. Which innovation pathways can deliver the improvements and breakthroughs needed to deliver enhanced ThriveAbility to all our stakeholders?

3. How can we measure True Value in everything we do?

4. How can we get our organization to begin the ThriveAbility Journey?

5. In what ways can advantages in 1-4 above be translated into competitive advantage versus other organizations that are not on the ThriveAbility Journey?

ThriveAbility is descriptive, prescriptive, and predictive- it *describes* the emerging edge of leading practice in strategy, innovation, sustainability and design, while *prescribing* an approach which includes an equation, decision framework, process and ThriveAbility Index. ThriveAbility is *predictive* in the sense that it enables us to calculate the costs and benefits of different options and trade-offs in the design, development and scaling of new products, services and experiences, along with the human and social transformations needed to achieve ThriveAbility.

The purpose of this book is to provide you and your colleagues with a practical, how-to guide on how to embed ThriveAbility in your organization. It will also come in handy for investors, advisors, consultants, financiers, facilitators, regulators and academics seeking to move beyond the confines of the limiting mindsets we are stuck in with current sustainability and shareholder value added approaches.

# Reviews of A Leaders Guide to ThriveAbility

"The amount of information in there is fantastic and I would say it is a masterpiece with a new holistic theoretical framework that could support innovation and transformation in business and society."

"The ThriveAbility approach makes a valuable and refreshing contribution to current debates and policy developments to go beyond economic growth, prosperity and sustainability. The new holistic theoretical framework and strong connection with practice, stresses the importance of eco-effectiveness while creating beneficial additionalties. The authors were daring enough to renew language in order to create the possibility for positive thinking and the adding of true quality in our life. Hopefully it will inspire people and organizations to renew things in a progressive and pragmatic way. Leaders, small and great, can realise the so needed ThriveAbility transition and bring humanity back."

*Dr Michael Braungart - Co-Founder of Cradle to Cradle*

"The investment community and big business need "integrated thinking" at every level. This is central to delivering a sustainable, positive and regenerative role in the economy. It is also fundamental to capitalism's social license to operate. The ThriveAbility operating system is a serious first step toward that."

*Dr Steve Waygood - Chief Responsible Investment Officer at Aviva Investors*

"Amidst rising global expectations of what constitutes responsible business, incremental improvement must give way to a transformational approach to corporate valuation and value creation. In the future, the valuation of a company must accord parity to all forms of capital. The ThriveAbility Index, which embraces integrated decision-making and innovation, is a potentially major contribution toward closing the gap between contemporary practices and societal expectations."

*Allen White - Co-Founder and Former CEO of GRI, (Global Reporting Initiative), Founder and Cochair of Global Initiative for Sustainability Ratings*

"ThriveAbility brilliantly captures what every leader, every business and every change-agent should embrace - a positive vision of how we can flourish as enterprises, as communities and as people. ThriveAbility is what I would call one of the "sustainable frontiers", where we let go of industrial models and cultural norms that are no longer fit-for-purpose; where we re-imagine organisations and redesign technologies to turn bureaucracies into holocracies and limits into innovations. ThriveAbility is the opposite of denial; it is positive engagement with challenges and proactive creation of solutions."

*Dr Wayne Visser, Director of Kaleidoscope Futures and author of Sustainable Frontiers*

"When Interface started its journey in 1994 to become a restorative enterprise — meaning to achieve business success with no negative impact — there was no handbook to help us find our way towards that outrageous goal: the top of Mount Sustainability, as our founder Ray Anderson used to call this. We think the, Leaders Guide to ThriveAbility' helps today's leaders to climb their own Mount Sustainability, and support the thriving of their own employees and organisation, as well as the world."

*Geanne van Arkel, Head of Sustainable Development, Interface Benelux*

"I am excited about this book. For the past 15 years, I and my teams have been working alongside many others to help drill into the heads of everyday business people that 'business and consumption as usual' is not sustainable, and that innovating our way out of the dead end we're headed toward represents a huge opportunity for those companies seeking to build real and lasting relationships with their customers in the future. Our effort has not been to suggest that the goal is simple sustainability, as that would be less than fully human. Our goal – once people understand that the status quo is on the verge of breaking down – is to enable the world forward toward a flourishing future for all of us. More and more of us around the world are coming to understand that our current reality is unsustainable and are now anxious to answer the question: "what do we do about it?" *A Leader's Guide to ThriveAbility* offers a sound theoretic and technical roadmap to help us achieve the real goal, which is for companies to learn how to 'enhance the ThriveAbility of itself and all its stakeholders." Deeply well researched and a remarkable synthesis of the front edge of our knowledge about ecosystems, and businesses' impact on them, as well as about what it means to aspire to a world where we are each encouraged to be truly human and truly thriving, *A Leader's Guide to Sustainability* joins my list of must reads for anyone entertaining the prospect of being involved with 21st century business – and that means everyone!"

*Koann Vikoren Skrzyniarz, Founder/CEO, Sustainable Life Media & Sustainable Brands*

# Foreword

We are delighted to share with you the fruits of our collaboration over the past few years with regard to how we can accelerate sustainability (and help shift capitalism into a healthier mode), so that all humanity can all live in a thriving civilization on a thriving planet in the centuries to come.

Following the in-depth research carried out in the Renaissance2 Foundation by myself and my colleagues between 2007 and 2013 on what it would take to co-create a thriving future, and the work Ralph and his colleagues had been conducting on sustainable innovation in his roles at the Global Reporting Initiative, the Sustainability Context Group and Deloitte over the same period, came an AHA! moment, when we both realized we each had some of the key parts of the solution, and should bring them together as one.

Thanks to the contributions of the participants In the Embedding ThriveAbility workshops and webinar series between 2012 and 2014, as well as engagement with several major conferences and dialogues with thought leaders in the fields of sustainability, finance and economics, psychology, business strategy/design, education and innovation over this period, we also added ideas and models from each of these fields to what appears to be emerging as a new, integrated field of research and practice in its own right: ThriveAbility.

During this time Paul, the founder of integralMENTORS, and Greg, co-founder of Boardex, both became involved as trustees of the ThriveAbility Foundation, bringing their own perspectives and insights to bear on this book. Bill joined us in autumn 2014, bringing a North American voice plus a sustainability context perspective to the conversation, as well as his superb communication skills.

Following the Integral European Conference in May 2014, Gyöngyi also joined the team as a researcher and personal assistant to Robin, helping pull together all of the distinct pieces of the puzzle and making sure there was a place for everything and that everything is in its place.

Many hundreds of leaders and experts have kindly given of their time to give us their thoughts and feedback on the concepts and ideas in this book, and it would be impossible to thank all of them here. Some of those more closely involved have been acknowledged at the end- to those whose names do not appear, you know who you are- we wish to thank you each from the bottom of our hearts for your time and support. It means a lot to us.

Very brief bios of each of the ThriveAbility Core Team members are also included at the end of the book. This team has done an amazing amount of work in a very short time, and is to be congratulated on their selfless contribution to a very demanding but worthwhile cause. To all of our families, a very big thank you for your support during this period of intense focus in 2014 and 2015.

We also wish to thank you, dear reader, for taking the time and trouble to read this labour of love, and trust that it will bring thriving and ThriveAbility to you and yours.

**From:**
Dr Robin Lincoln Wood and the ThriveAbility Foundation Team:
Ralph Thurm, Bill Baue, Paul van Schaik, Greg Wood and Gyöngyi Bolbas
*June 2015*

# The ThriveAbility Foundation

## THE VISION

To catalyse the achievement of a truly thriving global society by the middle of the 21$^{st}$ Century and beyond.

## OUR PURPOSE

To help create a regenerative, inclusive economy and close the sustainability gap by enabling organizations to manage their impacts on multiple capitals in ways that support stakeholder wellbeing and thriving.

## THE KEY OUTCOME

A **ThriveAbility Index** sponsored by the Foundation as a global public good that incentivises transformative change, led by licensed partners and supported by educational programs.

## THE ULTIMATE GOAL

To provide leaders with frameworks embedded in the **ThriveAbility Index** that enable them to allocate resources to initiatives that maximise the thriving of organisations and their stakeholders within a sustainable footprint that regenerates vital social and ecological resources.

**The initial goals** of the **ThriveAbility Program** include working with industry leaders, standard setters, information providers and investors to develop the principles and framework for a ThriveAbility Index based on the ThriveAbility Principles by:

- **Integrating** leading global sustainability and socially responsible investment criteria through the Six Capitals Equation and True Future Value instruments developed by the Foundation;

- **Piloting** these instruments with leading sustainability innovators in key industry clusters;

- **Providing** frameworks within which leading sustainability innovators can:

  o set the benchmarks for what is possible in those key industry clusters, with an emphasis on transformation and breakthroughs through collaborative innovation pathways;

  o evolve decision rules and accompanying instruments that provide industry specific contexts for thriveable resource allocation decisions;

- **Hosting** the co-development of industry specific open architectures and platforms for those decision rules and accompanying instruments.

# Contents

# 1. Introduction

> *"The purpose of the corporation is to enhance the ThriveAbility of itself and all its stakeholders."*[1]

ThriveAbility entails maximizing the thriving of an organization and its key stakeholders while achieving a sustainable (or even regenerative) footprint, where:

- *thriving* means "prosperous and qualitatively growing; the flourishing of each stakeholder", and
- *footprint* measures the amount of productive air, land and water as well as social systems needed to sustain the resource consumption, waste production and social impacts of the organization and
- *organizational stakeholders* include any entities that impact or are impacted by an organization's activities, such as employees, shareholders, key suppliers and the communities that buy the organization's products/services and sustain its activities.

It is the central thesis of this book that organizations that maximize the thriving of their stakeholders within a sustainable footprint will be those that endure into the future, and that those that fail to do so will wither and gradually disappear into the footnotes of history. Furthermore, we believe in aggregations of effects and interrelationships of systems in the age of the Anthropocene, such that society collectively must achieve a critical mass of sustainable organizations in order to survive, and a preponderance of ThriveAble organizations in order to truly thrive as a global civilization.

How can you, as a leader, use ThriveAbility to build a vibrant future for your organization or business as part of a ThriveAble world? Some of the key questions that you will need to grapple with include:

1. What are the *unique capabilities* needed to maximise the thriving of my organization and its stakeholders for the smallest footprint?
2. Which *innovation pathways* can deliver the improvements and breakthroughs needed to deliver enhanced ThriveAbility to all our stakeholders?
3. How can we measure *True Value* in everything we do?
4. How can we get our organization to begin the *ThriveAbility Journey*?
5. In what ways can advantages in 1-4 above be translated into *competitive advantage* versus other organizations that are not on the ThriveAbility Journey?

---

[1] We introduce a new way of thinking about stakeholders and shareholders further on in Diagram 28: "ThriveHolders",that transcends *and* includes these concepts, offering a much more comprehensive definition of what it means to be responsible for generating ThriveAbility. We decided that one new term would be challenging enough for this first page.

ThriveAbility is descriptive, prescriptive, and predictive- it *describes* the emerging edge of leading practice in strategy, innovation, sustainability and design, while *prescribing* an approach which includes an equation, decision framework, process and dashboard for ThriveAbility. ThriveAbility is *predictive* in the sense that it enables us to calculate the costs and benefits of different options and trade-offs in the design, development and scaling of new products, services and experiences. It also identifies the internal and external human and social development and transformations necessary to achieve ThriveAbility.

The purpose of this book is to provide you and your colleagues with a practical, how-to guide on how to embed ThriveAbility in your organization. It will also come in handy for investors, advisors, consultants, financiers, facilitators, regulators and academics seeking to move beyond the confines of the limiting mindsets we are stuck in with current sustainability and shareholder value added approaches.

Business, governments and civil society all have a key role to play in closing the thrival[2]/ survival gap. We at the ThriveAbility Foundation believe that the genius for innovation and enterprise to deliver the breakthroughs required is needed more than ever to ensure we make it through to a thriving world in 2050. May you find in these pages a richer and more engaging way of co-creating a thriving future for all of us!

## What Does it Mean to be a ThriveAble Leader?

*Humans have been and are today most delicately poised as the **fastest evolving species** on the planet and now play a role as the **most sensitive transducer** of what it means to be alive and well with purpose and joy. ThriveAbility focuses on the flourishing of all human beings so that they are able to fulfil their individual potential to the fullest and promote a positive state of wellbeing in a sustainable environment beneficial to all life.*

A precondition for being a ThriveAble Leader is that you yourself are Thriving in your own life. What, then, does thriving mean for each of us, and how is it arrived at?

"Thriving" describes a dynamic, interactive state in which one or more people experience wellbeing, happiness and a sense of satisfaction with their lives. Yet, "Thriving", by its very nature, also means very different things to different people, who are living in very different life conditions at very different stages of development.

Given the diversity of the human species geographically, culturally, linguistically and developmentally, any definition of thrival is likely to only cover the "basics" of what it means to live a good life that does not cost the earth.

---

[2]  We use "thrival" here in the sense that thriving on its own could be achieved at great cost to our planet and other people, whereas thrival is thriving that also enhances the survival of others around us, hence thriving + survival of all = thrival.

In the developed world we frequently find ourselves stressed out and unhappy despite the fact that from a material perspective most of us have "never had it so good". Recent research also shows that despite being better informed and educated than any previous generation, many struggle to find meaning and purpose in their work and their lives.

Recent research from the Gallup organization shows that only 13% of employees are actively engaged in their work, while 24% are actively disengaged and the balance simply unengaged. The bulk of employees worldwide -- 63% -- are "not engaged," meaning they lack motivation and are less likely to invest discretionary effort in organizational goals or outcomes.

The 24% who are "actively disengaged," are unhappy and unproductive at work and liable to spread negativity to co-workers. In rough numbers, this translates into 900 million not engaged and 340 million actively disengaged workers around the globe. That is a mind-blowing statistic for any leader believing they need motivated and engaged employees to succeed, let alone transform their enterprise.[3]

The 13% of engaged employees in the 2011-2012 study has ticked upward from the 11% in Gallup's previous global workplace assessment, conducted in 2009-2010. Furthermore, the proportion who are "actively disengaged" has dipped from 27% to 24%. However, low levels of engagement among global workers continue to hinder gains in economic productivity and life quality in much of the world.

Engagement levels among employees vary across different global regions and among countries within those regions. At the regional level, Northern America (that is, the U.S. and Canada) have the highest proportion of engaged workers, at 29%, followed by Australia and New Zealand, at 24%.

Regardless of region or industry[4], businesses seeking to adapt to rapidly changing global economic conditions must learn how to maintain high-productivity workplaces and grow their customer bases in widely varying social, cultural, and economic environments. Systems for reliably measuring and improving employee engagement across industries and regions worldwide are vital to that goal.

---

[3] Only 13% of employees worldwide are engaged at work, according to Gallup's new 142-country study on the _State of the Global Workplace_. In other words, about one in eight workers -- roughly 180 million employees in the countries studied -- are psychologically committed to their jobs and likely to be making positive contributions to their organizations.

[4] Not all economically developed regions fare as favorably; across 19 Western European countries, 14% of employees are engaged, while a significantly higher 20% are actively disengaged. However, the highest proportions of actively disengaged workers are found in the Middle East and North Africa (MENA) and sub-Saharan Africa regions, at 35% and 33%, respectively.
The findings also reveal differences among employees with different job types and at different education levels within countries. Recognizing these differences can help managers understand how societal factors could affect workplace characteristics and help them identify specific barriers they must overcome to build more engaged workforces. See the full report for results by job type and education level.

People spend a substantial part of their lives working, whether in a high-tech start-up in Singapore, a financial institution in Australia, or a garment factory in the Dominican Republic. As a result, the quality of their workplace experience is inevitably reflected in the quality of their lives. Gallup's finding that the vast majority of employees worldwide report an overall negative experience at work -- and just one in eight are fully involved in and enthusiastic about their jobs -- is important when considering why the global recovery remains sluggish, while social unrest abounds in many countries.

Business leaders worldwide must raise the bar on employee engagement. Increasing workplace engagement is vital to achieving sustainable growth for companies, communities, *and* countries --- and for putting the global economy back on track to a more prosperous and peaceful future. That is how critical it is to learn how to become a ThriveAbility Leader, from a human perspective, let alone the success of the business and the thriving of our species and biosphere.

Thriving and ThriveAbility will mean different things to different stakeholders. Suppliers, customers, business partners and regulators will all demand very different things from an organization, and the metrics for each stakeholder group will vary accordingly. Yet, at our core, human beings also share some common deeper needs and motivations which have been exhaustively explored by scientists and psychologists over the past century.

For example, one of the world's leading experts on human flourishing, Dr Martin Seligman, asks in his latest book, "Flourish[5]":

"What is it that enables you to cultivate your talents, to build deep, lasting relationships with others, to feel pleasure, and to contribute meaningfully to the world? In a word, what is it that allows you to flourish?

Happiness (or Positive Emotion) is one of the five pillars of "PERMA":

- Positive Psychology
- Engagement
- Relationships
- Meaning, and
- Accomplishment.

While the science and measurement techniques for Thriving are still being tested and developed, this does not prevent decision makers from using their own proxies for Thriving based on whatever data they can lay their hands on. This is, in fact, what consumer research and marketing surveys do all the time to establish the desirability of new products, services and experiences. Thriving applies this kind of evaluation to larger numbers of people for

---

[5]    Dr Martin Seligman, "Flourish A Visionary New Understanding of Happiness and Well-being" Paperback – Free Press, February 7, 2012

decisions with bigger consequences- macro-economic and political policy making for example.

Flourishing and thriving are hot topics today - world leaders are currently considering its implications for the criteria they use for policymaking. Businesses can certainly begin to do so immediately, at all levels, as they are so much closer to real people making everyday decisions about quality, sustainability and relative value.

## The Great Acceleration Need Not be the End of the Road

The gap is widening between what needs to be done to enable 9 billion people to thrive on Earth by 2050, and the current business as usual outcomes we generate. Closing this gap will make the difference between a thriving human civilisation on a thriving planet by the end of this century and the end of human civilisation, as we know it.

Scientists call the age we are now entering into the "Anthropocene"- the age shaped by man. The scale and speed of change in the last 60 years have been momentous - events since the 1950s have been called the 'Great Acceleration'. The human population has tripled, and the global economy exploded through new technology and a new global system of cooperation and investment.

Having spent 500 years perfecting modernism since the first Renaissance, more people alive today are experiencing greater levels of comfort and security than ever before in history, despite the brutally tough conditions of a billion or so in the developing world who have not yet benefitted from the material comforts of modernism. That is a not insignificant achievement of science and technology, together with the political and intellectual breakthroughs that yielded democratic systems of government for a few billion people.

At the same time, this system is built on a clockwork model of the universe in which mankind is lord and master of all he surveys, and nature is simply there to provide him with whatever he needs, without limit. We are going to need advanced levels of consciousness and capability in our leaders in the decades ahead, as we become like gods in our ability to shape the world around us, while possessing feet of clay that make us highly vulnerable to catastrophic risks.

Modernism's technocratic way of thinking combined with the ethno-centric, nationalist systems of government that peaked in the 20th century, left a deadly legacy in the first part of that century. Modernism is still peaking in the developing world so China, India, Africa and the Middle East are flashpoints for this mixture of advanced technology and highly nationalistic thinking.

Over the past century here in Europe and in many of the world's great cities, we have evolved beyond the modernist worldview into the post-modernist worldview. This communitarian value system expresses solidarity and social harmony, and has led to the creation of the European project that has avoided a third world war and dramatically expanded our economies and standard of living. It has also made Europe the greenest continent on earth relative to its economic output, and a leader in both sustainability and sustainable development worldwide. This is a heritage we can be very proud of, but which also demands that we ensure that Europe's transformative potential is realised in the next few decades in conjunction with other developed economies.

We must now move beyond the relativism and self-satisfaction of post-modernism to embrace a new synthesis that is emerging in integral[6] (or "whole systems") consciousness. There are many brilliant integral leaders around the world, though they are still a rare exception in the leadership teams in most organisations.

Such leaders are uniquely capable of transcending and including earlier levels of consciousness. Worldwide, tens of millions of leaders are now developing the early stages of such whole systems consciousness and capabilities. This represents a unique moment in history as we find this capability becoming significant in our best young leaders, fuelling what could be a great leap forward for our species if catalysed in time.

Completely separated from this miracle of science, technology and democratic mixed economies, we find belief systems of all kinds neatly sealed in millions of water tight compartments: religious believers, agnostics, atheists, mystics, spiritualists, complexity theorists- any and all attempts to explain the much bigger picture of which a tidy clockwork universe forms a very small part are all in there, pretty well sealed from the basic assumptions and mechanisms of modern life.

Of course, we cannot but help notice that our modernist, ethnocentric system is fraying around the edges, and slowly morphing into the equivalent of the butterfly emerging from the caterpillar cells in the chrysalis. While the caterpillar's business model is eternal growth: simply eat as much as possible, for as long as possible, the butterfly that emerges through the imaginal cells dissolving the caterpillar's cells for its nourishment has a different goal: to explore and pollinate as many flowers as possible, while searching for food, a mate and a new home. The butterfly is how the caterpillar adapts to changing life conditions.

Since the Club of Rome report over four decades ago, thought leaders around the world have agreed that we need to become more sustainable. Sustainability has been measured as the reduction of negative impacts on the environment, society and governance through reductions in population and consumption, divided by technological progress. Despite 40 years of hard work and massive investment, we find that today sustainability is failing to

---

[6]   We use the word "integral" in two senses here: the first to mean a function which integrates the key elements needed for a healthy whole to emerge; the second, to refer to integral theory and practice which has been developed by a wide variety of twentieth century thinkers and practitioners who have co-created a systemic way of transcending the ancient and modern ways of human thinking and being, such that a truly global, world-centric consciousness capable of dealing with the full complexity of our 21st century challenges might help us shape a better future for all of mankind.

deliver the results needed to transition us from a fossil-fuel based, consumption driven linear economic model toward a future where 9 billion plus people can thrive.

We are now using over 1.5 planets worth of resources[7]. The path set out by the UN Environment Program, intended to limit global temperature rises to 2°C above pre-industrial times, implies a 4.2% fall in world greenhouse gas emissions between 2010 and 2013. Yet greenhouse gas emissions by the world's top 500 companies rose 3.1% from 2010 to 2013, far off the cuts urged by the United Nations to limit global warming. The top 500 firms by capitalization accounted for 13.8% of world greenhouse gas emissions and 28% of gross domestic product in 2013, according to the report.[8]

Our current political and economic systems are entirely focused on the caterpillar business model: eternal growth. There is not a politician in a major country who would ever speak out against economic growth as measured by GDP: gross domestic product. We must build the adaptability of the butterfly's function into our institutions, if we are to build green, inclusive, ThriveAble economies in time.

## From Sustainability to ThriveAbility

How can we catalyse a thriving, sustainable future? In order for business to be a key engine of transformation to post-materialist, green, qualitative growth economies, business leaders must change the game, change the rules and change their goals.

The ThriveAbility Approach has evolved to integrate strategy, human development, innovation, sustainability and design in a way that simplifies the task and gets the job done while creating shared advantage and value. ThriveAbility describes how the emerging edge of leading practice in these fields is being integrated into a powerful set of transformative models and methods, while prescribing a pragmatic approach which includes a calculus/equations, decision framework, transformative process, a ThriveAbility dashboard and a ThriveAbility Index that will help shift markets to invest in ThriveAble organizations and projects.

ThriveAbility is predictive in the sense that it enables us to calculate the costs and benefits of different options and trade-offs in the design, development and scaling of new products, services and experiences. The key question is how to most effectively embed ThriveAbility into organisations, and alongside that, how to develop the methods, tools and management systems required to put this into practice.

---

[7]   Data courtesy of the Global Footprint Network- see http://www.footprintnetwork.org/en/index.php/GFN/

[8]   Drawn up by the information provider Thomson Reuters and BSD Consulting, a global sustainability consultancy.

## Table A – From Suffering to Thriving

| | Reacting | Improving | Sustaining | Net Positive | Thriving |
|---|---|---|---|---|---|
| **Desire** | Survive! | Comply! | Repair! | Recalibrate! | Thrive! |
| **Define** | Continue to live or exist, especially in spite of danger or hardship | Experiment with ways to improve CSR performance<br><br>Doing less bad | A system that maintains its own viability by using techniques that allow for continual reuse<br><br>Meet thresholds | Achieving new balance by optimizing performance within broader ecological and social systems<br><br>Net Positive | For all life to develop vigorously, prosper, and flourish within planetary boundaries<br><br>ThriveAble |
| **Response** | React | Mitigate | Balance | Adapt | Innovate & Breakthrough |
| **Focus** | Basic needs | Incremental improvements without limits and demand on social and environmental resources | Mitigate damage, sacrifice, austerity, obligation, externalities | Network structure of complex flow systems. Natural & Human Eco-system mapping | Key leverage points in global systems that align the Six Capitals for ThriveAbility |

As you can see from table A above, there are at least four clear differences between Sustainability-as-Usual and ThriveAbility. Our critique of existing models and ways of doing things is done solely with the intent of creating even better models, in the humble acknowledgement, based on empirical evidence, that 90% of what is being done in the name of sustainability today is applying the older, "meet thresholds" approaches, while only 10% of practice is currently heading in the direction of a ThriveAble world. And encouraging that good/better practice is the entire purpose of this book, and the ThriveAbility Foundation[9].

The further advantages of a ThriveAbility Approach will be outlined in the chapters that follow. Before we get into the details, we need to demonstrate the "golden thread" of logic that runs through this guide, which can help you transcend the detail and complexity inherent in the breakthrough challenge from "less bad" to "good enough" to "ThriveAble".

This way, if you ever feel lost in the many trees of the forest on your ThriveAbility Journey, you can jump into this strategic psychological helicopter to see the big picture, remember your goal and "see the wood for the trees".

---

[9]  We would like to thank Jonathon Porritt of the Forum for the Future for his observation that we were misrepresenting the spirit of sustainability and the best practice in the field with the left-hand column of Table A above. We would like to honour those sustainability pioneers who are actually already thinking much more strategically and holistically, and who are essentially already "ThriveAbility Leaders", as we point out in Chapter 5.

## Why ThriveAbility- Can we Reinvent Capitalism?

The first question running through your mind might be: "What exactly is ThriveAbility"? A new management fad? Another clever approach to "greenwashing? Just another utopian attempt to change the world based on "harnessing human potential?" Or is it cunning left-wing plot to get us greedy capitalists to change our ways? Let us examine this concept more closely.

The co-creators of ThriveAbility have each been engaged in a quest to transform business and corporations into a force for good over several decades. The research and fieldwork we have conducted with leaders across every industry sector and civil society has led us to the inescapable conclusion that if we wish to reinvent capitalism, _we need to reinvent capital and the organizations that generate and apply that capital._[10]

Why? At the end of the day, we need to look at who ultimately judges what is "good" in capitalism, so that more resources and rewards are allocated to good companies and good investments, while fewer resources are allocated to "bad" companies and investments. These ultimate judges would include stock markets, investors, asset managers, pension funds, sovereign wealth funds and insurance companies. Of course other stakeholders such as consumers, employees, business partners and, to some extent, suppliers will act as intermediate judges of the relative goodness of a company and its products and services, along with regulators, the media and governments. But at the end of the day it is financial capital that can really make or break a company or industry the fastest.

This is why we are co-creating a _ThriveAbility Index_, which will serve as a reliable guide to the ability of a company or organisation to generate the maximum amount of thrival for the smallest unit of footprint possible. From our experience and research, we believe that financial capital ultimately wields the greatest power (and responsibility) in capitalism, and that by helping the holders of financial capital make more thriveable decisions, we will help create a more thriving, sustainable world.

Financial capital does not exist in a vacuum, however. Natural and manufactured capital are the means by which we satisfy our basic needs and wants, while intellectual and human capital form the foundation for our knowledge and service economy, as well as the driving force behind innovation and the evolution of markets.

---

[10] The global supply of financial capital currently invested in the global economy has most recently been calculated to be $305 trillion- www.unep.org/inquiry/. Thanks to double entry bookkeeping, we know that such financial "assets" will have been invested mainly in natural/manufactured capital and infrastructure and other real assets.

### DIAGRAM 1 – The ThriveAbility Six Capitals Equation

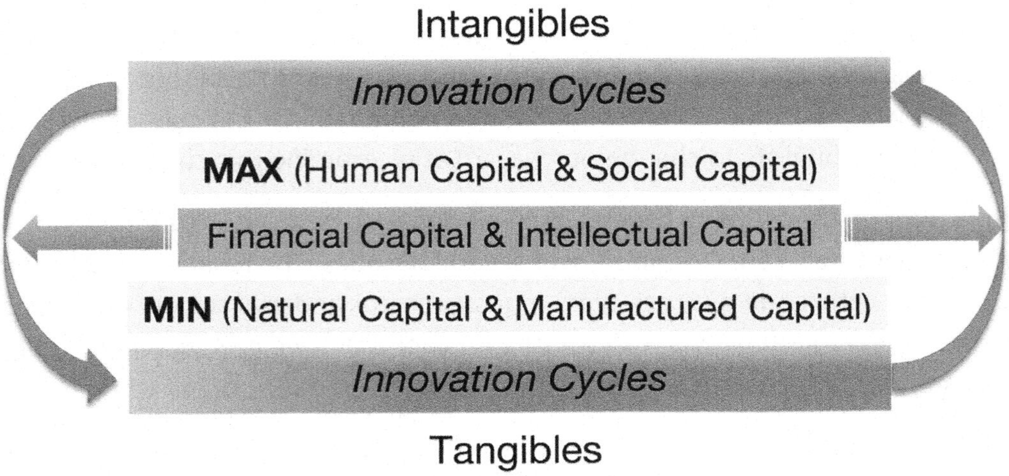

## Intangibles

*Innovation Cycles*

**MAX** (Human Capital & Social Capital)

Financial Capital & Intellectual Capital

**MIN** (Natural Capital & Manufactured Capital)

*Innovation Cycles*

## Tangibles

The way in which these six capitals inter-relate is shown in Diagram 1 above. These six capitals were agreed upon by the International Integrated Reporting Council[11] as part of the standard for integrated corporate reporting. There has been considerable confusion around where one capital begins and another ends, as well as how these capitals are inter-related. From a ThriveAbility perspective, it is rather straightforward:

- **Natural and Manufactured** capitals comprise anything one can see from Google Earth- they include our biosphere, hydrosphere, lithosphere and technosphere; natural capital is predominantly a commons regulated by legal systems, though land can be owned, while manufactured capital is owned by and large, (though the "sharing economy" is changing that to some extent);

- **Human and Social Capitals** are observable as human beings and the quality and quantity of relationships between them; there is now considerable insight into what makes for thriving in individuals, organizations and societies, and in the ThriveAbility Equation the objective of decision-makers is to maximise the thriving of human and social capitals for the minimum footprint possible;

- **Financial and Intellectual Capitals** are symbolic entities represented in the computer systems of financial sector players (including "virtual currencies"); intellectual capital comprises both the implicit and explicit knowledge and competencies of the individuals and groups involved in innovation and co-creation, as well as in the official records of patent, trademark and copyright protectors worldwide.

---

[11]  See http://www.theiirc.org/ for further details. An integrated report is a concise communication about how an organization's strategy, governance, performance and prospects, in the context of its external environment, lead to the creation of value in the short, medium and long term.

Our human systems are bigger, more complex and dynamic than we had ever imagined possible. Our US$75 trillion global economy is financed by US$305 trillion of financial assets, powered by over 100 terrawatts of energy we use annually. Scaling rapidly is a feature of the current world. Between 1983 and 2014 mobile phone subscriptions grew from zero to almost 7 billion, and are set to overtake the number of people in the world. In 2014 the five-year-old instant messaging company Whats App was valued at US$19 billion, more than Sony. China overtook the US to become the world's largest economy at US$17.6 trillion, an extraordinary feat achieved in less than half a century.

*UNEP Inquiry - Design of a Sustainable Financial System- Aligning the Financial System with Sustainable Development: Pathways to Scale. January 2015.*

The goal in a thriving, green inclusive economy should be to *maximise the thriving of human and social capital*, for the *least amount of natural and manufactured capital*, through the *value adding activities enabled by intellectual and financial capital*. This would appear to be unarguable common sense as well as impeccable economic, social and ecological logic.

The **ThriveAbility Six Capitals Equation** offers us a way to think in an integrated way about every decision we make as leaders, managers and individuals – this integrated thinking can then lead to the integrated decision-making and reporting that ensure that we create *True Value* that is thriveable now and in the future.

The purpose of the corporation therefore becomes to continually *enhance the numerator of this equation and reduce the denominator via innovation*.

## What are the Principles that Inform the Development of ThriveAbility?

If we are going to bandy grand phrases such as "reinventing capitalism" about, you deserve to know something about the principles that informed the development of ThriveAbility. Given that the co-creators of ThriveAbility have backgrounds in economics, psychology, architecture, finance, engineering as well as the social and hard sciences, you would not be surprised to know that our work has been animated by a simple set of five basic ideas:

1. *Incentives* - are key to understanding how our modern world functions, and how it can be changed for the better;
2. *Values* – (or "coping mechanisms"), implicit in our worldviews and mindsets, play a vital role in determining what we regard as an incentive, and how we will prioritise different sets of incentives in different circumstances (known as "stratification");
3. *Measurement* - knowing what to measure, and how to measure it, can change the way we create and value incentives to solve some of the harder problems to which

we urgently need beneficial solutions. As the old saying goes: "You cannot manage what you cannot measure";

4. *Intuition* - and hunches are a great way to generate insights, new thinking and models to understand a problem better, but there is no substitute for smart data when it comes to making better decisions that will provide better solutions to those harder problems;

5. *Alignment and Synergy* – any human activity involving two or more people requires both alignment and synergy to work, at many levels: physical, emotional, mental and spiritual. Depending on how long-lasting and deep the relationships of the people involved in the activity are intended/likely to be, alignment and synergy will need to embrace "higher" levels of functioning, ranging from the physical to the emotional, mental and ultimately, spiritual. Incentives also operate with increasing force along the same range.

This Leader's Guide to ThriveAbility has been designed to help you address three intertwined challenges whose combined effects are known to create "wicked", very hard to solve problems. The solutions to these wicked problems, not surprisingly, are also complex in themselves, though the right kinds of leadership in the right kinds of organisational structures and processes is capable of delivering the right kinds of solutions and breakthroughs, when the ThriveAbility approach is applied.

## The Logic of ThriveAbility – Transcending and Integrating the Key Ingredients for Organizational Success and a Thriving, Green Inclusive Economy

As we said earlier, ThriveAbility is not a new fad or magic bullet designed by management consultants, nor is it a hyper-complicated academic theory stuffed full of arcane details. You can breathe easy – it is a highly pragmatic, yet deeply credentialed approach to transcending and integrating the key ingredients needed for a successful strategy that can take you and your organization from "less bad" to "good enough" to "regenerative thriving".

The research and practical experience upon which the logic you are about to discover is based, goes back many decades, drawing on both hard data from the scientists and experts in many different fields, as well as the practical experience of leaders in sustainability, strategy, innovation, leadership and design[12]. In its own way, the curriculum for ThriveAbility is what they will hopefully be teaching in business schools and universities a decade from now.

The first key point to note is that the ThriveAbility Approach is based on an integrated logic that spans ecology and climate science, economics and finance, psychology and leadership theory, together with the science and art of design and innovation. None of these disciplines

---

[12]   For examples of the kind of hands-on experience we are talking about, take a look at the 50 Activists/ Advisors, Entrepreneurs and Intrapreneurs featured in Chapter 5. Also check out the backgrounds of the ThriveAbility Foundation team members at the back of the book.

on their own is adequate to solving the massive challenges we face today, yet the power of their logic when integrated is impressive.

Moving beyond sustainability with its focus on *impact minimization*, to ThriveAbility with its focus on *thrival maximization*, is becoming an urgent imperative if we wish to ensure 9 billion people living well on earth in 2050. Businesses and policymakers must radically simplify the task while accelerating investment into sustainable innovation, design and strategy.

The battle to prevent catastrophic climate change will be won or lost in our cities that account for 80% of Greenhouse Gas ("GHG") emissions globally and are home to nearly 60% of the world's population. Copenhagen, Curitiba, Barcelona, Stockholm, Vancouver and Paris are leading the pack of cities aiming to become resilient.

Business is a key driver in this shift to resilience. Based on the research carried out by the Renaissance2 Foundation, some of the imperative "must haves" we will need for a thriving world in 2050 include:[13]

## A. Resilient Environment

i. Doubling agricultural output without increasing the amount of land or water used;

ii. Halting deforestation and increasing yields from planted forests;

## B. Renewable Energy

iii. Halving carbon emissions worldwide (based on 2005 levels) by 2050 through a shift to low-carbon energy systems;

## C. Resilient Habitats

iv. All new buildings zero net energy,

v. Up to a tenfold improvement in Eco efficiency of materials

vi. Providing universal access to low-carbon mobility.

## D. Wise Culture

In social terms, we must create wiser cultures that take a longer-term perspective. To do this we must offer people incentives for behaviour change, so that sustainable living becomes mainstream within a decade.

**E. Human Development** - This also demands that we build trust, entrepreneurialism and inclusiveness into our organisations and societies, enabling enterprises and ecosystems to create value and help meet the basic needs of all.

---

[13]  For example, the "Vision 2050" report by the World Business Council for Sustainable Development's (WBCSD), lays out a pathway to a world in which nine billion people can live well, within the planet's resources, by mid-century. The report features a set of "must haves", which are included in outline here.

**F. Enlightened Enterprises & Integral Governance -** will help to redefine progress, drive more inclusive markets and take a true value, true cost approach to arrive at true profits and *True Future Value*. In economic terms, this requires that we incorporate the costs of externalities, starting with carbon, ecosystem services and water, into the structure of the marketplace.

The barriers to the kind of changes we need in the corporations of the world are powerful. What can be done to accelerate and deepen the changes we need for every corporation and major industry on earth to do what it takes to ensure we do not exceed the two-degree warming limit so that future generations can survive and thrive?

## Transforming Risks into Opportunities

As the international corporate community rethinks the way it conducts business to address global challenges, perhaps the most important mindshift needed is the shift *from* seeing our current global ecological, economic and social crises as risks to be mitigated, *to* opportunities to be taken advantage of, to "do well by doing good". Just how business leaders plan to address these challenges and where they see the best opportunities could hint at where the next big innovations may happen.

A variety of studies over the past decade have identified a range of opportunities created by our out-of-control growth model, ranging from the low trillions of dollars per annum to ten trillion dollars or more, a sizeable chunk of the global economy. The most recent, the *Global Opportunity Report* [14] released in 2015, surveyed 200 sustainability experts and 6,160 business leaders in 21 countries on their views on building a safe and sustainable future. Together, the respondents have shown how five major global risks can be turned into opportunities.

The risks identified are:

- lack of fresh water,
- unsustainable urbanization,
- continued lock-in to fossil fuels or energy dependency,
- non-communicable diseases, and
- extreme weather.

And in response, the 15 opportunities identified included:

- Early Warning and Forecasting Systems
- Energy Autonomy
- Rural Growth Initiatives
- Combat Non-Communicable Diseases with Mobile Technologies

---

[14] The organizations behind the Global Opportunity Report said they hoped the study, to be conducted annually, will provide "an open innovation platform" where people worldwide can explore and capture sustainability opportunities, and be able to use the more than 120 readily available solutions identified.

- Attractive Investments in Extreme Weather Resilience
- Green Consumer Choices
- Water-efficient Agriculture
- Innovation Finance for a Healthy Generation
- Cost-effective Adaptation
- Compact, Green and Connected Cities
- Fresh Water Production
- Everyday Health Enablers
- Regulation for an Energy Transition
- Smart Cities
- Smart Water Regulation

## Water and Green Consumer Choices

Solving water scarcity and managing water use could be the top untapped opportunity that will have the biggest positive impact on societies. Overall, development in water-efficient agriculture is the opportunity that inspires most confidence among leaders. Some 37 per cent think that this opportunity will bring benefits for society and consider their country to have great capacity to do something about it.

Water efficient agriculture is estimated to be able to improve rainwater management techniques that can multiply crop yields by a factor of 2 to 4 in parts of Africa and Asia. In arid regions, supplementing natural resources with purified or desalinated water can go a long way to ease water shortages.

Opportunities related to dependency on fossil fuels are also rated highly. Here, green consumer choices can also make a difference. This includes innovations to encourage consumers to use more renewable energy or buy more products made with renewable materials.

In solving the energy dependency issue, advances in distributed renewable energy generation provide off-grid areas with rapid access to electricity. In areas with established energy grids, the same technology allows homeowners or companies to save money and make their own clean energy.

Healthcare is another area of opportunity. This tackles the rise of non-communicable diseases such as cardiovascular diseases, cancers, and diabetes that pose a significant threat to lives, by, for example, making it easier and cheaper to choose the healthy option when buying groceries or thinking about transport options.

Other big opportunities are the building of "smart" cities by employing advances in sensor technology and Big Data analytics, or using existing city infrastructure more efficiently for safer, green environments. For example, collecting data about traffic and its effects on air quality can help governments decide where to invest to mitigate pollution.

## Developing Nations, Manufacturers Most Optimistic

The manufacturing and financial sectors are the most positive about making money by using technology to prevent or adapt to climate change. The most optimistic people are the Chinese and Indians, who rank top in spotting sustainability opportunities, with South America following closely. Europeans rank, perhaps surprisingly given their commitment to "green" technologies and lifestyles, at the bottom of the optimism scale.

Forty-eight per cent of Chinese managers, 44 per cent of Indian managers, 37 per cent of South American managers and 33 per cent of North American managers were positive. Meanwhile, the young and women are markedly more optimistic than everyone else.

## Yet Governments are Reluctant Participants

Governments are often expected to take the lead in realizing the opportunities highlighted above. What's worrisome is that the public sector is consistently less optimistic than the private sector about how the opportunities can positively affect society and its ability to pursue them. The key role that governments can play is by issuing regulations that support both sustainability and business ventures, though they seem reluctant to get involved more often than not.

Despite the massive uncertainties we face in the 21st century, there are two assertions we can make with a degree of disconcerting confidence: the first is that we will have exceeded the carrying capacity of earth; the second is that the price we pay for doing so will rise dramatically the longer we wait to take radical action to remedy this situation. In 2050, it is increasingly likely that the 9 billion people then alive will be struggling for survival, along with a crippled biosphere, if we continue business-as-usual.

On a more positive note, there is a great deal of evidence to suggest that our species is in the middle of a major evolutionary leap, which could transform the relationship between our species and our planet. Whether we can harness this shift to co-create a thriving world for all, or whether it is squandered in a series of regressive, "too little too late" gestures, will depend on whether our leaders have the courage to grasp this opportunity and all it implies for the our shared future.

The goal of this guide is to answer such questions and provide several powerful ways in which you can deploy ThriveAbility to ensure your organization is part of the solution and not part of the problem.

## Transcending Business and Reporting as Usual

During the past five decades Shareholder Value Added has become the holy-grail for most investors, businesses and corporations. Global capital markets and financial institutions have been allocating investment to firms, nation states and projects using a measure known to economists and investment professionals as "Economic Value Added" (or "EVA"). This concept and its measurement have been helpful in distinguishing between investments and firms that are "losers" (which are value destroying) and those that are "winners" (which are value enhancing), which has helped make the process of capital allocation more efficient over time.

EVA was a valuable tool to measure investment effectiveness in an industrial economy with no limits to growth, but in a world constrained by a need to become sustainable very rapidly, it is unable to distinguish between investments that are life and biosphere destroying and those that are life and biosphere enhancing.

There have been two responses to this challenge from two very different directions:

- Social and environmental activists and NGO's have demanded that we apply criteria to investments that include social and environmental impact measurements (thereby addressing what is known as the "sustainability context gap"),
- Ethical investors have demanded and co-created funds that enable socially and environmentally conscious investors to place their money into vehicles that apply social and environmental measures to select investments that meet their criteria.

The consequence is the rapidly growing field of impact or ethical investing, which is able to draw on a large number of social and environmental measures recognised and approved by a wide variety of standard setting bodies, regulators, ratings agencies, aggregators and auditors. In response, many organisations have implemented sustainability and corporate social responsibility ("CSR") programmes which generate an increasingly complex series of reports and management dashboards that enable them to ensure compliance and, in some cases, substantially improve their sustainability.

While such programs are to be welcomed, they are for the most part incremental in nature and failing to deliver the transformations we need for a thriving future. For example, the leading global standard for sustainability and ethical reporting, the Global Reporting Initiative ("GRI"), has over 4 000 members from 60 countries who are mainly large multinational or global corporations. This is a great start, but there are nearly 80 000 transnational companies in the world with $49 trillion of revenue, amounting to 65% of world GDP of $75 trillion[15]. In other words, 19 out of 20 companies traded in the world's capital markets and two-thirds of global economic activity do not report according to these standards.

Many critics of corporations and stock markets argue that the focus of markets on quarterly earnings is inhibiting investments in sustainability and preventing companies from taking a longer-term view. These critics provide a ready-made excuse for many CEO's who argue that they cannot afford to invest in longer-term measures such as sustainability or disruptive

---

[15] 63 000 companies are listed on listed on stock exchanges according to Bloomberg, and 7 000 traded in over the counter or "grey" markets in the US alone. CreditRiskMonitor's estimate is 78 480 companies globally.

innovations, as they will be "punished by the markets". This is a dramatic over-simplification of reality:

- At least half of publicly traded companies are either state-owned enterprises, particularly in places such as China (80% of market value), Russia (62% of market value) and Brazil (38% of market value); or family controlled conglomerates. Both SOE's and family conglomerates are capable of taking longer-term decisions and very often do so, making massive strategic investments in the process;
- Large and medium sized privately held companies account for tens of trillions of dollars in revenue globally, and are not held hostage by public markets at all[16] - for example, Richard Branson's Virgin Group, which has made a strong public commitment to sustainability, backed by major investments;
- Visionary CEO's such as Paul Polman of Unilever (who has committed to doubling Unilever's revenues while halving its footprint) and Tim Cook at Apple (who has also made a major commitment to sustainability), have made it clear to short-term investors and hedge funds that they are not welcome as investors in their shares;
- Sustainability leaders such as Interface, Patagonia, Natura, Puma and others have seen their share prices benefit from their leadership over long periods of time, and are better positioned than most of their competitors in their industries with a unique competitive advantage from sustainability leadership.

In 2012 a total of 5,500 companies produced sustainability reports worldwide[17] Yet a recent article in The Guardian by one of sustainability's leading gurus, John Elkington, is entitled: "Time to Forget Sustainability Reporting". Elkington correctly celebrates the move by leading organisations such as Nike and Puma toward integrated reporting, in which the language of sustainability is jettisoned, although recent research shows that the companies in 16 countries that make sustainability reporting mandatory do better those in the 42 countries that do not[18]

Although the benefits of sustainability reporting as a management tool for businesses can be significant, they tend to be limited to incremental improvements that will not deliver the breakthroughs we need in time for true ThriveAbility. The process of reporting highlights weaknesses and calls attention to areas of improvement that actually enhance their performance if management acts on this information. The measurement and tracking procedures that must be put in place to gather data enable analysis of energy, water, waste, and purchases. These data are in turn accessible for making decisions on capital expenses, retrofits, and programs. Sustainability reporting can prompt continual improvement and better data management, which in return improves business performance, operational

---

[16]  Witness the radical strategies of Richard Branson's Virgin Group and its biofuels development program.

[17]  According to CorporateRegister.com

[18]  Serafeim G. and Ioannou I.- The Consequences of Mandatory Corporate Sustainability Reporting Harvard Business School Paper 2011

efficiency and cost savings, which is a step toward where we need to be, but still falls short of what is needed to create a thriving future.

So, what can de done to address these challenges? Welcome to this Leader's Guide to ThriveAbility, where we intend to persuade you that an integrated, transformative, incentives-based approach to solving these challenges has a better chance of succeeding than our current incremental, linear solutions. Let us begin with an overview of some of the existing initiatives which will help make that a reality.

## Integrated Reporting and Thinking - From Linear Sub-Optimisation to Integrated, Simultaneous Equations

*"If you change the way people think, nothing will ever be the same".*
*The late Steve Biko, leading anti-apartheid activist*

Much has been made of the need for Integrated Reporting over the past decade, as the work of the Global Reporting Initiative (or "GRI"), United Nations Global Compact (UN Global Compact or "UNGC"), the International Integrated Reporting Council (or "IIRC") and others have made abundantly clear. The challenge? In order to develop integrated reporting, we need integrated thinking, and that is precisely what we are not doing at present in 99% of organizations.

What happens today in most organisations is that sustainability is treated as a separate function from the rest of the business, with its own head (the Chief Sustainability Officer, or "CSO"); if this functions exists at all. In less advanced organizations, the head of Environment, Health and Safety takes responsibility, indirectly for sustainability.

Sustainability is often seen to be just another filter to be passed over projects and investments, along with all the other functional stovepipes from finance to human resources to the strategy and marketing people- if an organization is reasonably advanced in its approach to sustainability.

In the laggards, sustainability is very much an after thought in developing strategy and new products and services, and is usually treated as an extension of Corporate Social Responsibility, or "CSR". At its worst, such an approach is basically "greenwashing", where the maximum amount of publicity is squeezed out of some minor changes in the way a product or service is made, packaged and labelled, to make it appear more "sustainable" and "green". Most journalists and the general public still find it difficult to dig beneath the surface of such claims to establish whether there is any real substance to them.

So it should come as no surprise then, that most of the 80 000 publicly traded organizations on our planet are either not reporting on sustainability at all (circa 70 000 of them by our own very rough estimates), or if they are reporting a little on sustainability (roughly 5 000 of them) or using a standard such as the GRI to report (another 5 000 of them, or so), then they are adding sustainability into their annual report in a largely linear, additive fashion.

This means that the 5 000 or so companies using the GRI standards to report on 84 or so "disclosure items" tend to take a piecemeal approach to putting their report together, having to work across many different organisational functions and geographies to pull together the data needed for their integrated report, largely after the fact. Here is how the G4 Sustainability Reporting Guidelines from the GRI are introduced:

"An ever-increasing number of companies and other organizations want to make their operations sustainable. Moreover, expectations that long-term profitability should go hand-in-hand with social justice and protecting the environment are gaining ground. These expectations are only set to increase and intensify as the need to move to a truly sustainable economy is understood by companies' and organizations' financiers, customers and other stakeholders.

Sustainability reporting helps organizations to set goals, measure performance, and manage change in order to make their operations more sustainable. A sustainability report conveys disclosures on an organization's impacts – be they positive or negative – on the environment, society and the economy. In doing so, sustainability reporting makes abstract issues tangible and concrete, thereby assisting in understanding and managing the effects of sustainability developments on the organization's activities and strategy."

While this is a great start, following such reporting standards can at most ensure that an organizations is seeking to be "less bad", and that it will over a period of time approach a set of operating parameters that represent "good enough", over a time frame that the organization gets to determine as "reasonable".

*The co-creators of ThriveAbility are fans of anything that can help us create a more sustainable, thriving world, so for the sake of clarity we hope you will appreciate that when we critique some of the shortcomings of current approaches, we do so with a great deal of appreciation and respect for the work being done by the organisations we are discussing. Many of those leading organisations have concurred with our diagnosis in private, and we are committed to standing on the shoulders of these giants to help us all see further.*

Even with the greatest goodwill in the world and the accurate disclosure of up-to-date information of the 84 or so "disclosure items", this piecemeal approach can, on its own, simply never hope to achieve significant shifts in strategy and the innovation breakthroughs required to limit global warming to two degrees, or to reverse ocean acidification, species/ biodiversity loss, deforestation and other "red zones" we have now ventured into thanks to uncontrolled industrialisation.

What is needed is a robust way in which breakthroughs can be incentivised and scaled rapidly through large organizations and investors driven by smart data and wiser leaders who can see beyond the "tragedy of the horizon" our current myopic systems encourage.

## Three Key Elements that will Ensure Longer-Term Organisational Survival

At its simplest, ThriveAbility describes the way we can thrive individually while flourishing together by imaginatively and systematically changing three things and closing three gaps. Right now we are attempting to close the sustainability gap on its own, with various "silver bullets", but we can see that this is not working. Why? Because unless we also close the organisational and cultural/leadership gaps, and provide the incentives to do so, we will not close the sustainability gap in time to avoid runaway global warming and irreversible damage to our biosphere and us.

1. **Changing the way we think about sustainability** (closing the **Sustainability Gap)** - the *mental shift* we need to make, *from* seeking to "shrink our way to sustainability", *to* harnessing the innate human drive to live a better life, in ways that need not cost the earth – in short to "Thrive";

   - **The Sustainability Gap** – what lies at the core of our current unsustainable trajectory really isn't that hard to understand: The Great Acceleration[19] that created unprecedented wealth and progress since the Industrial Revolution is now overtaxing the very ecological and social systems that undergird the business-as-usual pursuit of perpetual growth. Many companies recognize this threat, but their response – doing things "less bad" – is not fit-to-task. Most of the ecological, social, and economic problems we face require more than incremental band-aids; indeed, they demand *transformative change*.

2. **Changing the way we run our organisations** – (closing the **Organizational Gap)** a *journey from* being in denial about the serious negative impact the 80 000 or so largest multinational organisations on our planet are having on our environment and social infrastructures, *to* looking for ways in which all organisations from the smallest to the largest can design and deliver innovative products and services that rapidly reduce negative impacts while also generating much greater positive impacts;

   - **The Organizational Gap** – Such transformational change needs to scale across the gap that spans from the core of an organization to the way the industry it is in embraces the transformative challenge. This kind of shift needs to be seeded deeply in the organization, taking root to grow until it encompasses the entire enterprise as well as its key stakeholders. Such organizational transformation needs to scale across industries as new processes and practices spread across entire sectors.

3. **Changing the way we develop leaders in business and for-impact organisations** (closing the **Socio-Cultural Gap)** – a way of developing the leaders in our organisations who can think systemically and creatively about complex challenges, while engaging and aligning the political, technological and economic forces needed to deliver the shifts needed to delight our key stakeholders through innovations and breakthroughs that help them flourish now and in the longer term.

   - **The Socio-Cultural Gap** – Individuals within organizations can similarly span very different socio-cultural stages of development, shifting from less developed

---

19   http://anr.sagepub.com/content/early/2015/01/08/2053019614564785.full.pdf+html

mindsets to frames of thinking capable of managing increasing complexity. Closing the sustainability and organisational gaps requires increasing numbers of leaders who can think and act across larger spans of space and longer spans of time with much greater depth. Being able to harness this natural development trajectory can help open individual minds to the kinds of systemic thinking necessary to create the breakthrough innovations that can deliver ThriveAbility.

### DIAGRAM 2 – The Three Gap Problem

In order to close the Sustainability Gap, the Organizational Gap and the Cultural/Leadership Gap, we need to apply integrated thinking and measurement to the activities and decisions made at every level in an organization. That is the purpose of the ThriveAbility Approach and the ThriveAbility Index, to embed this integrated way of thinking about an organizations and its positive and negative impacts into every decision.

To do so, we need to move from the optimisation of each of the six capitals using a "linear equation" approach, to optimising the ThriveAbility Equation as an integrated, simultaneous equation, thereby helping close the Three Gap Problem.

At the same time as we develop individual leaders who can work with and integrate such complexity in systemic and creative ways, we also need to pay attention to building organisational cultures and systems capable of aligning the human, economic and ecological forces needed to power the journey from "less bad" through "sustainable" to "thriveable".

## From Denial to ThriveAbility – The ThriveAbility Journey

Over the past few decades it has become clear that industrial organisations go through several stages of development as they transition from being highly polluting, socially toxic yet economically "profitable" entities, to more caring and sustainable, economically enduring beings. Governments, charities, NGO's and socially entrepreneurial organisations have emerged over time to deal with the shadow side of irresponsible capitalism, yet despite all their efforts they have not yet managed to stem the tide of negative impacts nor have they succeeded in shifting the way most of these organisations think and operate to any great degree.

These five stages of the ThriveAbility Journey are shown in the diagram below:

### DIAGRAM 3 – The Five Stages From Denial to ThriveAbility

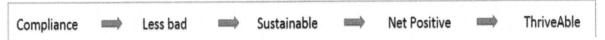

Compliance ➡ Less bad ➡ Sustainable ➡ Net Positive ➡ ThriveAble

## 1. Compliance

Most organisations on our planet today are either in denial about the need to become more sustainable, or simply at a level of development where they cannot actually see the problem, and if they have heard of climate change, "green" branding and so on, they imagine that it is "someone else's problem". This is one of the main reasons that we are not seeing the progress we need to close the sustainability gap in time before we inflict serious damage on ourselves and our planet.

That means that of the roughly 80 000 multinational corporations listed on stock exchanges or large enough to be publicly owned, perhaps 70 000 are not even aiming for "Less Bad" - they are simply somewhere between "Bad" and "Less Bad". In other words, they are contributing (in many cases, mightily), to the fact that we are using up the resources of 1.5 planets every year when we only have one planet worth of resources available.

Many of such organizations in the denial category are candidates for divestment or closure, and not considered in the ThriveAbility Approach as they are simply not interested in sustainability, or actively resisting it through lobbying and disinformation campaigns. The only thing that might change their minds is ever harsher environmental legislation, a carbon tax, a plummeting share price, a massive lawsuit or a series of disasters that trigger a change in management.

## 2. Improving

Due to pressure from governments, NGO's, industry bodies, customers and the like, many organisations wake up to the fact that they are generating negative impacts and need to do something about that. The decision is made to become "less-bad" in the areas the pressure is being applied, and some attempt at conforming to the new rules or standards beyond the bare minimum required by most legal systems, is made.

Perhaps 20%[20] of the 80 000 multinational organisations on our planet are making an effort to become less bad, though mainly in an incremental way which will require several decades for them to actually become sustainable. They still do not report on their sustainability efforts, but at least they have made a start to stop their worst excesses.

## 3. Sustainable

Over the past few decades many organisations have made the journey from bad through less bad to aiming at sustainability. Perhaps 10% of the 80 000 multinational organisations on our planet are now measuring aspects of sustainability in their organisational systems and key performance indicators, and also reporting on their progress in many different ways.

From the members of the UN Global Compact that submit CoPs to the Global Reporting Initiative reporters and beyond, we find examples of companies that are willing to also explore, define and submit information about the positive impacts of their products and / or services. They are not yet putting that into context with the remaining negative impacts, but they enlarge the scope to the lifecycle (LCA) or value cycle (circular economy concept) in order to start building data around a more systemic understanding of value (e.g. shared value concept).

## 4. Net Positive

Net positive organisations aim to not only reduce their negative impacts, but aim to more than offset these negative impacts with the positive impacts the organization generates in other areas. Leading organisations such as InterfaceFlor are already close to achieving zero negative impacts, though this journey will still take several more years to complete.

A tiny percentage[21] of large organisations today are aspiring to being somewhere in the scale from "Zero Impact" to "Net Positive", though the exact details of how Net Positive will

---

[20]  See statistics quoted in Chapter 1.

[21]  Less than a few dozen companies in total have publicly announced a commitment to Net Positive.

be measured in each industry is still being worked out by some pioneering working groups comprising the leading organizations aspiring to Net Positive status[22].

It is worth quoting in full a part of the report by Forum for the Future on the advantages of a "Net Positive" approach:

"The report – <u>Net Positive: A new way of doing business</u> – captures, for the first time, the principles of what it means to take a Net Positive approach and provides a route map to help businesses engage with the concept. It calls for the ambition of business to change from 'doing less harm' to becoming 'Net Positive' to have a **positive impact on the world**.

The authors explain that a strong sustainability strategy helps businesses in many ways; **enhanced reputation**, **increased sales**, **cost reduction** and **engaged staff.** The report identifies that a Net Positive approach – where businesses demonstrate positive environmental or societal impacts in key areas of their operations – adds further benefits, including competitive advantage, supply security and the space to innovate products and services through moving the organization into a leadership space[23].

## 5. ThriveAble

This is a very positive development indeed, as it creates the conditions in which the next level of aspiration, "Thriving", can emerge. "Thriving" would mean that all the key stakeholders of an organisation would be positively impacted by the organization's activities, with zero negative footprint. In other words, such organisations would be "gross positive". This may still be a distant dream for most organisations today, however there are already some small scale examples of Thriving organisations in existence already[24].

## Closing the Three Gaps - The ThriveAbility Index Generator and Delta

We live in a world of big data, and overwhelming amounts of information where the signal to noise ratio is usually so low that potentially valuable knowledge and insights are missed completely through information overload. This challenge prompted the ThriveAbility team and its innovation partners to build several versions of the ThriveAbility logic over a number of years, and the latest "release version" you see in diagram 4 below is designed to offer a golden thread for the ThriveAbility Journey.

---

[22]   See http://www.theclimategroup.org/what-we-do/news-and-blogs/net-positive-approach-key-to-future-business-success-new-report-by-forum-for-the-future-the-climate-group-and-wwf-uk/ for more details.

[23]   The benefits of a Net Positive approach are already being felt by businesses, including BT, Capgemini, Coca-Cola Enterprises, The Crown Estate, IKEA Group, Kingfisher and SKF. Leaders of these businesses came together with the report authors to share their experiences and help define the Principles of a Net Positive approach. They concluded that failure to deal adequately with environmental and social issues will result in "exposure to supply chain risks and missed opportunities".

[24]   For example, Sanergy builds healthy, prosperous communities by making hygienic sanitation affordable and accessible throughout Africa's informal settlements. The Sanergy Model takes a systems-based approach to solve the sanitation crisis sustainably. (Further information www. saner.gy)

The ThriveAbility Index Generator describes the way in which organizations engage with the ThriveAbility Approach, to assess where they are on the five stage ThriveAbility Journey, and to determine how they can move from the stage they are at to what is next for them and their industry. They do this by aligning their strategic opportunities, leadership talents and responses to sustainability challenges in a series of innovation pathways that move them at the right pace from where they are to where they need to be, using a transformation process known as the ThriveAbility Delta.

The data and insights generated in this process are then fed into the Benchmarking and Indexing processes that over time will generate a ThriveAbility Index for each industry, and ultimately, the whole economy.

In diagram 4 below, "The ThriveAbility Delta", we can see an origin point in the centre and three triangles framing three different positions on the radar screen behind the triangles. These positions are determined by the way in which organizations respond to the three key instruments in the ThriveAbility Assessment, which cover the three key gaps we need to close through integrated thinking and practices.

**Origin Point to Less Bad-Improving**

Here we find organizations either stuck or moving slowly from the "Bad" (very high negative impacts with few positive impacts) through the compliance stages through to "Less Bad". At their best, such organizations will have reached Stage 2 in the 5 stage ThriveAbility Journey mentioned above.

**Less Bad-Improving to Sustainable**

Here we are likely to find several thousand organizations working to improve their performance according to UNGC, GRI and/or other sustainability reporting frameworks. The leading companies in this space are boldly aiming to go where few organizations have gone before, including some of the leaders mentioned later on in this book. Here we are looking at organisations moving from stages 3 to 4 in the ThriveAbility Journey.

**Sustainable to Thriving**

Here we find those organizations aiming to be "Net Positive" – in other words, those that are starting the journey between stages 4 and 5 of the ThriveAbility Journey. Amongst the larger corporations, there are only a handful of organizations at this stage at the time of writing, though we believe they are capable of accelerating their progress rapidly through the use of the ThriveAbility Assessment and its corresponding methods and tools.

Amongst smaller organizations, especially the socially entrepreneurial types, there are likely to be thousands already in existence who would qualify for inclusion into this category, as it is much easier to build a thriveable organization from scratch than it is to transform an existing leviathan. The shift organizations make over time from "Less Bad" to "ThriveAble" is what we call the ThriveAbility Journey. What does such a journey look like?

**DIAGRAM 4 – The ThriveAbility Delta**

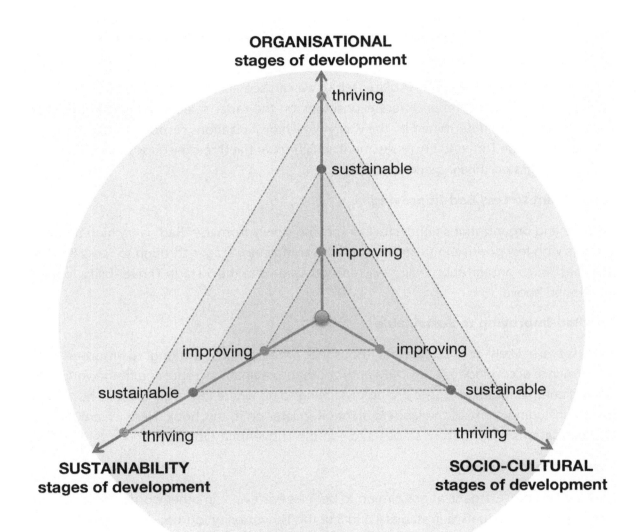

## 2. The ThriveAbility Journey

### What Does a Thriving, Green, Inclusive Economy Look Like?

Imagine a world powered by renewable energy, where all human beings thrive in resilient habitats; where businesses operate in a circular economy that regenerates natural capital, without a particle of waste, and are led by enlightened leaders whose goal is to maximize the ThriveAbility of all their stakeholders; where each individual is empowered to pursue their passion and make a living in service to others; where governance systems are transparent, effective and wise in the ways in which they deliver their services to their communities and populations; and where intercultural appreciation and insight enriches the exchanges between the diverse worldviews and cultures embraced by humankind.

Does that sound like an impossible dream, or pie in the sky? The co-creators of ThriveAbility would point out that every single one of these "pockets of the future" is currently observable in the present, right here and right now, somewhere in the world. It is just that the future is distributed unevenly, and sometimes hard to see when one is up to one's neck in alligators and trying to drain the swamp.

Before we begin our exploration of the ThriveAbiity Journey, let us take this desirable future scenario of a thriving human civilization on a thriving planet, and convert it into practical outcomes that are measurable and manageable. What would such a future look like?

### The Six Desiderata of ThriveAbility

Based on the pioneering work being done by the thought and practice leaders in each of the six-pillars explored later on in this chapter, we can frame six desiderata by which we can measure the endpoint of the ThriveAbility Journey set out in Table B below.

#### Table B - The Six Desiderata of ThriveAbility

| **Sustainability:** Natural Capital; Manufactured Capital | |
|---|---|
| 1. | A Circular, regenerative economy |
| a. | Natural and man-made materials and ecosystems are regenerated through circular economic processes |
| b. | All impacts are managed proportionately to the carrying capacities of the multiple capitals |
| 2. | Long term resource planning for intergenerational equity |
| a. | Technologies, Products, Services and Businesses designed for durability to continue serving future generations |
| b. | Innovations are inspired by natural systems by engineers, designers, entrepreneurs and others working with the grain of nature. |

| | | |
|---|---|---|
| | **Organizational:** Intellectual Capital; Financial Capital | |
| 3. | | A transparent and level global playing field that delivers True Value |
| | a. | Apply true accounting principles that measure true costs including externalities, and calculate true returns with full transparency |
| | b. | Level the playing field towards renewable and regenerative industries through true taxation and incentives |
| 4. | | Strategic Decision-Making to Scale-Up to ThriveAble Sectors |
| | a. | Nurture multi-stakeholder collaboration to amplify and scale up positive impacts |
| | b. | Investment decisions based on the ThriveAbility Index |
| | **Socio-Cultural:** Human Capital; Social Capital | |
| 5. | | Holistic Education to Develop Complex Systems Thinking & Leadership |
| | a. | New open business models for education that integrate physical wellbeing, mental depth, emotional maturity and spiritual development. |
| | b. | Developmental pathways based on co-working and co-creation between disciplines and sectors that are aspirational and compelling for future generations |
| 6. | | Governance Systems Aligned to Inclusive Stakeholder Wellbeing |
| | a. | Radically inclusive and transparent governance structures that serve the different priorities and needs of different developmental levels |
| | b. | Innovative structures for and approaches to interworking between governments, NGO's, businesses and academia that focus on Stakeholder ThriveAbility. |

These six desiderata may seem a very long way from the current state of play. Indeed, they will need transformation and breakthroughs at every scale in order to become a reality in the 21st century.

## Looking over the Horizon - Imagination, Innovation, Transformation & Breakthroughs

*"Stakeholders and experts alike are beginning to see business-led solutions as pretty much all we have got to work with, in the absence of government and of really effective NGO's".*
*Doug Miller – Chairman of Global Polling Firm GlobeScan*

Human imagination and ingenuity have been at the forefront of our evolution as a species since time immemorial. What we call creativity and innovation today could not exist without our imagination and ingenuity. "What if...", "How might we...", "Imagine that..." are phrases which can make a very big difference in the way we perceive and work with current reality to create previously unimaginable future states.

Historically it has been down to entrepreneurs to turn new discoveries and inventions into innovations that changed the world. Sometimes the scientist, discoverer or inventor also played the role of the entrepreneur, such as was the case with Gutenberg, Edison, Zeiss, Ford, Marconi, Benz, Hewlett and Packard, Gates and Jobs, and many, many others.

From a corporate perspective, the research and development function took over the discovery and invention role, while product and service developers and designers worked with applied researchers to develop new products and services, which were then launched by the marketing department and sold by the sales department.

In large organizations the need for transformation is always present, given how rapidly we human beings become comfortable in our roles. Our ability to habituate to a norm and then keep it "steady as she goes" is both a great strength as well as a massive weakness when faced with change, particularly the kind which creeps up slowly on us but in the longer term can be massively disruptive- for example, climate change, species loss, peak oil, peak soil, and so on.

Hence the need for imaginative, often heretical individuals who have become adept at sticking their necks out without getting them chopped off in an organizational context. The ability to align the forces in and around an organization to support such individuals and their ideas and investment proposals is critical to enabling the very large, often slow moving beasts we know and love as multinational corporations, to adapt, transform and innovate in time.

The critical challenges facing our natural and business ecosystems are a result of both ecological limits to growth for current levels of human population and consumption, and an evolutionary innovation challenge. Economics and sustainability theory and practice are both based upon a core assumption about a limited supply of resources that fails to account adequately for the transformative nature of human development, creativity and innovation.

Innovation theory and practice demonstrate that *what* is considered a resource, and *how* resources are generated, changes regularly in evolutionary terms as natural, human and technical systems evolve. Thriveable innovation and design is such an evolutionary force. The focus of sustainability on reducing negative environmental and social impacts is an important starting point, but lacks the motivators that drive innovation and design to create the breakthroughs we need for Thrival.

The future survival and Thrival of the human species depends upon our ability to co-create win/win/win social and organisational structures and habits that ensure that we can scale sufficient sustainable innovations to meet our basic resource needs globally, while reducing our impact on the hardest to replace resources through reduced population growth and harmful consumption.

Transformation integrates existing disciplines in creative ways, leading to innovative outcomes that are game changers. Personal and organisational transformation is the key to a Thriving Future.

In their book "The Breakthrough Challenge", John Elkington and Jochen Zeitz describe 10 ways to connect today's profits to tomorrow's bottom line. In his foreword to this key contribution to our thinking and practice, renowned entrepreneur and co-founder of *the "B-Team", Sir Richard Branson* says:

"Success and sustainability are two sides of the same coin. Where the priorities of business and society align, everyone stands to gain. Better still, there are countless stories of entrepreneurial spirit and energies that help make the impossible possible".

Making the impossible, possible. That pretty much sums up the challenge of breakthrough and innovation. The beauty is that history demonstrates that previous generations have consistently overestimated what is impossible, and underestimated what is possible, due to the nature of the human mind and certain inbuilt cognitive limits.

History demonstrates that the vast, silent majority of human beings prefer the safety and comfort of the known to the risks and uncertainties of the unknown. Yet all progress has come about through entrepreneurial, risk-taking souls who have dared to challenge the status quo and received wisdom to create the new.

In his monumental work: "Ideas – A History of Thought and Invention from Fire to Freud"[25], the renowned author and historian Peter Watson surveys the 10 000 ideas that have created modern civilization over the past 10 000 years. From deep antiquity to the present day, he shows how the invention of systems of thought such as writing, mathematics, science, philosophy and the rise of concepts such as the law, sacrifice, democracy and the soul, have shaped our modern worldview.

In amongst these lofty concepts and systems of thought are also the prosaic basic inventions which enabled us to transcend the resource limitations we faced at different points in our human history, from fire, agriculture, the wheel, the ship, and cities to vaccines, fossil fuels, antibiotics, electricity, plastic, computers, telecommunications to genetics and many more.[26]

The key point is that all of these ideas, systems, concepts and technologies were invented and discovered by the most powerful tool of all time, the human mind. And at every stage of our development as a species, the mainstream of popular thought would have found the next generation of ideas, systems, concepts and technologies to be inconceivable. We are no different, but the good news is that there are more innovators, transformers and creatives on our planet right now than have ever existed in the history of mankind, and by drawing on this unprecedented resource we can make more breakthroughs now than ever before. That is guaranteed.

What is less clear, is the extent to which such breakthroughs and innovations will become commonplace – in the parlance of Silicon Valley, how fast they will SCALE into the mainstream. And this is where psychology and the sociocultural understanding of change and transformation

---

25   Peter Watson, Ideas – A History of Thought and Invention from Fire to Freud, Harper Perennial, 2005.

26   For a more detailed exegesis of these ideas and their connection with human development in general, see "The Trouble with Paradise", Robin Wood, AuthorHouse, 2014.

become invaluable, as well as a deeper understanding of the true complexity of what we all (often rather glibly) refer to as "innovation".

**What is Sustainable Innovation? Or Thriveable Innovation?**

Innovation is a complex and multi-facetted phenomenon, which is why it is obligatory to make it as simple as possible in all of its dimensions if we are to get anywhere defining the difference between *sustainable* and *thriveable* innovation, and *incremental* and *breakthrough* innovation.

First of all, most innovation fundis know that there are many different kinds of innovation, from incremental improvements to existing technologies, products, services and business models, to radical breakthroughs (often known as "disruptive") which result in very new and different technologies, products, services and business models. In the end the incremental innovations usually end up being used to extend the lifespan of sunset industries, while breakthroughs generally tended to accelerate the sunset.

For example, we all know that the minicomputer disrupted the mainframe, and that the PC disrupted the minicomputer, and now there are very few mainframes left, no minicomputers and mainly glowing internet servers in data centres around the world and laptops/ tablets/ smartphones in the hands of a few billion smart users. Any firm that did not adapt to this saw its life cut short very swiftly. Even the mighty IBM almost died, and had to be resuscitated through radical surgery in the 1990's.

So, disruption is definitely good for users and consumers- but is it sustainable or thriveable?

Take the Apple range of products – brilliantly designed, user-friendly (if a little expensive) devices that make life easier, on a good day. But is it sustainable to have an average replacement cycle of, at best, a few years? Where do smartphones, tablets, laptops and iMacs go to die? Today, mainly in landfills, where in developing countries they are disassembled by small children who are exposed to their many toxic ingredients. Not so sustainable, even if Apple and all the other manufacturers manage to make their entire supply chain "less bad" in terms of the classic sustainability "zeros" for water, waste, carbon, human and social impacts and so on.

## Creating True Future Value - A Backcast from 2020: the Ubiphone

Let's conduct a brief thought experiment, based on a what-if scenario of the first company to develop a circular economy, regenerative mobile device model- and let's call this thriveable device the "UbiPhone".

So, let's begin, by asking: "What if the mobile device industry were to shift to a circular economy business model, where success was to be measured by the value of the assets in the flow of materials, as well as by the growth in number and value of devices sold?"

What if Apple or Samsung was to be valued for all the irreplaceable rare earth minerals and other precious materials it owned in the circular materials flow? Indeed, why not sell mobile devices as a service, on a monthly rental, where the device is never owned by the user but simply leased from the provider, along with device sharing options for backup, emergency recovery and other situations where a specific device is in harm's way for whatever reason?

Of course, such a thriveable device would have to be designed from the concept stage up, and would also be a major competitive advantage to whomever could get generation y and z to shift to that business model.

A more modular product, with interchangeable parts, sold as a service, and instantly traded to another user if the original user upgrades to another device, and which is also fully recycled and upcycled at the end of its life in true circular economy fashion. Why not?

Such an innovation could be made to be thriveable by innovating simultaneously along the three axes of ThriveAbility.

We are not saying this will be easy, or could happen overnight, but it is definitely doable for those who believe in making the "impossible possible":

1) **Sustainability** – integrating technological, product, service and business model breakthroughs by applying the following two key principles:

   - Designing a circular, regenerative business model for the Ubiphone

     o Man-made materials in the Ubiphone plus the natural ecosystems involved in their extraction are regenerated through circular economic processes – a modular and fully recyclable/upcyclable phone and spare parts;
     o All impacts are managed proportionately to the carrying capacities of the multiple capitals, especially natural and manufactured capitals- this entails full application of the ThriveAbility Six Capitals Equation to Ubiphone suppliers in Scope 1, 2 and 3.

   - Creating a business system that values long term resource planning for longer term value-added benefitting current and future generations

     o All Ubiphone technologies, products, services and business models designed for durability to continue serving future generations;
     o Innovations for the Ubiphone are inspired by natural systems by engineers, designers, entrepreneurs and others working with the grain of nature.

2) **Socio-Cultural** – making the UbiPhone desirable and cool through social "pull" marketing both inside the organization and in the distribution channels by applying the following two key principles:

- Aligning people, values and culture in the organization and its business ecosystems using governance systems aligned to make all the stakeholders feel part of this thriving new UbiPhone idea, offering no hassle voluntary simplicity

    o Apply inclusive and transparent governance structures that serve the different priorities and needs of different developmental levels in the business ecosystem
    o Innovative structures for and approaches to interworking between governments, NGO's, businesses and academia that focus on Stakeholder ThriveAbility.

- Implementing talent and market development approaches that develop complex systems thinking & thriveable leadership capabilities

    o Experimenting with new open business models for innovation and training/ development that integrate physical, mental, emotional and thriving needs and aspirations for Ubiphone users;
    o Shaping developmental pathways based on co-working and co-creation between disciplines and sectors that are aspirational and compelling for future generations, with particular reference to the specific target markets that will be early adopters of the Ubiphone.

3) **Organizational and Business Ecosystem** – Laying the groundwork for a transparent and level playing field that eventually delivers True Value in both the new Ubiphone business model and the mobile phone industry eventually by:

    o Applying true accounting principles that measure true costs including externalities, and calculate true returns with full transparency;
    o Levelling the playing field towards renewable and regenerative industries through true taxation and incentives negotiated with sympathetic governments, including locating Ubiphone manufacturing in such jurisdictions;
    o Nurturing multi-stakeholder collaboration to amplify and scale up positive impacts wherever possible as the Ubiphone is designed, developed, manufactured, sold and recycled;
    o Encouraging investors in the mobile phone/smart handset industry to base their investment decisions on the ThriveAbility Index metrics.

To even begin the journey implied by the UbiPhone case study above, one would need to understand the massive difference between incremental and breakthrough innovation. The very first, and most important difference begins with mindset and differences in managerial style. This critical difference will be covered in great detail later on, but we will make one key observation here.

Although we will refrain from over-simplifying things in this leader's guide, we will make one very simple observation here: there are some people who really love incremental innovation (called a *preference for linear change)*, and other people who much prefer breakthrough change (called a *preference for non-linear or transformative change*).

On the one hand, the *linear change managers* are the ones you really need on the operational front fine-tuning the six-sigma program and perfecting the improvements to the new sustainability environmental profit and loss program. On the other hand, if you want breakthrough, transformative change that will disrupt existing patterns and ways of doing things, you will definitely need leaders who have a *high preference for transformative change* and actually love the chaotic, rollercoaster highs and lows of the disruptive innovation process.

Yet, it is simply amazing how many organisations think that by putting a "safe pair of hands" senior executive in charge of a highly risky disruptive innovation program, will somehow magically reduce the risk. Yes, it will certainly reduce the risk that your disruptive innovation program ever gets off the ground or that a product/service ever gets out the door. But you will kill the golden goose well before it can ever begin to lay any fresh eggs. Do not go there, at any cost.

So, how do we connect this brave new world of transformation and breakthrough to current reality and management practice? There are a number of successful initiatives that have begun to have a positive impact on the world of sustainability, even if they will be the first to admit that their focus currently does result in largely incremental change toward sustainability goals that are generally unambitious and not defined in terms of how the impact of an organization on a specific capital needs to change to meet the real limits on those capitals.

These current initiatives do not yet provide the incentives to create a thriving world that might motivate bolder leadership and breakthroughs. But they are a good beginning.

## Laying the Social, Economic and Financial Groundwork – The Six Pillars

The starting point for the ThriveAbility Journey begins with those 80 000 organizations that are slowly becoming aware of the challenges they face in both preventing/adapting to a world of two to four degrees warming, together with the 7 000 organizations which have begun the sustainability journey but are still at the earlier stages of being "less bad", with their major focus being on impact reduction and efficiency generation wrapped in a layer of corporate social responsibility and green marketing efforts. Out of those 7 000 organizations that are on the sustainability journey, a few hundred are now focused on the next major leap into becoming "net positive".

In order be measurable and manageable, the ThriveAbility Journey has to plug into the existing ways in which we measure progress in our organisations and institutions, and then stretch those management systems toward some future desiderata that are common cause for any leader who cares about improving the state of our world.

Luckily, there are several organisations that have already established some baselines from which we can create the "future pull" that can inspire and support leaders and managers everywhere to move in the right direction.

To begin with, the transformations taking place in the disciplines of economics and accounting are very encouraging. A variety of projects and organisations have been busy for at least a decade building a framework within which the ThriveAbility journey can take place. What follows is a brief summary of those organisations and projects.

The central pillars upon which the journey toward ThriveAbility can begin include:

- **Thriving, Wellbeing and Engagement - The Gallup Approach** as embodied in the Macroeconomic Path, a leadership model for successful societies, and the Microeconomic Path framework by which leaders and companies can understand and work with human nature to accelerate organizational performance;
- **The Six Capitals Approach** to measuring Value-Added, championed by the International Integrated Reporting Council (IIRC);
- **The Ten-Sector/80 Industry Approach** to developing Sustainability Accounting Standards being developed by the Sustainability Accounting Standards Board (SASB);
- **The Sustainability Reporting Framework** pioneered by the Global Reporting Initiative (GRI);
- **The Vision 2050 and Action 2020 Programs of the** World Business Council for Sustainable Development (WBCSD);
- **The Ten Universally Accepted Principles** embodied in the Guidelines of the United Nations Global Compact (UN Global Compact or UNGC).

Let us take a quick tour through what each of these six pillars contributes to laying the foundations on which the ThriveAbility Journey is based.

- **Thriving, Wellbeing and Engagement - The Macro & Micro-Economic Paths to Thriving & Performance – Gallup International**

Gallup developed both of its macro and micro frameworks based on global surveys that include the key concepts of Thriving, Wellbeing and Engagement, as a key part of its work to delivers analytics and advice to help leaders and organizations solve their most pressing problems. Combining more than 80 years of experience with its global reach, Gallup is extremely knowledgeable about the attitudes and behaviours of employees, customers, students and citizens.

**World Poll and World Path** - In every corner of the Earth, the Gallup World Poll tracks the opinions that matter most. Using data available nowhere else, Gallup can analyse over 100 crucial world issues affecting people's lives -- issues such as the global economic meltdown, the Arab Spring, the earthquake in Haiti, good jobs and bad jobs worldwide, confidence in institutions, and societal instability.

The World Poll is based on a framework called the Gallup Macroeconomic Path, a leadership model for successful societies. Each step on the path links to a set of survey questions that Gallup asks across each country. This approach makes it possible to track historical trends and make direct cross-country comparisons.

Gallup conducts nationally representative surveys face to face or via telephone in more than 160 countries and in over 140 languages, covering the emerging and developed world.

Many well-known organizations and influential academics use the World Poll to enhance their research and shape their work, either by accessing World Poll raw data, interacting with advanced aggregate data through Gallup Analytics, or adding questions to the global survey to create a new global data set for a specific set of indicators. Gallup also conducts custom analytics for organizations on a proprietary basis.

Gallup developed the Microeconomic Path as a framework by which leaders and companies could maximize human nature to accelerate organizational performance. Their consultants and analysts apply their knowledge of this path to address the right steps in the right order, improving the way organizations create strategy and operate.

This approach has led to the creation of unique tools and techniques for achieving the highest levels of organizational performance and organic growth. In the late 1990s, Gallup pioneered the employee engagement movement and introduced the premier tool for measuring and managing employees, the Gallup Q12: 12 actionable workplace elements with proven links to vital performance outcomes. Gallup remains at the forefront of employee engagement and has partnered with thousands of organizations to help them create a sustainable culture of engagement.

*More information at: www.gallup.com and http://www.gallup.com/services/170945/world-poll.aspx*

- **The Six Capitals Approach to measuring Value-Added - IIRC (International Integrated Reporting Council)**

The International Integrated Reporting Council (IIRC) is a global coalition of regulators, investors, companies, standard setters, the accounting profession and NGOs. Together, this coalition shares the view that communication about value creation should be the next step in the evolution of corporate reporting.

The IIRC is the global authority on <IR>(Integrated Reporting). Its mission is clear: to enable Integrated Reporting to be embedded into mainstream business practice in the public and private sectors.

Their long-term vision is a world in which integrated thinking is embedded within mainstream business practice in the public and private sectors, facilitated by <IR> as the corporate reporting norm. The cycle of integrated thinking and reporting, resulting in efficient and productive capital allocation, will act as forces for financial stability and sustainability.

*More information at: www.theiirc.org*

- **The Ten-Sector/80 Industry Approach to developing Sustainability Accounting Standards - SASB (Sustainability Accounting Standards Board)**

SASB's mission is to develop and disseminate sustainability accounting standards that help publicly-listed corporations disclose material factors in compliance with SEC requirements. Through these standards, along with associated education and outreach, SASB is working to increase the usefulness of information available to investors, and improve corporate performance on the environmental, social, and governance issues most likely to impact value.

- The Sustainability Accounting Standards Board is an independent 501(c)3 non-profit.
- Through 2016 SASB is developing sustainability accounting standards for more than 80 industries in 10 sectors.

- SASB standards are designed for the disclosure of material sustainability issues in mandatory SEC filings, such as the Form 10-K and 20-F.

- SASB is accredited to establish sustainability accounting standards by the American National Standards Institute (ANSI). Accreditation by ANSI signifies that SASB's procedures to develop standards meet ANSI's requirements for openness, balance, consensus, and due process.

(SASB is not affiliated with FASB, GASB, IASB or any other accounting standards boards.)

*More information at: www.sasb.org*

- **The Sustainability Reporting Framework - GRI (Global Reporting Initiative)**

GRI has pioneered and developed a comprehensive Sustainability Reporting Framework that is widely used around the world.A sustainability report is a report published by a company or organization about the economic, environmental and social impacts caused by it's everyday activities.

A sustainability report also presents the organization's values and governance model, and demonstrates the link between its strategy and its commitment to a sustainable global economy.GRI's mission is to make sustainability reporting standard practice for all companies and organizations.

The GRI Framework is a reporting system that provides metrics and methods for measuring and reporting sustainability-related impacts and performance. With their new emphasis on materiality the G4 Guidelines should help organizations to address the sustainability gap that exists between what is being committed to in the reporting process, and what is actually required in each industry to deliver according to the real natural capital constraints being faced today.

*More information at: www.globalreporting.org*

- **The Vision 2050 and Action 2020 Programs - WBCSD (World Business Council for Sustainable Development)**

The Vision 2050 and Action 2020 Programs of the WBCSD have integrated some of the best thinking and intelligence on what is required to create a thriving future for our planet through businesses. The WBCSD is a CEO-led organization of forward-thinking companies that galvanizes the global business community to create a sustainable future for business, society and the environment. From its starting point in 1992 to the present day, the Council has created respected thought leadership on business and sustainability.

The Council plays a leading advocacy role for business, through leveraging strong relationships with stakeholders, and helping drive debate and policy change in favour of sustainable development solutions.

The WBCSD provides a forum for its 200 member companies - who represent all business sectors, all continents and combined revenue of over $US 7 trillion - to share best practices on sustainable development issues and to develop innovative tools that change the status quo.

Although some of the WBCSD members in the non-renewable resources sector have been laggards in their implementation of sustainability programs that can actually meet the goals set out by world bodies and governments, there is hope that under its new leadership it will be able to help its members in the non-renewable resources sector to get to grips with the major challenges they face in surviving in a future world of carbon taxes and pressure for divestment driven by realpolitik of stranded assets.

The Council also benefits from a network of 60 national and regional business councils and partner organizations, a majority of whom are based in developing countries. By thinking ahead, advocating for progress and delivering results, the WBCSD both increases the impact of its members' individual actions and catalyses collective action that can change the future for the better.

*More information at: www.wbcsd.org*

- **United Nations Global Compact (UN Global Compact)**

The United Nations Global Compact is a strategic policy initiative for businesses that are committed to aligning their operations and strategies with ten universally accepted principles in the areas of human rights, labour, environment and anti-corruption. This set of principles asks companies to embrace, support and enact, within their sphere of influence, a set of core values in the these four areas.

By doing so, business, as a primary driver of globalization, can help ensure that markets, commerce, technology and finance advance in ways that benefit economies and societies everywhere.

*More information at: www.unglobalcompact.org*

These six pillars provide us with a strong base on which the development of the ThriveAbility Approach and Index can be developed. The most important principles and methods applied in each of these six pillars have been integrated into the initial version of the ThriveAbility Approach and Index so as to provide a robust and accessible framework within which we can progress from "Version 1.0" to each of the next stages of development with confidence.

So, what would an integration of all of the key ingredients in these six pillars look like? In order to give you some idea of what the goal state of ThriveAbility would look like, we have pulled together Six Desiderata of ThriveAbility.

## Transforming the Sustainability Reporting Ecosystem – The ThriveAbility Ecosystem

There are seven key roles that underpin the sustainability reporting ecosystem as it is constituted today, as illustrated in Diagram 5 below. These roles include:

- the *Standards Organizations*: IASB, FASB, IIRC, GRI, SASB, GISR, Science Europe, OECD Guidelines, ICC, UN Global Compact, Global Research and The Prince of Wales Trust;
- the *Assurers* of these standards (for example, the Big Four and other accounting firms and assurance organizations); PWC, KPMG, Ernst & Young, Deloitte, Grant Thornton and many others;
- the *Aggregators* of the data: for example, Bloomberg, Standard & Poor's and Moody's;
- *Analysts*: for example, MSCI, EIRIS and Sustainanalytics;
- *Raters*: for example, GIIN, Vigeo and CDP;
- *Users* of this data, mainly *investors* and *regulators*; (e.g. Bank of England, FSA (Financial Services Authority), Investors: for example, Aviva, the Calvert Social Index Fund[27]; *Indexes*: FTSE, Stock Exchange: South African Stock Exchange, Bovespa) and finally we have
- *Disclosers* of that data, those companies that are doing their best to be more sustainable. (e.g. *Companies*: Unilever, GE, Kraft, Johnson & Johnson, *NGOs*: WWF, Greenpeace, *Media*: BBC, CNN, The Guardian).

---

[27] The fund has returned 13.75 percent over the past year, 21.38 percent over the past three years, 15.03 percent over the past five years, and 6.68 percent over the past decade.

**DIAGRAM 5 – How the ThriveAbility Ecosystem Might Help Accelerate a Rapid Evolution in the Sustainability Reporting Ecosystem Cycle**

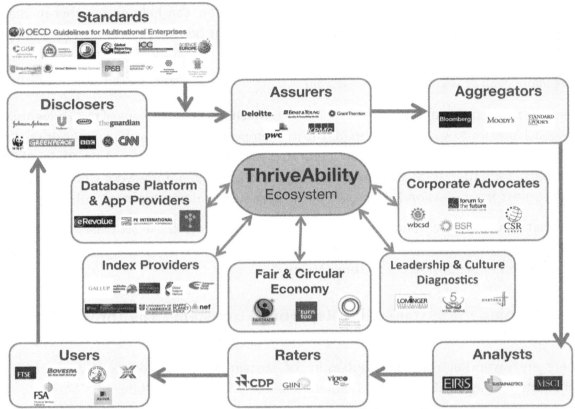

Note: This is a representative sample of keystone ecosystem players- not all players can be included due to limited space

These roles are all necessary to achieve '*less bad*' sustainability performance, but not sufficient to ensure a thriving global economy by 2050. We may achieve net positive in the best of all possible scenarios within this sustainability reporting ecosystem eventually, but net positive still generates massive natural, human and other costs.

To move as rapidly as possible from Stage One to Stage Six in the ThriveAbility Journey, seven of the key ingredients required include:

1. A **decision-making framework** that builds on existing sustainability reporting and financial reporting approaches while generating insights as to how to motivate key stakeholder groups to align around breakthrough innovations through appropriate incentives;

2. An **integration** of the natural, manufactured, financial, intellectual, human and social capitals needed to deliver the rapid adoption of a set of metrics and approaches that can deliver a green and inclusive economy by 2050;

3. A robust, globally accepted **industry classification standard** and system that can be used to build a common, open source database of the requirements for each stage of the ThriveAbility Journey to be met according to each of the six capitals;

4. A reliable and globally accepted way of measuring **socio-cultural development stages** at multiple levels from individual leaders to teams to larger groupings (units, divisions, categories, regions and so on) and whole organizations;

5. A reliable and globally accepted way of **measuring thriving and ThriveAble outcomes for different stakeholder groups,** together with an analysis of the life conditions which are conducive to thriving;

6. A **stratified approach** to designing irresistible, thriveable business propositions as well as socially innovative ways of doing things that offer a much more effective way to accelerate the rate of adoption of more thriveable business models & lifestyles;

7. A universally accepted way of **measuring the sustainability context gap** with regard to fair use of natural capital and the industry allocation methods needed to gain commitment to such an approach by governments and organizations.

In order to make a start in delivering these seven key ingredients required to move beyond Net Positive (and also to accelerate the journeys of those from denial/compliance through sustainability as usual to Net Positive), a catalytic ThriveAbility ecosystem is needed, as shown in the centre of Diagram 5 above. The key roles in this ThriveAbility ecosystem include:

- **Corporate Advocates** - WBCSD, Forum for the Future, BSR and CSR Europe;
- **Leadership and Cultural Diagnostic Service Providers** - 5Deep, Loevinger and Harthill;
- **Fair and Circular Economy Players** – Fairtrade, Turntoo and the Ellen Macarthur Foundation;
- **Database Platform and App Providers**- Verso, PE International and Erevalue;
- **Index/Data Providers** - Social Progress Index, Gallup, Happy Planet Index, Positive Psychology Centre, University of Cambridge, European Social Survey, NEF, Global Footprint Network and the Stockholm Resilience Centre.

## The ThriveAbility Index Generator

The ThriveAbility Index Generator shown in diagram 6 below enables us to measure three key aspects of an organization's progress on the ThriveAbility Journey:

- **The Sustainability Gap** – organizations must contribute their fair proportionate share to closing the Sustainability Gap between current incremental aspirations and the transformative change needed to respect the boundaries (ecological ceilings and social foundations) needed to achieve true sustainability at the planetary and societal levels. Initiatives such as the Future Fit Business Benchmark and the MultiCapital Scorecard measure organizational operation within their fair share of the floors and ceilings of social and natural capitals;
- **Organizations' Stage on the ThriveAbiity Journey** – here we measure the four key domains (using 95 indicators) demonstrated by decades of research to be accurate

predictors of the six stages of development on the ThriveAbility Journey. In each domain there are a few key principles used to generate the key indicators and statements that form a multiple choice question from which respondents are asked to select their favourite statements. An assessment of the current stage of development an organization is at with some useful feedback on strengths, areas for improvement and new opportunities for innovation, breakthroughs and better practices is then delivered to decision makers[28];

- **Sociocultural Stages of Development** – of the organization and its leaders, at multiple levels from individual leaders to teams to larger groupings (units, divisions, categories, regions and so on) and whole organizations. This includes a survey that looks at the current levels of values of the leading individuals of an organization and provides recommendations as to how to become a thriving individual and create an aligned, thriving leadership team within that organization capable of taking it to the next level in the ThriveAbility Journey.

The three axes of the ThriveAbility Index Generator, (also represented in the ThriveAbility ix Capital Equation through the six capitals) are:

- **The Sustainability Gap - Closing the Gap Between what a Thriving Ecology Requires and What the Organization is Currently Consuming (Z Axis) –** *The Denominator of the ThriveAbility Equation - Natural and Manufactured Capital*

Impact reduction is the focus of sustainability today. However we are all aware that there is a 'context gap' because the global figures and the numbers that scientists are producing tell us that in terms of global and regional ecosystems, the natural capital costs of just the top 100 worst companies are $5 trillion a year.

The latest IPCC report to the UN suggests that with 90 trillion dollars of green focused investment we can contain climate change to a 2 degree warming scenario. That $90 trillion of investment includes the transition from fossil fuels to renewable energy, the shifts in industry, transport and agriculture that are needed, as well as water and everything else associated with this transition.

The challenge today is that each industry has only a vague idea to what extent it is part of the solution or part of the problem on the Z-Axis that measures the context gap - there is

---

[28]  The FOUR key domains covered by the ThriveAbility Assessment are:
   1. PLANET To what extent is your organization taking into account its true ecological footprint.
   2. PEOPLE & PRINCIPLES To what extent does your organization motivate and align the people in an around your organization fully realize their potential contribution to your sustainability and other strategic initiatives?
   3. PURPOSE AND TRUE PROFIT To what extent does your organization participate in integrated reporting initiatives and the application of inclusive business models? To what extent does your organization support true cost, true pricing and true taxation initiatives and emerging standards?
   4. ACCOUNTABILITY AND RESPONSABILITY To what extent does your organization integrate all of the activities outlined above, to support more effective decision making for sustainability and ThriveAbility?

still not enough data to really pinpoint exactly how we help the 'bad' organizations – the ones costing 20 trillion a year – to become much less bad. The same applies to the 'good' organizations with whom we want to work -how can we accelerate their progress toward ThriveAbility, rather than becoming 'just less bad'?

- **The Organizational Gap - Accelerating an Organization's Stage on the ThriveAbility Journey through Innovation and Investment Pathways (Y Axis) –** *The Middle Line of the ThriveAbility Equation: Financial and Intellectual Capital*

The ThriveAbility Journey describes the journey taken by organizations from reluctant compliance with environmental, health and safety regulations, through six stages ending with a ThriveAble organization. A ThriveAble organization is one that not only produces zero harmful impacts on any of the six IIRC capitals, but also generates very high levels of thrival in its key stakeholder groups.

Thrival is a measure of how well an individual stakeholder is thriving using survey and census metrics derived from a number of global suppliers. ThriveAbility is the measure of the ratio of thrival creation divided by the associated footprint.

**DIAGRAM 6 - The ThriveAbility Index Generator**

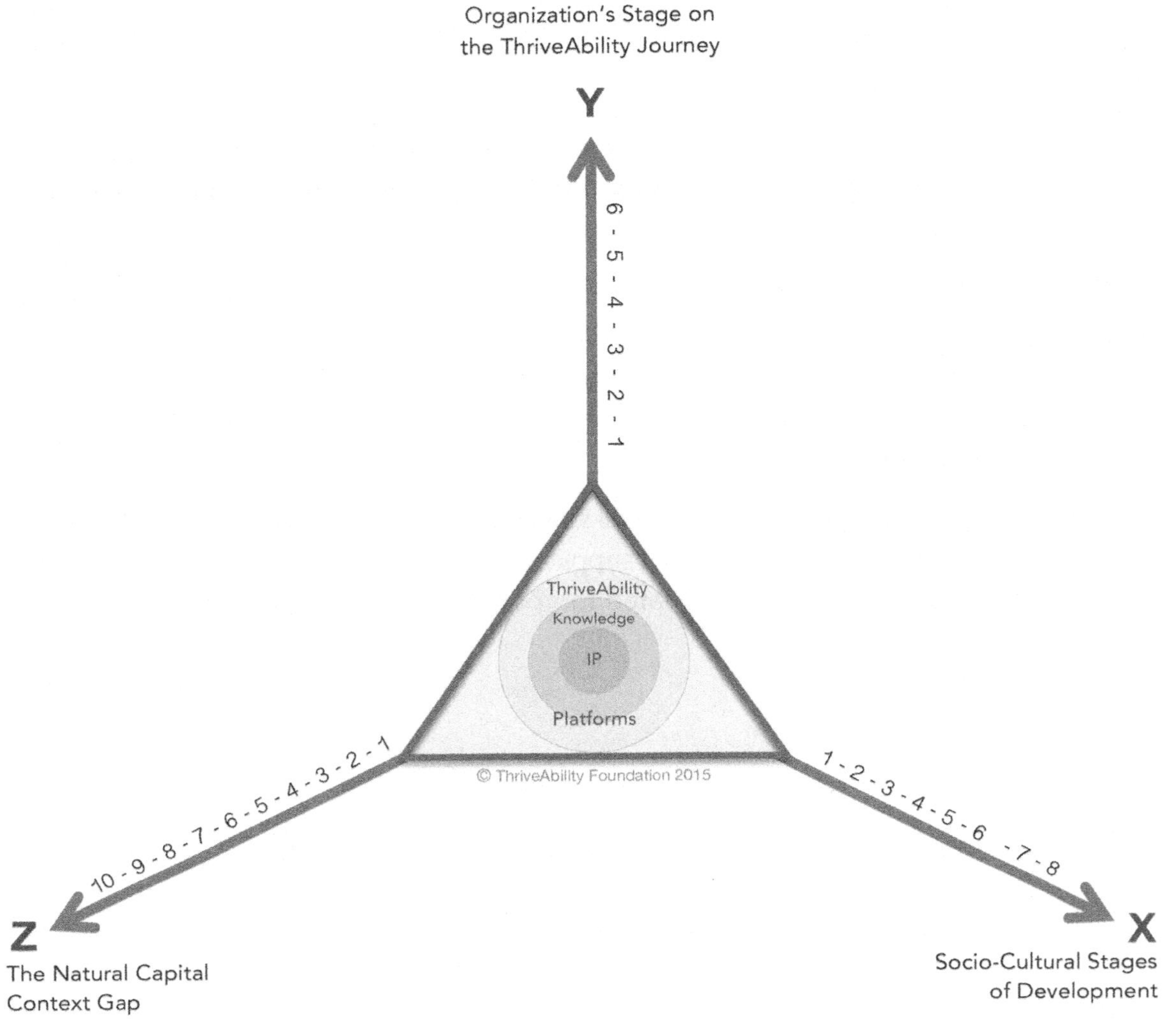

Organization's Stage on
the ThriveAbility Journey

**Y**

6 - 5 - 4 - 3 - 2 - 1

ThriveAbility

Knowledge

IP

Platforms

© ThriveAbility Foundation 2015

10 - 9 - 8 - 7 - 6 - 5 - 4 - 3 - 2 - 1

1 - 2 - 3 - 4 - 5 - 6 - 7 - 8

**Z**

The Natural Capital
Context Gap

**X**

Socio-Cultural Stages
of Development

- **The Socio-Cultural Gap – Aligning Stages of Human/Leadership Development (X-Axis) –**

  *The Numerator of the ThriveAbility Equation: Human and Social Capital*

Today economics and sustainability do not take into account the key developmental stages and motivating factors of human beings – apart from behavioural economics, psychology is largely absent. Today almost all sustainability reporting and plans place a low or zero emphasis on the X-Axis - they may talk about culture change and behavioural change models, but these are still in the very early stages of knowledge about how we should be motivating stakeholders to align to co-create thriving companies, communities, products and services.

We are able to accurately measure eight distinct stages of personal and socio-cultural development on the X-Axis. This is important because developmental stages are key drivers of innovation and transformation as well as highly correlated with progress on the other two axes.

Recently, behavioural economics began the journey with Kahneman, Seligman and others demonstrating the impact of psychology on economics. Yet, at each stage of development, thriving has a different meaning. Various frameworks such as "Memenomics" [29] point out the crucial role mindsets and cultures play in shaping our business models and systems.

We build on that scientific base together with subsequent work by organizations such as Gallup – for example, while recognizing the importance of Seligman's work on Flourishing and the PERMA framework for wellbeing, we will also build on Gallup's global thriving databases.

All of which demonstrates how absolutely critical it is to take such psychological insights seriously, even though most sustainability approaches don't take that into account at all. The change programs we see in major organizations are still applying very basic approaches.

The ThriveAbility Approach applies models of stratified behavioural change and incentives that are proven to accelerate progress towards breakthrough that include innovation acceleration methods and technologies alongside logical evaluations supported by data from companies like Gallup who have already pioneered many of these measurements.

Given the primacy of the mindsets and worldviews leaders use to develop and implement their strategies, later on in this book we will dive into a further level of detail on this topic to illustrate how critical it is that the different developmental stages are recognised and taken into account in developing ThriveAbility strategies.

But first, we need to examine the current state of the art in capitalism and business, to define the starting point for the transition the ThriveAbility Approach and Index seek to deliver.

*In short, how can we get smarter, wiser capital, to help reinvent Capitalism?*

*Or for those of you familiar with financial markets and investing: "What is the Delta that drives the True Value Alpha?"*

---

[29]   http://www.memenomics.com/

# 3. Toward a Socio-Economic System that Generates True Value

> "The highest use of capital is not to make more money but to
> make money do more for the betterment of life."
> *Henry Ford*

One of the keys to successfully changing the system we are currently in is to shift money flows toward thriveable innovations and corporations, and away from damaging and toxic technologies and industries. In the process we also shift money flows away from corrupt oligarchic systems of governance that feed off of industries such as fossil fuels and unethical producers of foods, chemicals/whatever, and to a fairer system, rewarding more distributed sets of producers who are beneficial to all life and each other.

Current measures of value vary widely, depending upon the underlying motives, values and incentives of the investor category in question. While it is popular to repeat the mantra: "Let's do well by doing good", what is meant by "well" and "good" vary widely, as one observes when spotting the very different outcomes that result from the individuals spouting this pop wisdom.

The health and stability of our businesses and economies are dependent on the health and stability of both the natural environment and the people living within it rather than the other way around. In order to create and maintain value into the future, organizations therefore need to integrate ThriveAbility into their overall strategy and decision-making processes.

We are in an epoch in which we are moving from Shareholder Value to True Value. This also means we are moving from playing the games of Monopoly and Oligopoly to playing a new game called "Co-Creating True Value". This involves getting investors and fund managers managing the 80% of global assets under management not currently concerned with issues of sustainability, to transition to playing a new game we might call Capitalism 2.0.

As we put it in chapter 1 – "To reinvent capitalism, we must reinvent capital, and the organizations that generate and use those capitals". What would this mean in practice? There appear to be a number of pathways that need to be pursued in parallel to reinvent capital for a thriving future:

- Make Capital Smarter, Wiser and Capable of Complex Systems Thinking
- Shift the Values and Perspectives that Prioritise the Incentives for Investing
- Apply the ThriveAbility Approach and Index to accelerate the transformations and innovations that drive ThriveAble investments.

We will begin by examining the current state of the art of Socially Responsible and Impact Investing, before exploring how each of these three pathways toward thriveable capital and investing can be embodied in current institutions and practices.

## The Current State of the Art – Socially Responsible and Impact Investing

It is encouraging to note that figures for Socially Responsible Investment ("SRI") are growing rapidly. _22% of total global assets under management (i.e. USD 13.6 trillion invested in SRI) are currently influenced by some kind of responsible investment strategy._[30]

The sheer scale of the total value of assets under management today is over $80 trillion.

**DIAGRAM 7 – $68.7 Trillion under Management in 2013**

From an international perspective, there is strong evidence that "green" investments are significantly different from SRI investments in terms of financial performance and underlying firm characteristics. Green equities outperformed SRI equities between 2003 and 2007, whereas they underperformed between 2008 and 2012 with absolute multi-factor alphas of more than 1 per cent per month in both directions. Green portfolios mainly contain stocks of

---

[30] The most common strategy used globally is negative exclusionary screening (US$ 8.3 trillion), followed by ESG ("Environmental/Social/Governance") integration (US$6.2 trillion) and corporate engagement/shareholder action (US$ 4.7 trillion).

low quality with weak business models that are highly capital-demanding but unprofitable, whereas SRI portfolios are principally characterized by stocks with well-conceived and profitable business models. Green investments can be considered as a sector bet on the renewable energy industry shaped by massive governmental subsidies during the mid-2000s.

The global SRI market using ESG considerations is driven by Europe, representing almost two-thirds of the total SRI ESG investments. Europe, the USA, Canada and Japan account for 96% of global SRI investments.

There is growing evidence that SRI strategies are outgrowing the traditional investment market. Investors are now more willing to take non-financial factors into account in their investment decisions. The differences vary considerably per European country. For example in the Netherlands, the SRI market grew by more than 25%.

The total US-domiciled assets under management using SRI strategies expanded from $3.74 trillion at the start of 2012 to $6.57 trillion at the start of 2014, an increase of 76 per cent,. These assets now account for more than one out of every six dollars under professional management in the United States. The assets engaged in sustainable, responsible and impact-investing practices at the start of 2014 represent nearly 18 per cent of the $36.8 trillion in total assets under management.

**DIAGRAM 8 – Socially Responsible Investment Trends in the USA 1995 - 2014**

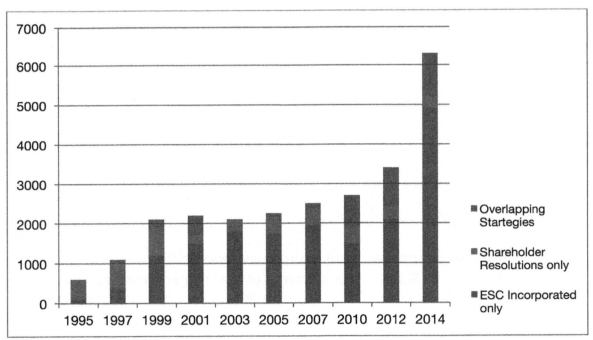

Investors have two good reasons to invest in SRI funds or services. Firstly, the financial return. A growing number of international studies show that SRI portfolios outperform mainstream portfolios. Secondly, retail investors increasingly seek social return, which Socially Responsible

Investments can deliver. For example, a major ethical bank recently confirmed that their SRI portfolio outperformed on Environmental, Social and Governance indicators by respectively 25, 15 and 19 percent.

Despite this impressive progress in the worlds of SRI and ESG investing, there is still a huge gap that needs to be closed between the small number of leading firms driving this trend, and the vast number of firms just getting to grips with the basic challenges ahead. Progress toward basic sustainability has been highly uneven across companies- most are held hostage to short-term investor pressures and a myopic view of wealth creation that is dominated by a focus on financial capital to the exclusion of other "capitals" indispensable to long-term, inclusive wealth creation. Namely: natural, human, social, and intellectual capital.

Another major challenge is that investors all take different perspectives on what sustainability excellence means. For example, mainstream investors, social investors and NGO's apply very different criteria, leading to opaque, inconsistent sustainability and CSR measures. This is not made any easier by the variety of players and roles that are involved in setting, disclosing and assuring standards, from the standard setters themselves to the disclosers, assurers, aggregators, analysts and rating agencies.

A survey by Deloitte (Zero Impact Growth, ZIG)[31] of 65 of the leading sustainability advocates in ten industries around the world also demonstrated how far we have to go to get to the point where even the leading organisations are all able to bring about the transformations required in their industries to meet the 2 degree warming scenario requirements.

---

[31] Deloitte: Zero Impact Growth Monitor - Strategies of leading companies in 10 industries

## DIAGRAM 9 – The Deloitte Zero Impact Growth Survey Results

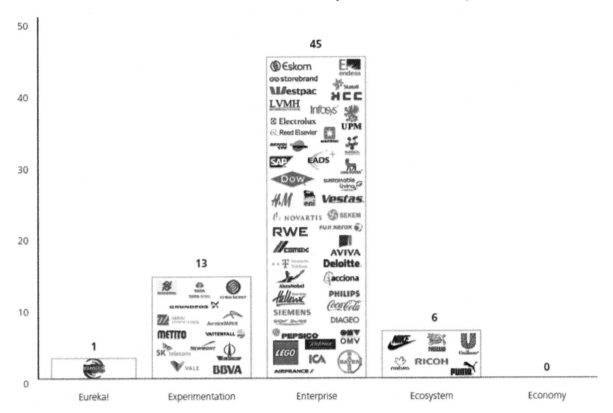

The Zero Impact Growth survey found that only 6 of the 65 "sustainability leaders" were operating at the business ecosystem level of transformation. Puma, Unilever, Nestle, Nike, Natura and Ricoh are all collaborating with their industry supply chains and competitors to transform industry their value chains, along similar lines to the initiatives recommended by the WBCSD in its Vision 2050 recommendations.

48 of these sustainability leaders were optimising their value chains at the enterprise level, while 13 were still in the early stages of experimentation with sustainability initiatives. Clearly a whole new language and set of concepts and skills need to be learned by organizations to make sustainability breakthroughs more likely.

If we are to move to the sustainable economy and thriving future, a new frame of reference for decision-making is required, involving new ways to measure progress at global, national and corporate levels. A measurement framework that incorporates economic growth, social equity and well-being, and environmental sustainability, is needed; one that, at the same time, provides a common set of goals for action by business and governments at the local, national and international levels.

This emerged as a key theme of the United Nations Conference on Sustainable Development, 'Rio+20' held in June 2012. The outcome document from Rio+20 includes references to performance measurement systems at each level of an economy:

- The **global level**: agreement to develop a set of global Sustainable Development Goals (SDGs) in key priority areas to complement the existing Millennium Development Goals after 2015. It was recognized that once set, progress towards the achievement of the goals needs to be assessed and accompanied by targets and indicators.

- The **national level**: recognition of the limitations of GDP as a measure of well-being and sustainable development. Launch of a programme to develop new national indicators that go beyond GDP.

- The **corporate level**: acknowledgment that the implementation of sustainable development will depend on active engagement of the private sector; recognition of the importance of corporate sustainability reporting and encouragement of companies, where appropriate, especially publicly listed and large companies, to consider integrating sustainability information into their reporting cycle.

The Deloitte Zero Impact Growth ("ZIG") report reveals 4 major gaps that were visible through the ZIG Monitor:

- a major comparability gap (that is why all rankings and ratings tell us different stories about best-in-'their'-class performance),
- major gaps between the overall strategy of organizations towards Zero Impact Growth and furthermore the real capabilities of sub-strategies to deliver on the organization's overall strategy (it simply doesn't add up in many cases), and finally
- gaps in the balance of sub-strategies and major performance gaps in and between industries.

And all of that while the report only assessed companies that see themselves as leading in sustainability.

The Zero Impact Growth report offers us a baseline picture of where we really are, and also assesses the brakes, accelerators and options for a 'joint flight' towards adapting Zero Impact Growth as the new basic paradigm that we all need to agree on, if we are to deliver the regenerative or restorative growth we need to survive and thrive. It's a process that can be a door opener for cross-industry fertilization, for social entrepreneurship, for collaborative action to develop true costing, true pricing and true taxation initiatives leading to true valuation of resources, goods and services. This "North Star" reality check forms an essential part of the measures used for ThriveAbility evaluations.

The move to integrated reporting highlights an important trend: that sustainability and CSR need to be integrated into the core of what any organisation does. As Nike's Hannah Jones put it[32]:

---

[32]   in her acceptance speech at the 2011 Ceres-ACCA North American Awards for Sustainability Reporting as reported by John Elkington in the Guardian of 18 May 2011.

"Nike now believes that "the time is fast approaching when we will jettison the language of sustainability, and simply talk about value creation; NPV [net present value], ROIC [return on invested capital], market share, innovation portfolios and shareholder returns." "We have long said that things we have taken for free will become the new gold," she explained, "water, waste, carbon. Today, externalised costs are being forcibly internalised into cost structures, economies and incomes. The weather is not waiting to be regulated. We believe we have entered the era of climate adaptation, where we are no longer contemplating the potential, but beginning to grapple with the consequences."

"But," she continued, "here's the thing: to be able to deliver this transparency has required data, which in turn has the potential to trigger innovation. We're discovering how combining different data sets can be a tool for empowerment; social change; new insights; new solutions. What happens when we can mash up the data from these reports? How do we apply Silicon Valley, new-business-model thinking to the data we see emerging from the sustainability world? And in a world where open data is starting to create new businesses, new solutions to intractable problems, how do we reap even create value from the world of reporting? How does reporting actually become the start of an innovation story, not only the crowning of an accountability story?"

Finally, she noted that, "When we talk about sustainability without the context of value creation we diminish the potential and the opportunity and the speed with which the transition will happen. How do we turn sustainability into a 'pull' function, not a 'push' function, within a corporation? The answer lies in viewing sustainability as a strategic prism through which to view the resiliency, future growth trajectory and value creation potential of a company."

This guide echoes Hannah Jones, and argues for a new measure to replace Economic Value Added- we call it "True Value" (about which much more will be said later on in chapter 4). It also argues for us to now move beyond the dominant role reporting has played in the field of sustainability to date, and to embed new management practices and tools based on a new theory of management and economics based on ThriveAbility thinking, logic and data.

## The Challenge of Changing the Game

One of the world's largest investors once described our planet as being on a journey to an unstable destination, through unfamiliar territory, on an uneven road having already used its spare tire. Leadership today must take innovative actions that generate new capabilities and resources. We must become much smarter and more disciplined about every investment we make, whether it is time, energy or money.

Many leaders around the world understand all too well that the game we have been playing for several centuries is over, and that a new game is emerging that requires a significant change in the rules that govern how we conduct ourselves, our businesses and our governance systems.

These new rules are still emerging, as are the goals that they shape for each of us, and our businesses and institutions. Yet they are slowly emerging and beginning to be articulated.

Despite this understanding, it is proving difficult for most leaders to operationalize the changes they know are needed, due to a great deal of uncertainty around what that might mean for their most important stakeholders and the natural resistance to change that is inherent in human systems. There is also reluctance to damage or risk what is still working until it is definitively broken, unless there are other real options on the table.

There are many different opinions as to what must be done. Some say that the "system" is beyond repair, and that we must get outside of it to change it. Others believe we can accelerate what is already working in the new, more sustainable game, and that this simply requires a better market, culture or technology to make the old game obsolete. There is an element of truth in both of these propositions- we certainly must shift our mind-sets to change the game, and we also have to preserve and promote the best of what is already working to survive and thrive in the process.

The most important attribute of all at this time, is to maintain an open mind and to be as agile and creative as possible in finding and promoting the radical new opportunities our current situation offers to innovative, entrepreneurial minds.

## A Multi-Level Game in Transition

In every era, how we make a living and who gets to lead the system changes as knowledge, culture, technology and innovation co-evolve. Chieftains rule agrarian tribes, while CEO's rule corporations and Presidents and Prime Ministers rule countries. Civilisation has always been built out of exchanges between different peoples living in different biomes and life conditions with different natural advantages and needs. There have always been good and bad leaders, healthy and unhealthy cultures, and this remains part of the evolutionary process. What is certain is that the game we have been playing for the past few centuries has to change and is changing dramatically.

Underlying all of these variables are some fairly stable pathways of human development which describe the journey individuals and take from power-driven and conventional ways of being and investing, to more rational, pluralistic and integral ways of being and investing.

When observing our businesses, institutions and economies in action over time, we can recognise a broad spectrum of value systems ranging from:

- the animal spirits of the opportunists such as Gordon Gecko in "Wall Street I and II" and Jordan Belfort in "Wolf of Wall Street" to
- the diplomats in charge of highly conservative, risk averse bond-market and institutional investor operations as well as traditional forms of corporate and sovereign lending (including many of the regulators), to

- the rational achievers running large investment funds complemented by the expert hedge-fund and data driven investors, to
- the rugged individualists in venture capital and socially entrepreneurial and impact investing, to
- the strategists such as Warren Buffett and his approach to value investing at a much more strategic level, based on in-depth analyses of entire industries.

The worldview of each of these different levels of investor psychology becomes capable of handling greater complexity and diversity, thus enabling the higher levels of investor thinking to inhabit more complex decision spaces with many more variables and longer time spans than those at lower levels. Thus the individualist and strategist investors are capable of detecting variables and trends that are invisible to expert, achievers, diplomats and opportunists, as well as capable of thinking much further ahead into the future of organizations and industries.

Such Complex Systems Thinking capabilities enable the more highly developed investor to play a much bigger game across a much wider playing field, which in turn opens up many more new opportunities than are visible to less complex players.

The most remarkable—and encouraging— finding from the research of Rooke and Torbert on the Action Logics underlying such behaviours, is that leaders (and hence investors) can transform from one action logic to another. They have documented a number of leaders who have succeeded in transforming themselves from Experts into Achievers, from Achievers into Individualists, and from Individualists into Strategists. Finally, Alchemists capable of large system and society wide transformation are now emerging in greater numbers and will be critical to shifting us into ThriveAbility.

Given that the kinds of investors we have in our societies tend to shape the organisations and societies they invest in, it should come as no surprise that the dominant social logic of Capitalism 1.0 shares most of the characteristics of the Opportunists and Expert Achievers making those investment decisions.

This goes a long way to explaining why our systems of business and governance in the 20th century were driven by the perception that competition for scarce resources and winning the race for advanced technologies were the real drivers of progress. If a little "collateral damage" was inflicted along the way as "externalities", then that was the problem of government and regulators, because the job of business was to produce the maximum output with the minimum input, on the largest scale possible, thus yielding the largest profit and shareholder return possible, with no regard for externalities.

Diagram 10 below shows how the confluence of the life conditions and developmental stage a leader/investor is centred in, are usually closely associated with their strategic perspective and strengths. In other words, opportunists, diplomats, experts, achievers, individualists and strategists will tend to stick to their particular investment approach unless there is a significant shift in their life conditions (outside-in change), or they grow into the stage of development that is next for them (inside-out change), and change the incentives they respond to based on the corresponding shift in their values. ThriveAbility is the very first approach to innovation and transformation designed from the action logic of the outer turquoise capsule, enabling it to be applied to all levels of development and life conditions as appropriate. This is what we mean when we refer to a "stratified approach" to incentives and to change applicable at all levels.

**DIAGRAM 10 – Mapping Rooke and Torbert's Dominant Action Logics of Corporate Leadership to Worldview and Decision Space Complexity in Investing**

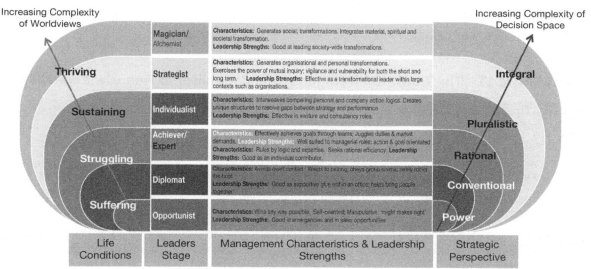

While Capitalism 1.0 produced unprecedented material prosperity for the emerging middle classes, and massive surpluses for successful investors, it also re-created a highly income-stratified world on a global scale. Insiders in business, government and finance became the new "masters of the universe", while outsiders experienced diminishing wealth as Capitalism 1.0 began to unravel, producing reactions ranging from the World Social Forum to the Occupy movements.

What began as colonisation in the 18th and 19th centuries ended up as Coca-Colanisation in the 20th century, as corporations extended their reach into developing markets. The "1%" ended up owning not only the best properties on the Monopoly Board with the highest rents, they also ended up owning the banks and having a limitless supply of "Get Out of Jail Free" cards, with which they could finance this game on a much larger scale globally.

According to Said Dawlabani, author of "Memenomics"[33], between 1950 and the Great Crash of 2008, one of the key drivers of our current malaise has been the rise of financial

---

[33] MEMEnomics: The Next Generation Economic System, Said Elias Dawlabani 2013

engineering as the dominant source of economic growth, in contrast to the product and service engineering that drove earlier stages of growth between 1950 and 1995. The dot.com bubble and bust was also an early product of this financial engineering driver, along with the massive scams at Enron, Worldcom, Lehman Brothers and AIG Insurance, among many thousands of others between 1998 and 2008.

In diagram 11 below, we can see some of the characteristic of the shift in the US economy from 1950 to 1995 that laid the foundations for the current global crisis we have been in since the great Crash of 2008. In the transition from industrial to financial capitalism, we saw the financial sector hypertrophy from 1.2% of the economy to 18.6% in 2008, an astonishing growth rate of 1 442%. Along with the shenanigans of the Federal Reserve Bank and Wall Street's major players, this hypertrophy of financial engineering wreaked havoc with the "real" economy, the fortunes of the middle classes and the state of our environment, legitimising Gordon Gecko's famous line in "Wall Street": "Greed is good".

**DIAGRAM 11 – The Transition from Industrial Capitalism to Financial Capitalism**

| 1950'S – 1970'S | 1980'S-MID 1990'S | MID 1990'S -2007'S |
|---|---|---|
| ➤INDUSTRIAL ECONOMY | ➤INDUSTRIAL –SERVICE | ➤ SERVICE-INFORMATION |
| ➤PRODUCT ENGINEERING | ➤SERVICE ENGINEERING | ➤ FINANCIAL ENGINEERING |
| ➤INDUSTRIAL OUTPUT DETERMINES STOCK VALUE | ➤BREAKING CO's TO SMALLER PIECES CREATES VALUE | ➤ SPECULATION ABOUT FUTURE PREFORMANCE CREATES VALUE |
| ➤QUANTIFIABLE MARKET- VALUE ASSETS | ➤LESS MEASURABLE SERVICE -VALUE ASSETS | ➤ HIGHLY SPECULATIVE VIRTUAL VALUE - NOTIONAL VALUE ASSETS |

| US LABOR FORCE IN TRANSITION | | | % CHANGE |
|---|---|---|---|
| ➤ INDUSTRIAL SECTOR : 28% | 18.0% | 10.5% | -62.5% |
| ➤ SERVICE SECTOR: 28% | 35.0% | 51.5% | +83.0% |
| ➤ FINANCIAL SERVICES: 1.2% | 5.30% | 18.6% | +1,442% |

Dawlabani's "Memenomics" framework builds on the Spiral Dynamics[34] values research of the past two decades, which in turn builds on the pioneering work of Professor Clare Graves from 1950 to 1980 at Union College in Albany, New York. Graves was a contemporary of Abraham Maslow, whose "Maslow's Pyramid" is well known to every student of psychology and most business school and economics graduates today. Though Graves and Maslow collaborated from time to time, Graves' work is much less well known than that of Maslow, although it deserves a much wider audience along with the other (surprisingly convergent) approaches articulated in this guide.

So, to return to the question with which we began this chapter on True Value:

"How can each of the three pathways toward thriveable capital and investing be embodied in current institutions and practices in order to reinvent capital for a thriving future?:

---

[34]  http://www.spiraldynamics.net/

- Make Capital Smarter, Wiser and Capable of Complex Systems Thinking
- Shift the Values and Perspectives that Prioritise the Incentives for Investing
- Apply the ThriveAbility Approach and Index to accelerate the transformations and innovations that drive ThriveAble investments."

## The New Game – Toward Regenerative, ThriveAble Capitalism?

"Taking a longer view and aligning with deeper currents in the markets will require business leaders to shift their focus. A key element of this shift, as players like Didas and Generation Investment Management conclude, is that focusing much more carefully on key social and environmental trends – and the economic and political eddies and currents that are forming around them – can provide real long-term dividends."
*John Elkington and Jochen Zeitz – The Breakthrough Challenge*

As the above quote from "The Breakthrough Challenge" suggests, there are some investors and organizations out there playing a winning, more sustainable, longer-term game that appears to be invisible to the opportunists and diplomats who have been allowed to wreak such havoc on our common wealth in the past four decades. It is sobering to realize that opportunistic sociopaths now "own" the best democracy money can buy in the USA, and will be running as the billionaire's party in the 2016 elections using any politician who could use their cash- (about two-thirds of them, apparently, at the latest count). Only a presidential veto now stands between tar sands oil flowing through the KXL pipeline to Houston, Wall Street removing the regulations designed to prevent another Great Crash, and the crucial powers of the EPA being undermined by opportunistic legislation.

In order to unravel the Gordian knot that appears to underlie the wicked problems being generated by the underlying value systems and Action Logics driving Capitalism 1.0, let us begin with two of the three pathways embedded in the "How can we reinvent capital?" question we began this chapter with:

- **Pathway One** - Make Capital Smarter, Wiser and Capable of Complex Systems Thinking
- **Pathway Two** - Shift the Values and Perspectives that Prioritise the Incentives for Investing

*Pathway One* - Wiser capital that fully grasps the complex inter-relationships and feedback loops between business, nature and society is emerging worldwide, but it is only capable of attracting funds from investors who wish to play a longer term, value-investing kind of game. Whatever the new game that is emerging will end up being called by future historians, it is certain that it will recognise limits to growth and prioritise people over money and material wealth. The big question is what kind of system/s and organisations will become the dominant species in this new game. While it is clear that the corporations, governments and banks that have played keystone roles in Capitalism 1.0 will have to transform into different animals or become extinct, there are still few role models for the new game with any longevity.

Capitalism 2.0 is basically a massive social, organisational and economic science experiment, as well as a work in progress that continues to surprise. As with all radical historical and evolutionary shifts, the transition from the old game to the new will see an accelerated cycle of creative destruction as relatively unknown technologies and players emerge overnight to become leading players, and the incumbents in every industry struggle to remain relevant. The playing field will become very uneven, and certainly favour bold innovators rather than timid tinkerers.

*Pathway Two* – In order to shift the values and perspectives that prioritize the incentives for investing, we need new, systematic and transformative ways of leading and managing the world's 80 000 major corporations.

One of the key differences between the 20th and 21st century attitudes to nature will be that instead of merely preserving what little is left after industrialisation, we will find and apply exciting new ways to enhance nature that can avoid the plague of side effects brought about by a poor understanding of natural, living systems we demonstrated in the 20th century. In this synergy zone between ecophiles and technophiles, we will find an increasingly win-win-win game being played between humans and our biosphere[35].

> **PRACTICAL TOOL – The ThriveAbility Journey Profile instrument** is used in the ThriveAbility Assessment, to assess the stage a company/organization is at in its Journey from Denial/Compliance through to Less Bad, Sustainable, Net Positive and ThriveAble. This ThriveAbility Journey Profile enables an organization's leaders to appreciate where their organization is leading and lagging in its current sustainability/CSR perspectives, practices and systems, helping to resolve misalignments and blockages.

Another major difference between this new game in this new century and the one we played in the 20th is that for the first time in the two millennia since Aristotle pronounced happiness to be what humans strive for, we will have reasonably accurate measures of human wellbeing and happiness. This will empower people to make better decisions in their lives and careers based on accurate assessments of their potential, values and strengths, not just their material needs and wants.

## The Transition

There is a great deal of evidence to suggest that sustainable companies outperform their counterparts over the long-term in both stock market and financial performance. The authors

---

[35]   Jeremy Rifkin points this out well in all of his books, in particular "The Zero Marginal Cost Society" (Palgrave Macmillan 2014) and "The Empathic Civilization" (Polity 2012).

of a recent working paper from Harvard Business School[36], found that superior performance for sustainable firms is 4.8% higher than unsustainable firms. $1 invested in 1993 in a sustainable firm would have grown to $7.1 by now as opposed to $4.4 with a portfolio of traditional firms.

The transition from the old game to the new game is being shaped by three mutually reinforcing drivers:

- **Growing Negative Outcomes** for Business as Usual - The accelerating impact of the *ten megaforces* that are driving the three *high risk outcomes* of *climate change*, resource shortages and *ecosystem decline*, and the serious consequences these three outcomes have for all businesses and societies, will create unprecedented challenges (and opportunities) for organisations of all kinds. This driver influences decision makers to act through a healthy dose of fear, caution and a desire to survive and protect what they cherish;

- **Accelerating Global Innovation** - the biggest gift of capitalism 1.0 has been the scientific, technological and knowledge revolutions that emerged as a result of the first Renaissance and the Enlightenment. The impacts of this revolution are still reverberating around the world especially in developing countries, whose growth will shift from being fuelled by carbon heavy sources of energy and polluting industrial technologies, to renewable energies and biologically friendly technologies. The political and social impacts will follow next as forces for democratisation and social justice gather pace. This driver influences decision makers to act through a passion for excellence, innovation and new opportunities;

- **Breakthroughs in Leveraging Human Potential** - our species is educating and developing itself at a historically unprecedented pace. Such development is driving not only scientific and technological breakthroughs, but also social, ethical, spiritual and organisational breakthroughs. As our species matures from its difficult teenager phase into early adulthood, we find new levels of responsibility and empathy emerging around the world in billions of people. As the profile of our leaders shifts from autocratic to servant to integral values, we can imagine a future in which the current civic-minded, "We" generation now starting their careers, matures into the leadership cadre of 2030, informed by a world-centric empathy that makes human thrival rather than profit and power the yardstick of human progress.

Imagine a world in which organisations have successfully motivated their key stakeholders to drive green growth through sustainable innovation. Imagine that the frustrations and multiple pressures for change we experience are actually early indications of the emergence of a new era and that many profitable, sustainable innovations are hidden in the turmoil, just waiting for enterprising, innovative leaders to reach out and catalyse them. This is the promise of ThriveAbility.

---

[36]  http://futurequotient.tumblr.com/

Embedding ThriveAbility into an organization's strategy and decision-making processes can help reduce future regulatory, resource and price risks and provide a vision of how business may be impacted by short, medium and long term environmental and social changes. It can also provide a more holistic view of the organization in terms of its operations, risks and opportunities to enable more sustainable management and value creation into the future. Yet this is still the rare exception rather than the rule.

## How Does this Transition Help Us Progressively Approximate True Value?

*"The purpose of the corporation is to enhance the ThriveAbility of itself and all its stakeholders."*[37]

The current six capitals framework proposed by the International Integrated Reporting Council (the "IIRC") has provided a good baseline on which the ThriveAbility Approach can build. The key to making the six capitals concept useful as a dynamic transition tool, is to convert it into an equation which helps us measure increments in ThriveAbility. In other words, we need to calculate the transformation that takes place in the business model shown below in diagram 12, using the ThriveAbility Six Capitals Equation shown below in diagram 13.

True Value calculations are always progressive approximations of what is possible with the current state of the art in an organization given the current state of the art of the six capitals in that organization and its industry. If an organization is an industry leader, then it will most likely possess some form of competitive advantage in one or more of the capitals, and this will show up in the data going into the ThriveAbility Six Capitals Equation.

The pace of innovation in the innovation cycle that surrounds the six capitals equation will be driven by a number of factors, ranging from the minimum permissible speed set by the nearest competitors in the industry, and by the underlying rate of innovation in the supply and demand sides of the organization's value chain and networks.

---

[37] We introduce a new way of thinking about stakeholders and shareholders further on in Diagram 28: "ThriveHolders", that transcends *and* includes these concepts, offering a much more comprehensive definition of what it means to be responsible for generating ThriveAbility. We decided that one new term would be challenging enough for this first page.

**DIAGRAM 12 - How an Organization Delivers Value from a Holistic Perspective**[38]

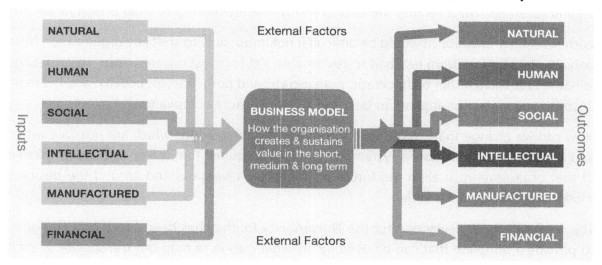

**DIAGRAM 13 – The ThriveAbility Six Capitals Equation**

The smarter, wiser investor will bring their own insights to bear on the role that different forms of financial and intellectual capital can be harnessed in the business model of an organization, so as to leverage the other four capitals in beneficial, thriveable ways. Equally importantly, ways in which the ThriveAbility Six Capitals Equation can be maximised can be explored based on possible changes to the business model itself, subject to the shifts this would necessitate in one or more capitals.

## What Drives the Delta that Shifts the Alpha?

The key question for anyone concerned about ensuring a thriving future for their organization and human civilisation, has to be:

---

[38]  IIRC Positon Paper September 2011

*"What will motivate enough people to change how they think and act sufficiently to shift their organization from the level they are at on the ThriveAbility Journey to what is next for them?"*

Without such motivation, it would be difficult if not impossible to shift any organization from denial to less bad, or from less bad to sustainable. Yet for most organisations, sustainability initiatives remain a rather technocratic, bureaucratic and non-strategic activity, and the main unconscious motivator appears to be avoid risk and ensure compliance.

How can we change that? In order to incentivise the innovations which are possible within and around an organization, a systematic process is required that will enable the leadership of that organization to align the forces for beneficial change in and around the business model and the key stakeholders.

The Six Step Model developed for the ThriveAbility Journey has been specifically designed to provide a template that can be used by an organization to map out the specific steps it will need to take to move effectively through the ThriveAbility Journey.

There are six logical steps[39] involved in driving the ThriveAbility delta, as follows:

1. **ASSESS** – this first step involves assessing the <u>internal drivers for change and transformation in an organization</u>, at multiple levels from individual leaders to teams to larger groupings (units, divisions, categories, regions and so on) and whole supply chains:

   a. **Organizational Stages of Development** - the current stage at which an organization is at on the ThriveAbility Journey. This is done with the help of the ThriveAbility Assessment, which measures 95 indicators based on the collective experience of dozens of sustainability professionals[40]. *(This is known as the "Y" Organization axis in diagram 6 above).*

   b. **Socio-cultural Stages of Development** – the current stage of development of the leadership team and culture in an organization, including Management Style preferences including first order (linear) and second order (transformative) change preferences.
   This includes a survey that looks at the current levels of values of the leading individuals of an organization and provides recommendations as to how to become a thriving individual and create an aligned, thriving leadership team within that organization capable of taking it to the next level in the ThriveAbility Journey. *(This is known as the "X" Socio-cultural axis in diagram 6 above);*

---

[39] Whose pneumonic is "ASATBI".

[40] Initially developed by ThriveAbility Co-Creator Ralph Thurm based on his experience at Siemens, Global Reporting Initiative and Deloitte, and subsequently updated in conjunction with Dr Robin Wood and the ThriveAbility team in 2014.

    c. **Sustainability Stages of Development** - the current stage of development of the metrics used by the organization and it's industry to measure its ecological and social footprints. Organizations must contribute their fair proportionate share to closing the Sustainability Gap between current incremental aspirations and the transformative change needed to respect the boundaries (ecological ceilings and social foundations) needed to achieve true sustainability at the planetary and societal levels.

    Initiatives such as the Future Fit Business Benchmark and the Multi-Capital Scorecard measure organizational operation within their fair share of the floors and ceilings of social and natural capitals. *(This is known as the "Z" Sustainability axis in diagram 6 above)*;

2. **SCAN for Innovation Drivers - Survey of External Drivers of Change and Opportunities for Innovation** – External data sources and surveys from organisations such as Gallup and providers of market research information, help to pinpoint _key external change drivers and opportunities for innovation for the organization_. This would include any new information generated during stage 1 above. This is a multi-stakeholder process in which key organizational stakeholders are involved at some level.

3. **ALIGN - Strategic Alignment – Leadership Development and Innovation Pathways** – this is where the alignment or misalignment between the three key components of the ThriveAbility Assessment- organizational, socio-cultural and sustainability stages of development, come together, and are in turn mapped onto the external change drivers and opportunities. The goal is to identify the key drivers of change that can be successfully aligned inside and around the organization, in such a way that pathways for leadership development and innovation emerge naturally and powerfully in the motivational systems of the leaders in the organization and its key stakeholders.

4. **TRANSFORM** – based on the set of innovation pathways which emerge in stages 2 and 3 above, a robust transformation process that allocates the right mix of talents to the appropriate breakthrough hotspots and guides more incremental/linear and risk-averse talents toward the incremental improvement agenda where they cannot frustrate the intrapreneurially and visionary talents needed for breakthroughs. This is also accompanied by a conscious de-risking process for hotspots based on multi-stakeholder working groups and processes;

5. **BENCHMARK** – sets of complementary organizations within and across industries are then connected for a benchmarking process for the basic ThriveAbility metrics applicable in specific industry groups/clusters. The Sustainable Accounting Standards Board (SASB) approach to industry classification known as "SICS" is used, together with a proprietary list of sector leaders compiled by the ThriveAbility Foundation;

6. **INDEX** – finally, the ThriveAbility Index indexing process begins, once a critical mass of organizations within each sector is attained. Indexing involves a testing and baselining process to gain the acceptance of the thought-leader organizations driving pilot partnerships in each industry, that eventually delivers the ThriveAbility Index components that can become industry standards.

---

**PRACTICAL TOOL – The Process Model for the Six Steps in the ThriveAbility Journey** is used to apply the findings from the ThriveAbility *Assessment* and the strategic *Scan*, to *Align* the organization and its key stakeholders in a way that enables a *Strategic Alignment Outlook* to be generated. This Outlook enables an organization's leaders to design and manage the innovation pathways and organization and leadership development pathways their organization needs to move on to the next stage for it in the ThriveAbility Journey. This organization specific process is completed in Step 4, *Transform*, where the innovations and breakthroughs become reality. Step 5, *Benchmark*, provides reliable comparative metrics for the industry benchmarking process which then leads to Step 6, the *Indexing* stage, where the components of the ThriveAbility Index are piloted in key industry sectors.

---

**DIAGRAM 14 – The Six Steps in the ThriveAbility Journey**

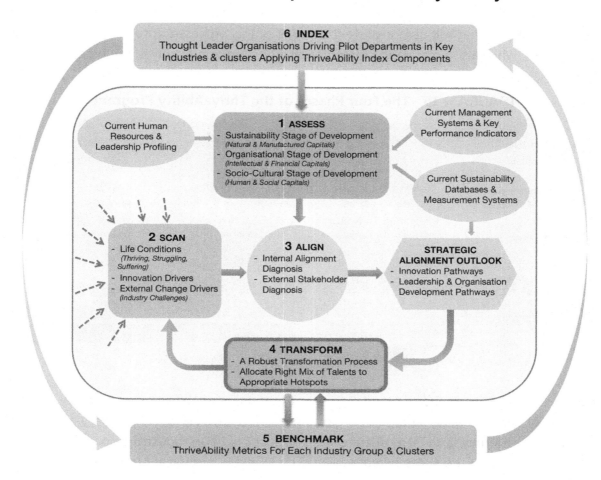

## The Four Phases of the ThriveAbility Program

As you can imagine, the six-step process outlined above is not an overnight phenomenon- in fact, it will likely be a multi-years process for any organization which chooses to embark on such a journey. This is why the Phases of the ThriveAbility program itself, the larger, over-arching program that supports and enables the Six Step process, is phased over a number of years.

*Steps 1 – 4* in this journey begin with **Phase One** of the ThriveAbility program, shown in Diagram 15 below. This is the *ThriveAbility Assessment,* a process which can be applied in any kind of organization anywhere, provided its leadership has a desire to take the next steps on its own journey toward ThriveAbility. In the beginning, this is likely to be confined to the more enlightened leaders who appreciate the benefits such a transformation could bring, but over time we expect that many others will be tempted to begin their own journeys, inspired by the example of leaders in their own industries who have managed to make significant strides in their own organizations.

Once the strategic alignment outlook has been produced through the alignment diagnostics in *Step 3*, the leadership of an organization is then in a position to embark on a transformative process in *Step 4*, that will demonstrate the power of this process to produce breakthrough innovations, while also accelerating incremental innovations currently in the pipeline.

### DIAGRAM 15 - The Four Phases of the ThriveAbility Program

| Phase 1 Enabling | Phase 2 Activation | Phase 3 Indexing | Phase 4 Thriving |
|---|---|---|---|
| ThriveAbility Assessment | Develop Industry Benchmarks  Instigating ThriveAbility Innovation Programs | ThriveAbility Index Measurement & Launch  ThriveAble Industry Assessments & Recommendations | ThriveAbility Index Annual Updates  ThriveAbility Innovation Portfolio Management |

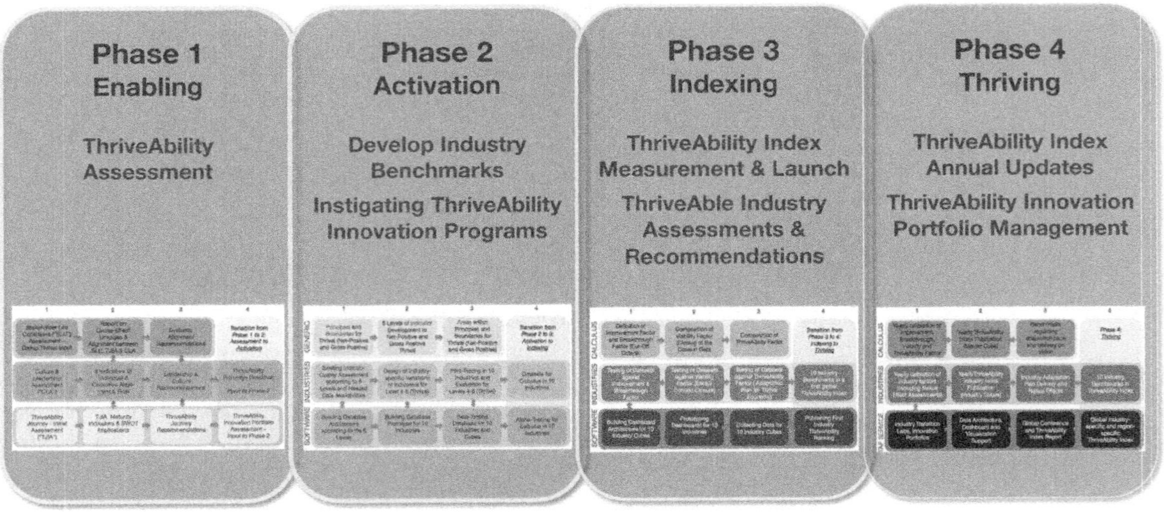

The interface between *Steps 4 and 5* in the six step ThriveAbility process is key, as the purpose of benchmarking a range of organisations who have engaged in *Steps 1 to 4* of the ThriveAbility Journey is to demonstrate what is possible in an industry or part thereof, as well as to celebrate the shifts being achieved by all those organizations who form part of the Benchmarking process.

In **Phase Two** of the ThriveAbility program, this benchmarking process is able to begin in any industry where at least 4 to 6 organizations have been through the ThriveAbility Assessment. *Step 6* of the ThriveAbility Journey starts once a critical mass of organizations has successfully completed the Step 5 Benchmarking process, and this is called **Phase Three** in the ThriveAbility Program- "Indexing".

**Phase Four** of the ThriveAbility program, "Thriving", begins when a critical mass of organizations in all ten industries (using the SASB industry classification) is achieved. The ThriveAbility Index now starts to act as an important signal to investors and markets about where the biggest and best opportunities are for thriveable investment. Perhaps we might even now reach a tipping point, where the current 20% of the market for socially responsible investment rapidly shifts to 80% of the market over a five to ten year period, as the massive gains in investing in thriveable companies and industries becomes apparent to all.

Specific benefits for specific stakeholder groups are built into each phase of the ThriveAbility Program. For example, **Phase 1** aligns and accelerates the key sustainability initiatives in and around an organization, while also aiming to generate one or more breakthroughs that were previously thought to be impossible.

After Step 3 in the ThriveAbility Six Step process, the Strategic Alignment Outlook is key to developing three value propositions that can help put companies on track to deliver a *ThriveAbility Pathways Roadmap* and an initial *ThriveAbility Innovation Portfolio Assessment*:

- **The ThriveAbility Journey Assessment** takes the gist of the three Sustainability, Organizational and Cultural/Leadership axes forward and allows for a first positioning in the cube for the company.
- **The Culture & Leadership Assessment** looks at the current levels of consciousness of the leading individuals of an organization and provides recommendations as to how to become a thriving individual and create an aligned, thriving leadership team within that organization. This also helps the organization deliver its stated positioning and innovation portfolio.
- **The Stakeholder Life Conditions Assessment** contextualizes the company's strategy within the Sustainability thresholds in order to become a thriving organization within thriving business, social and natural ecosystems.

Specific **Phase One benefits,** which would be realized with the production of the *Strategic Alignment Outlook in Step 3* of the ThriveAbility Six Step process, include:

- **Net Positive Potential Diagnosis**- Strategic insights embedded in an open source cloud based collaboration platform about the key learnings from the ThriveAbility Assessment
- **Leadership Team Alignment** Recommendations on how to best align a thriving leadership team with the organization's ThriveAbility Strategy
- **Stakeholder Alignment** of the organization and industry leader partners to go further faster together on the ThriveAbility Journey
- **ThriveAbility Strategy**- North Star Positioning on future sources of competitive advantage, and a set of Innovation Pathways for the organization toward its next step on the ThriveAbility Journey.

The combination of the use of these three tools will help generate the necessary outcomes to prepare an organization for **Phase Two** alignment in the development journey towards the ThriveAbility Index.

**Phase Two** then enables those companies participating in the Program to build industry-specific ThriveAbility Principles, Boundaries and Indicators to benchmark their results with the other partner companies, providing a powerful means to accelerate company and industry breakthroughs. These companies will benefit enormously from insights gained from Phase 1. The ThriveAbility Program incorporates a variety of Stakeholder Alignment Processes, helping organizations and industry leader groups go further faster together.

In the sports industry, for example, Nike and Puma collaborated to reduce their toxic impact and use of leather all the way back to Tier 1 suppliers, even while competing on their brands and products. As the Roadmap to Zero shows, this is just one of many examples of companies collaborating to achieve breakthroughs[41] Enhanced brand recognition with key stakeholder groups such as customers, employees, suppliers and investors can also be measured at this stage.

**Phase Two** helps create the necessary clarity to separate incremental from breakthrough innovations and helps clarify the continuum of various company maturities from denial to less bad to zero-impact based to net-positive to gross-positive - the litmus-test to finally be a thriving organization.

Companies involved will be able to assess their own performance against 6 levels of indicator qualities and will together design industry-specific indicators on mainly levels 4-6 in their industry-specific working groups, supporting companies on their net-positive to gross-positive journey to achieve ThriveAbility. They will be able to test those within their organizations and to provide feedback to their industry working groups. A multi-stakeholder approach will support the discussions. The datasets from the pilot-testing will support the development of **Phase Three calculus** and factor development.

Software partners will be able to assess the process and align through the development of database support. Companies in their different industry-working groups will be able to use those beta-versions and help develop them through to alpha-versions.

Specific **Phase Two benefits** include:

- Typical values + centre of gravity of a thriving leadership team at each stage of development;
- Companies are able to assess their own performance against 6 levels of indicator qualities;
- Companies can together design industry-specific indicators focused on levels 3-6 in their industry-specific working groups;
- The ThriveAbility Program supports companies on their net-positive to gross-positive journey with educational and collaborative opportunities;
- Companies have the possibility to involve Young Leader (Alpha) Teams in the challenge to discuss and develop thrival indicators;
- Software partners are able to assess the process and align their architectures and interfaces through the development of database support protocols;
- Companies in their different industry-working groups are be able to use those beta-versions of software and help develop them through to alpha-versions;
- Enhanced brand recognition with key stakeholder groups such as customers, employees, suppliers and investors can also be measured.

---

[41] http://www.roadmaptozero.com

**In Phase Three** companies share, learn and develop crucial factors that will feed into the ThriveAbility Index:

- The **Improvement Factor** and the **Breakthrough Factor** need proper boundaries. By setting principles and boundaries for zero impact, net positive and gross positive in **Phase Two**, a clear distinction can be applied with regard to the effects of a number of small $\Delta$[42]s vs. various big $\Delta$s. Also the assumptions about the necessary rate of adoption will need to be tested. The generic work stream and the 10 industry work streams will help clarify those boundaries.
- The **Viability Factor** needs to take into account the biosphere carrying capacity (BCC), the global socio-economic footprint (GSEF) and the sustainable technology intensity (STI). The latter will need to be discussed in the 10 industry work streams, and possible nexus phenomena and effects will need to be distilled. BCC and GSEF will need to be built from research and external data. Individual company factors and corridors for transformation can then be developed.

Specific **Phase Three benefits** include:

- Open source ThriveAbility process that can scale in organizations;
- The ThriveAbility Index can be developed for individual companies, industries, and regions
- Implications for political agenda setting, company-specific and aligned strategies and programmatic roadmaps can be developed as a result;
- The Young Leaders (Alpha) Teams in partner companies can support these developments through continued multi-stakeholder collaboration;
- Investors will start recognizing the leaders and start to put their money where the leaders are and divest out of the laggards, which has positive impacts on the share prices and valuations of the leaders.

**Phase Four** demonstrates to the corporate and foundation contributors to the ThriveAbility program how the ThriveAbility Foundation becomes a self-sustaining organization from 2019 onwards. With the existing and published ThriveAbility Index – the flagship product – of the foundation, we anticipate that a whole set of outcomes will be available and managed by us, amongst them:

- Flagship research for the development of the ThriveAbility Index in 10 industries based on the SICS classification
- Benchmark studies on industry breakthrough potentials and development roadmaps on how to get there
- Continuation of collaborative transition through Transition Labs and innovation portfolios

---

[42] The Greek symbol for "Deltas" is used here to represent discrete, measurable units of change in an organization.

- Continued development of market-based software solutions to build a new landscape of necessary platforms and apps.

Specific **Phase Four benefits** of the ThriveAbility Program include:

- Benchmark studies about industry breakthrough potentials and development roadmaps on how to get there;
- Continuation of collaborative transition through Transition Labs and innovation portfolios;
- Continued development of market-based software solutions that build a new landscape of necessary tooling;
- Educational curricula will be developed for universities, business schools and can be translated into multi-stakeholder formats with beneficial social impacts;
- A yearly Global ThriveAbility Conference that can deliver on transition action agreements;
- A new economic system paradigm, based on the enlightened wisdom that ThriveAbility leaders will advocate for;
- Build a win-win-win set of outcomes for all stakeholders.

This is clearly a major initiative, whose success will depend not only on the calibre of the organizations that participate in the ThriveAbility program, but also the degree to which the ThriveAbility Ecosystem can align within itself and also with the sustainability, CSR and reporting ecosystems within it operates.

To succeed, we will need a critical mass of thought leaders and practitioners to begin the ThriveAbility Journey with us, and we hope that if you have got this far in this book, your staying power already begins to recommend you as a budding ThriveAbility Leader. Thank you for staying the course!

In the next few chapters, we are going to explore the Intangible "Measures that Matter", that drive approximately 80% of corporate valuations in the 21st century knowledge economy. In particular, we will look at how human and social capital are pivotal in generating intellectual capital that drives the transformation processes of natural and manufactured capitals, ultimately resulting in superior returns on financial capital. Essentially, this is about how leadership & culture multiply true value through innovation & transformation.

To get to the heart of how this happens and motivates people to "reach for the stars", we need to get to grips with the deeper implications of Action Logics and value systems in leadership, organizational culture and the innovation process.

**To Sum Up**

*If we are to reinvent Capitalism, we need to reinvent capital and the organizations that generate and use the six capitals.*

In order to reinvent capital, we need to transcend and include true costing (including externalities), *true pricing* (relying on markets alone to price ThriveAbility), to *True Value*.[43] We also need to better define and develop *integrated thinking and reporting* in this process.

*True Value* is calculated using the six capitals in the <u>ThriveAbility Six Capital Equation</u>, where we maximise the thriving of human and social capital for the minimum footprint of natural and manufactured capital, through the power of intellectual and financial capital, driven by an accelerated innovation cycle.

There are three pathways toward embodying thriveable capital and investing in current institutions and practices in order to reinvent capital for a thriving future:

- **Making Capital Smarter, Wiser** and Capable of Complex Systems Thinking
- **Shifting the Values and Perspectives** that Prioritize the Incentives for Investing
- **Applying the ThriveAbility Approach and Index** to accelerate the transformations and innovations that drive ThriveAble investments.

The <u>ThriveAbility Approach</u> seeks to close the *sustainability gap* by closing the *organizational gap* that, in turn, requires closure of the *cultural and leadership gap* in organizations.

The <u>ThriveAbility Journey</u> maps the *five stages* from compliance through "less bad" through sustainable, net positive and thriveable, enabling organizations to navigate their transitions from one stage to the next more effectively.

The <u>ThriveAbility Approach and Index</u> have been designed so as to not only build on existing sustainability efforts and metrics, but also to address the *human and organizational factors* that bedevil most initiatives that seek to move beyond merely incremental change. In this way we seek to enhance the existing strengths we have in *innovation, design, transformation, leadership, strategy and psychology* to ensure a thriving future for us all.

We turn now to the human drivers of thriving and breakthrough to better understand how this is all integrated into the strategy and operations of an organization.

---

[43]  It would also be nice to be able to rely on true taxation and level playing fields for everything from renewable energy to resilient cities and habitats, but we are slightly cynical about the role of governments, given their poor performance to date.

# 4. The Drivers of True Future Value

*"The business world must become a powerful driver of human, social,
and planetary well-being. Terms like "holistic well-being" may seem
unconnected with financial well-being or corporate well-being, but they
are powerfully linked – <u>and will become even more so over time"</u>.
John Elkington and Jochen Zeitz – The Breakthrough Challenge*

<u>*Sustainability is as much a problem of changing our mental models as it is a problem of dealing with the flows of materials, energy and resources effectively and sustainably.*</u> ThriveAbility is in part a response to the failure of sustainability to address this critical psychological challenge, and to fully appreciate and measure the human and social capitals that lie at the heart of all innovation and progress.

The ability to design in and calibrate incentives in organizational and industry contexts is central to ThriveAbility- not only is the human being missing from sustainability, the "Why I should care/Why this matters" motivation is either missing completely or unconsciously assuming the same mental model as those advocating the change, versus meeting stakeholders and leaders where they are at, and helping them define the challenges in terms of what is logically next for them in their own development.

In addition, the ThriveAbility Six Capitals equation defines:

* **Specific Incentives** for each capital shift required, linked to/motivated by an accompanying *values profile* for those needing to make that shift happen. This is what we call the strategic alignment between the innovation pathways and the leadership capabilities needed to drive those innovations/breakthroughs between steps 3 and 4 of the Six Step ThriveAbility process.
* **The Productive Relationship** between the six capitals expressed as a function in which *human and social capital,* divided by *natural and manufactured capital,* is maximized through the innovative application of *financial and intellectual capitals*. This mirrors the objective of ThriveAbility to maximize human thriving for the lowest footprint possible through deliverable innovation pathways.

What drives the evolution of human beings is the interplay between the growth and development of individuals, and their environment. Historically our environment dictated our life conditions, and it is only relatively recently (in the past few millennia), that we have been able to modify our environment to any significant extent. Scientists and historians are sufficiently impressed by our 21st century environment modifying abilities to name the geological age we are in the "Anthropocene"[44].

We do indeed live in an extraordinary age, where all of the world's knowledge and cultures, are available to each of us. For the past few hundred thousand years a person was born into a culture that knew only of its own existence. For example, someone born in Africa, was raised as an African, married an African, and followed an African religion—often living in the same hut for their entire life, on a spot of land that their ancestors settled millennia ago.

We have evolved out of Africa from isolated hunter-gatherer bands like the Bushmen, to the tribal settlements and farms of the Xhosa, to the ancient nations of Africa, to the conquering feudal empires of the Zulus and other warring tribes. In the past five hundred years we have also witnessed the emergence of international corporate states such as the Dutch East India Company to modern multinationals such as Unilever, and the other inhabitants of the global village including the United Nations and hundreds of thousands of NGO's and charities. We are now witnessing the next stage in our evolution toward an integral global village that seems to be humanity's destiny if we can learn to thrive without costing the earth.

What has emerged globally over the past five centuries is a system of world trade between nation states dominated by markets, businesses and governments, with technological progress at the centre of the whole system. Ideally, this system lets the individual decide how they want to live, what they want to do to make a living, and provides them with the resources to get on and do just that. In such a system we make our progress in the world on the basis of our merit, and our ability to apply technology to add value or be of service to others. In other words, a technocratic meritocracy, on a good day, where each person has the freedom of choice to create their own life in their own way, believing whatever it is they wish to believe.

In the 21st century we are living in a time where most of the developed world has embraced a form of capitalism, ranging from the egalitarian social democracies of northern Europe to the semi-feudal dictatorships found in many developing economies. Capitalism is a decidedly non-Utopian system, which at its roots focuses primarily on economic growth and material wellbeing. Markets have no ethics or morals- only people do, and they differ widely in what they believe to be right and wrong.

Until the 20th century and the rise of psychology in the popular consciousness, no overarching model existed that could explain how it was that so many people could believe they alone

---

[44] Many scientists are now using the term and the Geological Society of America titled its 2011 annual meeting: Archean to Anthropocene: The past is the key to the future. The Anthropocene has no precise start date, but based on atmospheric evidence may be considered to start with the Industrial Revolution (late 18th century). Other scientists link it to earlier events, such as the rise of agriculture. Evidence of relative human impact such as the growing human influence on land use, ecosystems, biodiversity and species extinction is controversial, some scientists believe the human impact has significantly changed (or halted) the growth of biodiversity

were right, and that everyone else was wrong. The 20th century itself was characterized by clashing ideologies from capitalism to communism, from militaristic fascists to peace-loving hippies, and hundreds of millions of people died untimely deaths in the name of those ideologies. During the 21st century we have an opportunity to transcend these polar opposites, to move toward the syntheses of the clashing theses and antitheses so beloved of mankind. But how so?

## The Three Foci of Integrated Thinking – Inner, Other, Outer

There are new kinds of understanding which are becoming increasingly available to those who care about creating a flourishing world in the 21st century, rather than heading down into an apocalypse. For example, renowned psychologist Daniel Goleman delves into the science of attention in all its varieties in *Focus*[45].

In an era of unstoppable distractions, Goleman argues that now more than ever we must learn to sharpen focus if we are to survive in a complex world. He boils down attention research into a threesome: inner, other, and outer focus. Drawing on rich case studies from fields as diverse as competitive sports, education, the arts, and business, he shows why high-achievers need all three kinds of focus, and explains how those who rely on Smart Practices—mindfulness meditation, focused preparation and recovery, positive emotions and connections, and mental "prosthetics" that help them improve habits, add new skills, and sustain greatness—excel while others do not.

"Inner" focus refers to self-awareness and self-management: how well we can tune in to our guiding values, for instance, or know our strengths and limits – which in turn gives us a realistic sense of self-confidence—and also handle our distressing emotions so they don't interfere with getting things done, marshal our positive emotions to stay motivated in working toward our goals, and bounce back from setbacks.

"Other" focus describes how well we attune to people: our empathy, which allows us to understand how people perceive things, how they feel, and what we can do to help them be at their best. And tuning in to others this way provides the basis for skill in competencies like motivating employees, persuasion and influence, negotiation and conflict resolution, and — increasingly important – teamwork and collaboration.

Empathy[46] is a form of paying attention to others that enables us to connect with others no matter whom they are or where they come from. This empathic intelligence is now being

---

[45]   Daniel Goleman, Focus: The Hidden Driver of Excellence, Bloomsbury 2013.

[46]   For an overview of the literature on empathy see: Simon Baron-Cohen (2003): Empathy is about spontaneously and naturally tuning into the other person's thoughts and feelings, whatever these might be. There are two major elements to empathy. The first is the cognitive component: Understanding the others feelings and the ability to take their perspective ... the second element to empathy is the affective component. This is an observer's appropriate emotional response to another person's emotional state. The Essential Difference: The Truth about the Male and Female Brain, Basic Books (July 1, 2003)

cultivated from a very young age in major cities and places where the full diversity of mankind is coming together from nursery school through university and beyond into the workplace.

Such intelligent empathy is based both on a much more comprehensive awareness of the breadth and depth of the human experience around the planet, as well as direct experience of people from other cultures and races. At its best, this empathic intelligence also extends to nature and other species, though that is sometimes a real challenge for the increasingly urbanized populations of the world, whose experience of nature in the wild is increasingly limited.

"Outer" focus has to do with how well we can sense the large forces that shape our world – whether organizational dynamics, like whose opinion matters most for a decision, or economic forces such as how a new technology will roil a market, or environmental trends like the new value placed on lower-carbon processes. Outer awareness allows a leader, for example, to formulate a winning strategy that anticipates what's coming.

Integrated thinkers will view challenges from all three perspectives - inner, other and outer, or what integral thinking calls first, second and third person perspectives. We will see the importance of this as we examine how leadership evolves through different stages of development, and how the dynamics of "outside-in" and "inside-out" change operate in this process.

## Integrated Thinking and Leadership – Starting with Minds and Mindsets

In the field of sustainability, much hope is pinned on a mythical beast called "Integrated Reporting". The assumption is that if companies could only produce Integrated Reports, this would somehow help them think and act in a more integrated fashion, and therefore make better, more sustainable decisions. The logic in this chain of reasoning is exactly the wrong way around.

The pre-conditions for Integrated Thinking and Action (what we might call Strategic Vision and Leadership), begin in the deep, dark recesses of the human mind and value systems, in areas we only began mapping in the past century. There are several threads to this story:

- Industrial civilization has embedded _specialisation_ as its core strategy for progressing knowledge and innovation, leading to the "stovepipes" or functional hierarchies so characteristic of our large organizations;
- Experts and professionals (i.e. "specialists") come to dominate the management hierarchy as a result. In order to advance, they learn something called "Strategic Management" which (if one is lucky), helps them develop the capability to (as management guru Peter Drucker put it): "Get into their strategic psychological helicopter and transcend the problem";

- The ability to think strategically while accessing and integrating specialist knowledge is limited to less than half of senior managers/executives broadly speaking[47]- what are known as "Achievers", a classic CEO profile type;

- Yet this ability to integrate internal functions and knowledge does not mean that such Achiever executives have the ability to think strategically from an "outside-in" perspective- they are therefore focused on pushing "inside-out" strategies that may be maladaptive for the organization in complex, dynamic marketplaces. This requires a combination of "Individualist" and "Strategist" capabilities which are much more rare;

- Hence we rarely find the kind of integrated thinking required for integrated decision making that is either pro-active or adaptive, which goes a long way to explaining why we are in the mega-mess we are in right now, and why there are so few examples of truly transformative sustainable innovation initiatives (as exemplified by the 50 "ThriveAbility Leaders" in the next chapter).

To expect Integrated Reporting, let alone Integrated Thinking in such conditions is equivalent to praying for a miracle - comforting, but not terribly effective. This is why we need to put in place a systemic approach to the integration of such specialist knowledge, driven by complex systems thinking capabilities, at all levels in organizations. This is what lies behind the logic of the ThriveAbility Approach, and in particular, the ThriveAbility Six Capitals Equation.

## The Significance of the ThriveAbility Six Capitals Equation

The ThriveAbility Six Capitals Equation integrates the following key logical threads:

1. The need to focus on the maximization of the thriving of *human and social capital*;
2. For the smallest possible footprint in terms of *natural and manufactured capital*;
3. Through an accelerated innovation cycle driven by the harnessing of *intellectual and financial capital*;

---

[47] See Rooke and Torbert's 2006 Harvard Business Review article - What meaning-making capacities are necessary to enable managers to succeed at implementing change? It is my proposition that sufficient managers must have post-conventional meaning-making capacity (in Leadership Development Framework terms, Individualist and later). Research by Torbert in the US and by The Harthill Group in the UK has shown that the key stages for managers are:

| Torbert – USA (497 Managers) | Harthill Group – Europe (490 Managers & Consultants) |
| --- | --- |
| • Opportunist / Diplomat 11% | Opportunist / Diplomat 2.5% |
| • Expert 34% | Expert 21% |
| • Achiever 46% | Achiever 33% |
| • Individualist 5% | Individualist 23% |
| • Strategist 3.5% | Strategist 13.5% |
| • Magician <0.5% | Magician 7% |

The European sample includes mostly people engaged in developmental activities and undoubtedly contains more late stage profiles than compared with samples of Managers not engaged in developmental activities.

4. Making appropriate adjustments to the *different kinds of incentives* needed to motivate those responsible for taking strategic decisions;

5. Based on both the different kinds of incentives appropriate to each form of capital, as well as the different kinds of incentives appropriate to *each developmental level of the key stakeholders represented in the decision-making process*.

The key question arising from all of this is to what extent can the accelerated innovation cycles required to drive the breakthroughs we need, become a regular feature of the corporate landscape, rather than the rare exception?

**DIAGRAM 16 – The ThriveAbility Six Capitals Equation**

Intangibles

Tangibles

To begin to answer this question, we need to consider both the individual minds of those leading the innovation process, as well as the organisational context in which innovations occur. Innovation is probably one of the most studied yet least understood processes in the world. There are many reasons for this, which we will decode one by one. The first is that most models of innovation attempt to propose a universal, "one size fits all" model of innovation. The model we recommend in the ThriveAbility program is a hybrid of several underlying innovation models, as in our experience there are several levels and kinds of innovation which each need to be treated in different ways to be fully understood and successfully applied.

### How Leadership & Culture Multiply True Value through Innovation & Transformation

In 1997, Big 4 accounting firm Ernst and Young began research on how one might measure the value of intangibles in corporate balance sheets. At that time, 40% of the value of industrial corporations was intangible, and 50% of "hi-tech" corporations was intangible. The introduction to the E&Y report confirmed that intelligent corporate leaders seeking to meet the challenges of the future realize there is a *dangerous disconnect between the bottom line and long-term goals*. Sharing knowledge, wooing customers, and honing products that will reinvent their industries represent investments for the long-term — usually at odds with short-term financial reporting practices.

At the heart of this new thinking is a growing body of evidence revealing that reliance on financial measures alone will critically undermine the strategies leading edge companies must pursue to survive and thrive long term. Baruch Lev, professor of Accounting and Finance at New York University's Stern School of Business, argues that to say that tangible assets should be measured and valued, while intangibles should not — or could not — is like stating that 'things' are valuable, while 'ideas' are not.

The top 5 non-financial metrics investors valued most were:

1. Strategy Execution
2. Management Credibility
3. Quality of Strategy
4. Innovativeness
5. Ability to Attract Talented People

(Full Disclosure - I was privileged to see the "Measures that Matter" report presented by Tony Siesfeld in London while it was still hot off the press, shortly after joining E&Y in 1997 to co-found their business strategy group. I am amazed that this report was not followed up by further research efforts, given the magnitude of its implications for investors and corporate leadership).

In the 21st-century economy, traditional methods of business reporting simply do not reflect the full value of a company. In a 2010 report, the International Integrated Reporting Council (IIRC) explained that a growing share of companies' market value can be attributed to "intangible factors," rather than traditional assets, such as cash, securities and real estate.

The rise of extra-financial factors has been quite rapid. IIRC[48] asserted that, in 1975, more than 80 per cent of a company's value was linked to its physical and financial assets. By 2010, this figure had fallen to less than 20 per cent, with "intangible" assets and ESG ("Environmental, Social and Governance") factors playing an increasingly central role in driving market value.

Mainstream investors are increasingly aware that there are now numerous extra-financial factors that directly affect a company's performance. This fact is reflected by the growing number of major asset management firms that use ESG analytics to evaluate the unique risk profiles associated with different investment options.

For instance, in 2012, Mercer announced that it would begin to include ESG ratings in client reports by the end of the year.[49] In a press release discussing the rationale behind the company's decision, Mercer's Global Chief Investment Officer referred to ESG factors

---

[48]  http://www.theiirc.org/2010/08/02/formation-of-the-international-integrated-reporting-committee-iirc/

[49]  http://www.socialfunds.com/news/article.cgi?sfArticleId=3603

as increasingly important "risk-return drivers," and said that making use of pertinent extra-financial research would "result in better overall outcomes" for the firm and its clients.

McKinsey[50] expanded on this idea with a report discussing the link between growing global consumption of key resources and the need for companies to become more sustainable in order to remain competitive. The firm's analysts framed the issue of sustainability as a practical component of business planning, rather than an ethical consideration.

A pair of studies conducted by researchers at the University of California lend further support to this notion. Teams led by Professor Paul Griffin[51] looked at the link between corporations' disclosure of sustainability related information and changes in the value of their stock. On average, firms making pertinent disclosures experienced a 0.5 per cent increase in share value following a disclosure. As a whole, the sample group received an aggregate value increase of approximately $10 billion.

Leonard Nakamura[52] of the Federal Reserve Bank of Philadelphia provided three different measures of the magnitude of intangible assets in today's economy – an accounting estimate of the value of the investments in R&D, software, brand development and other intangibles; the wages and salaries paid to the researchers, technicians and other creative workers who generate these intangible assets; and the improvement in operating margins that he attributes to improvements to intangible factors. With all three approaches, he estimated the investments in intangible assets to be in excess of $ 1 trillion in 2000 and the capitalized value of these intangible assets to be in excess of $ 6 trillion in the same year.

So, if 80% of the value of the 21st century publicly quoted corporation is intangible, and the quality of the leadership team, strategy, innovativeness and governance (including ESG criteria) are now central to that 80% of the valuation of an organization's worth, where is the data in the reporting from corporations? The efforts of the GRI and IIRC toward Integrated Reporting have made substantial progress in the past decade, but the lack of integrated thinking and leadership appear to be the biggest stumbling blocks to generating integrated corporate reports that actually tell investors anything substantial.

Even more importantly, given that most of the reported data is at least 18 months old, how does the data on quality of the leadership team, strategy, innovativeness and governance (including ESG criteria), show up in the management reporting on a daily/weekly/monthly basis?

The ThriveAbility Six Capitals Equation ("TASCE") is a starting point to address this massive gap between what we know we should know, and what we actually know from corporate

---

[50] http://www.mckinsey.com/insights/strategy/
beyond_corporate_social_responsibility_integrated_external_engagement

[51] http://gsm.ucdavis.edu/carousel/stock-values-rise-when-companies-disclose-green-information

[52] http://www.philadelphiafed.org/research-and-data/publications/working-papers/2009/wp09-11.pdf

reports today. The TASCE should also ultimately become a standard feature in management reporting too. In fact this will be a central requirement of the ThriveAbility Index.

Given that the TASCE focuses on maximising human and social/relationship capital for the lowest unit of footprint of natural and manufactured capital, accelerated by an innovation process driven by intellectual and financial capital, we can now see the critical importance of leadership, governance, strategy, "sustainability" and innovation. ThriveAbility is the central concept that enables such an integration to be calculated with data, for the very first time.

The ThriveAbility Index will enable corporate stakeholders, investors and markets to use the TASCE to make better decisions about engaging with or investing in a firm, with a great deal less effort than is currently required to gather and make any sense of the voluminous quantities of data needed for a good-enough decision.

Let us revisit those five qualities that investors valued most in 1997:

"The top 5 non-financial metrics investors valued most were:

1. Strategy Execution
2. Management Credibility
3. Quality of Strategy
4. Innovativeness
5. Ability to Attract Talented People"

While today we would definitely need to add governance and "sustainability" (the "E" and "S" "environment" and "social" in ESG) to this list, the troika of leadership, strategy and innovativeness still remain at the core of what it will take to create ThriveAble organizations in a thriving world.

The 21$^{st}$ century list of "intangible" qualities valued by investors, (summed up, as one word, "ThriveAble"), would then be something like:

1. Quality of Leadership and Governance
2. Quality of Strategy and its Execution
3. Innovativeness and Design
4. Sustainability and Resilience
5. Ability to Attract Talented People.

Items 1 and 5 speak to *maximizing Human and Social/Relationship Capitals* (the numerator in the TASCE), while Item 4 speaks to *minimizing the Footprint of Natural and Manufactured Capitals*, (the denominator in the TASCE). Items 2 and 3 speak to the ability of an organization to adapt to and shape its world, which in turn generates both *intellectual and financial capital.*

*If the quality of leadership and governance in an organization and its ability to attract and retain talented people are one of the keys to maximizing human and social capitals, how can one incentivize the leaders of an organization to focus on thriving for their key stakeholders?*

We would have to know what "thriving" meant to each of those key stakeholder groups, as well as to the leaders of the organization and its management teams and people, to establish which incentives would be appropriate for whom and where/when.

*If the quality of strategy and its execution, along with the innovativeness and design capabilities of an organization are key to enabling it to adapt to and shape its world for the better, what incentives will help drive the quality of strategy and innovation upwards so as to be not merely sustainable, but ThriveAble?*

We would have to know what "strategy" and "innovation" meant to the leaders and stakeholders of an organization, to establish which incentives would be appropriate for whom and where/when.

Where would one start?

Let us begin with the individual minds and the levels at which they approach innovation. As we will explain, the first six levels of human development approach life, leadership, strategy and innovation in very different ways to the next three levels, which is known as the difference between "first" and "second" tier levels of development. But first, a little background on the psychological underpinnings for our assertions.

## The Role of Different Kinds of Minds in Leadership and Innovation

Psychology makes it clear that psychological and cultural development follows a pattern, and that pattern is always from more partial to more whole[53]. In the 21st century not only can we expect a continuation of this arc of development: we can also expect a great leap forward in human civilization, as we move through the conventional stages of development (the six "first-tier" systems mentioned above) to a new phase in human history characterized by empathic, integrated ways of being and doing that are global in perspective (the "second-tier" approaches mentioned above). Second-tier minds are essentially capable of integrated, complex and systemic thinking about global systems. First tier minds struggle to deal with such longer time-scales and larger-scale systems, finding it easier to be concrete and specific about their own more regional or local interests.

Right now we are caught in a life and death struggle between the relatively new second-tier consciousness, culture and systems that are emerging and the old first-tier ways of

---

[53] Since research began in the mid-20th century eminent scholars and psychologists have independently discovered similar stages of human psychological development. Building on the shoulders of giants such as Freud, Piaget, Kohlberg, Graves and Maslow, the latest research by Kegan, Loevinger, Wade, Beck and Cowan confirms the five to seven developmental levels in the original models while extending these models with a further two to three levels.

"business as usual" which is fighting what is emerging with great cunning, deception and massive amounts of money when the more global priorities conflict with their own narrowly defined interests. The current global crisis offers major business opportunities ranging from developing and maintaining low-carbon, zero-waste cities, to improving and managing bio-capacity, ecosystems, lifestyles and livelihoods. In today's dollars, the market opportunities created by adapting to the new global reality for sustainable living are somewhere between $3-$10 trillion USD per year in 2050.

If we are to realise these multi trillion dollar opportunities and ambitious programs such as the World Business Council for Sustainable Development's Vision 2050 and Action 2020 programs, we are going to have to harness the most profound motivation of our people. To do so we need to understand how Personal Action Logics & Collective Value Systems drive decisions, with particular reference to sustainability and ThriveAbility. What would get the people who lead our organizations and nations to powerfully commit to ThriveAbility? What would their dominant action logic need to be? And how can we translate "what's in it for them" for those whose action logics are firmly lodged in first-tier thinking?

All around us we can see that this great shift is a monumental struggle, not only between old and new ways of thinking and doing, but also between the "haves" and "have not's" in the old system and the new forms of wealth being created, and between those who have power in the old systems and those to whom power is shifting as the new systems gradually take hold. Yet evolution is an unstoppable force, and it has a clear direction, which in the case of human development, is "UP", even while the reactionaries are furiously stabbing at the down button in the elevator.

Psychology focuses on understanding our individual and collective interiors, starting with how our thoughts, feelings, motives, intentions and impulses translate into our behaviour. Such an understanding of ourselves provides us with a better understanding and appreciation of both the nature and motivations of others, as well as insights into our own nature and development.

There are a few hundred different versions of Psychology, each with its own particular vocabulary and biases. What is remarkable, however, is the extent to which all of these developmental models settle on _eight or so levels of human development_, irrespective of their origins. Our ability to see these different levels of development in our own personal history, and ourselves, provides us with a greater capacity to relate to and empathize with the place others are at, and where they are coming from.

We can then learn to appreciate not only where people have come from and where they are today, but also _what might be next_ for them in their own development and life journey. Of course, as with any science, we have to be careful that we do not use our knowledge to manipulate people or situations for our own ends in unethical ways, although this is probably inevitable with most human beings who would like to see one set of outcomes preferred over another. Even if you cannot use this knowledge completely objectively, one is honour bound to at least use it for the highest possible good for as many people as possible.

In the second tier, transpersonal phases of development, the pre-frontal and frontal cortices become new control centres[54] which enable individuals to activate their "strategic psychological helicopter", from which they are capable of getting an overview of the situation they are in and in which they are capable of being mindful and taking better decisions that benefit the greatest span of human beings while honouring the greatest depth in those individuals.

The ThriveAbility Program has been designed to work with leaders who are exiting first-tier thinking and entering second-tier modes of thinking and innovation, with the ability to deal with the truly "wicked", complex problems that arise when we get into the fields of sustainability, innovation, and thriving. Here we need to leave behind the "silver-bullet", one-size-fits-all solutions of first-tier thinking, and prepare for a momentous leap in our capability to navigate exceptional levels of complexity and uncertainty. At the same time, we have to also be able to motivate our colleagues and friends who still have a need for simplicity, and find the right approach and set of incentives for each of them.

## The Dominant Action Logics of Corporate Leadership

*"What most people want is not knowledge, but certainty"*
*Lord Bertrand Russell*

Most developmental psychologists agree that what differentiates leaders is not so much their philosophy of leadership, their personality, or their style of management. Rather, it's their internal "action logic"— how they interpret their surroundings and react when their power or safety is challenged. Relatively few leaders, however, try to understand their own action logic, and fewer still have explored the possibility of changing it. Leading researchers have found that leaders who do undertake a voyage of personal understanding and development can transform not only their own capabilities but also those of their companies.

The leadership model we apply in ThriveAbility is a synthesis of what the co-creators of the ThriveAbility Program have found to work in practice in large change programs in both public and private sector organizations and large public systems (national healthcare and education systems, for example), over the past two decades. This synthesis has three important components, each of which offers a unique insight into the logic of change and transformation in large-scale human systems:

- The *"Action Logic of Leaders"* work of Rooke and Torbert applying the research of psychologist Susanne Cook-Greuter[55] and others into how leaders evolve in a corporate setting;

---

[54]   The cognitive science behind this is dealt with in more detail in Appendix A.
[55]   http://www.cook-greuter.com/

- The *"Integral Psychology"* work of philosopher Ken Wilber, who synthesises some 400 different psychological approaches into his frameworks of human development. Wilber's analysis of adult human development is certainly the most profound of all the researchers, though it does require a great deal of study to fully appreciate the powerful logic of his frameworks[56];
- The *"Spiral Dynamics"* work of Professor Don Beck and Dr Christopher Cowan, whose pragmatic application of the research conducted by Professor Clare Graves into adult human development between 1950 and 1980 at Union College, New York, offers many practical examples of the way change and transformation can be better managed using such developmental approaches.

Let us start with the work on the *Action Logic of Leaders.* In their close collaboration with psychologist Susanne Cook-Greuter — and their 25 years of extensive survey-based consulting at companies such as Deutsche Bank, Harvard Pilgrim Health Care, Hewlett-Packard, NSA, Trillium Asset Management, Aviva, and Volvo — researchers Rooke and Torbert worked with thousands of executives as they've tried to develop their leadership skills. The good news is that leaders who make an effort to understand their own action logic can improve their ability to lead. But to do that, it's important first to understand what kind of leader you already are.

Rooke and Torbert's 2006 Harvard Business Review[57] article tells us that Experts and Achievers predominate in leadership positions in developed nations both in private enterprise and government. They tend to lead diplomats and opportunists lower down in the organisation. Individualists and Strategists already occupy leadership positions in large-scale systems with longer time horizons, and are emerging as the next wave of leadership for the future, offering great potential for ThriveAbility Leadership.

Different leaders exhibit different kinds of action logic—ways in which they interpret their surroundings and react when their power or safety is challenged. In their research of thousands of leaders, they observed seven types of action logics. The least effective for organizational leadership are the Opportunist and Diplomat; the most effective, the Strategist and Alchemist. Knowing your own action logic can be the first step toward developing a more effective leadership style. If you recognize yourself as an Individualist, for example, you can work, through both formal and informal measures, to develop the strengths and characteristics of a Strategist.

The most remarkable — and encouraging — finding from the research of Rooke and Torbert is that leaders can transform from one action logic to another. They have documented a number of leaders who have succeeded in transforming themselves from Experts into Achievers, from Achievers into Individualists, and from Individualists into Strategists. Finally, Alchemists capable of large system and society wide transformation are now emerging in

---

56    http://www.paulhelfrich.com/library/Helfrich_P_The_Five_Phases_of_Wilber.pdf

57    Rooke and Torbert, Seven Transformations of Leadership, Harvard Business Review 2006

greater numbers and will be critical to shifting us into ThriveAbility. Given that the kinds of leaders we have in our organisations tend to shape the organisations and societies they lead, it should come as no surprise that the dominant social logic in the developed world shares most of the characteristics of the Experts and Achievers who lead those organisations and nations.

**DIAGRAM 17  Stages of Development – The Dominant Action Logics of Corporate Leadership**

The leader's voyage of development is not an easy one. Some people change little in their lifetimes; some change substantially. Despite the undeniably crucial role of genetics, human nature is not fixed. Those who are willing to work at developing themselves and becoming more self-aware can almost certainly evolve over time into transformational leaders. Few may become Alchemists, but many will have the desire and potential to become Individualists and Strategists. Corporations that help their executives and leadership teams examine their action logics can reap rich rewards.

*Integral Psychology* frameworks & diagnostics are also key enablers to create the maps and pathways for the personal and organisational shifts required for ThriveAbility. Such tools help scan leadership and organisational value systems using models of organisational alignment to identify the pathways of change and transformation that are possible in specific organisations and business ecosystems. The ThriveAbility synthesis of both Integral Psychology and *Spiral Dynamics* combines the depth of Wilber's analyses with the pragmatic applications of Beck and Cowan in the field.

We have reserved the more complex, advanced aspects of integral psychology for Appendix C, though we will be applying some of the practical implications of the all-quadrants, all-levels, all-lines, all-states thinking in the main section of the Leader's Guide to ThriveAbility. You will also notice that we have used the "colour coding" of Spiral Dynamics for certain of our models, and the "colour coding" of Integral Psychology for others, based on whichever is the most useful in that context. The number of levels does not change (six levels in first tier systems, and three levels in second-tier systems), so you should be able to navigate these colour changes with relative ease.

Spiral Dynamics is named after the *Spiral of human development*, where each step up the spiral is an alternation from a more individualistic/expressive mode to a more communal/sacrificial pole. At each level, this fundamental dichotomy finds a more complex and sophisticated expression, but the alternation is consistent. The problems inherent in each worldview are partially resolved with a swing back to the other pole (the swing from the entrepreneurial spirit of ORANGE to communitarian GREEN resolves some of the destructive imbalances of excessive consumerism, for example). You will notice that we have applied these Spiral Dynamics colours to the Action Logic levels in Diagram 17 above, to illustrate the alternation between "warm" expressive/individualistic systems (red, orange, yellow and coral), and "cool" communally oriented/collective systems (blue, green and turquoise)[58].

The Spiral Dynamics value systems[59] can be thought of as broad orienting paradigms, a schema through which we interpret the world. These value systems fall into a series of eight levels, with the potential for higher ones emerging as we speak. Each level also has entering, peak, and declining phases. They avoid the most common pitfall of stage models by introducing a great deal of fluidity. First, situational factors encourage different value systems to "light up." We might rely upon one value system in the religious domain and another in intimate relationships. In times of intensive stress, previously submerged value systems often re-emerge.

Beck and Cowan argue that the healthy expression of each value system is essential to the health of the entire spiral of development. In this way, they allow for the kind of structural analysis that is so useful from stage models without the rigid (and alienating) process of just assigning people to boxes, stages, or roles. We can be encouraged or assisted to use more complex and evolved paradigms, but the goal of what they call "the spiral wizard" is to

---

58  For those sticklers for detail who will have noticed we talked about six first tier systems and three second tier systems, please note that for the purposes of leadership in large, modern organizations the "beige" and "purple" systems have been omitted from the Action Logics as they are rarely found in such contexts.

59  Or "V-Memes" as Beck and Cowan call them in their book "Spiral Dynamics

meet people, situations, and cultures where they are at, creating organizational and political models that are, at most, a ½ step ahead of the individuals involved.

The spiral wizard recognizes that the health of the overall spiral is paramount and that change can generally happen only in small increments. Beck and Cowan are more interested in lubricating change effectively than rejecting and overthrowing old structures.

Each value system leads to certain beliefs, social groupings, motivation patterns, organizational dynamics, and goals. If we try to impose solutions or structures that are too far ahead of the curve (that reflect or engage inappropriate value systems) the result is alienation and rebellion rather than transformation. In this way, Beck and Cowan model a way of being in the world that is eminently practical, sensitive and oriented towards transformation. Too often, we intuit a "better" or "higher" mode of being without respecting the stages of change and development that must happen before large numbers of people in an organization or society can enact such a mode. Spiral Dynamics avoids the use of the terms "better" or "higher," describing "more complex" value systems.

Spiral Dynamics also offers a model of change that describes the different ways in which shifts to a new worldview can occur. This is based on the degree of fit between how life conditions are changing, and the ways in which different individuals can respond to such changes. We should add at this stage that for ThriveAbility Leaders, this "outside-in" model of change is only one option. A great deal of change also arises from an individual out-growing a specific environment/set of life conditions, and choosing to move one to a context they find better suited to their needs based on where they wish to go next in their developmental journey. This is what we call "inside-out" change.

In the *alpha change condition*, the value system ably fits the predominant life conditions. As this changes, the *beta change condition* emerges in which the old value systems begin to be inadequate to deal with changing circumstances. This is a time of uncertainty, questioning, and doubt. From here, there are two possibilities:

- Reform (an evolutionary change) to create a new alpha fit with more sophisticated value systems or
- Revolt (a revolutionary change) that generally stems from a slow initial reaction to change. Revolt emerges from something they call a gamma trap, a zone of frustration and hopelessness.

If people are fortunate and savvy, a transformational pathway emerges (called the delta surge) to the next alpha fit. If not, regression occurs, or the organizational structure dissolves. Within this basic change model, they see seven main types of change: two horizontal, two oblique, and three vertical -

- The horizontal options are to 1) fine tune and 2) expand out, neither of which alters the fundamental value systems of the organization.

- The oblique alternatives (stretch-down and stretch-up) involve accessing higher or lower value systems on a temporary basis to deal with pressing circumstances.
- The vertical alternatives are 1) Break-out, which is revolutionary but runs the risk of regression; 2) Up-shift, which is an evolutionary shift to the next level, as with delta surge; 3) Quantum, which is when a number of value systems are shifting simultaneously. This kind of change is integral to success in nation-building and functioning in a global marketplace, and is seen in era shifts like the Industrial Revolution and the ecological/economic crisis we face in the 21st century.

Leadership promotes positive change and the health of all levels of the spiral and involves a sensitivity to meet where people are at. First, this involves seeing whether people are Open (capable of change), Arrested (change potential is present but hindered), or Closed (frozen in a value system). Rather than trying to dynamite arrested and closed individuals, the savvy "Spiral Wizard" tailors interventions and motivations to meet people where they are at. The optimum leadership style for open individuals is ½ step ahead of their centre of gravity.

For example, an ORANGE population mass is best led by a ORANGE (Expert-Achiever) / green (Individualist) or perhaps an orange/GREEN leader who can subtly lead them further while instinctively appealing to their fundamentally ORANGE (Expert-Achiever) worldview. Individuals who are more closed respond best to management and leadership that reflects their same level (e.g. fundamentalists listen best to other die-hard fundamentalists). Graves insisted that people have a right to live the way they want to live. It is our job to tailor organizations to suit them and motivate them with the most appropriate tools. Table C illustrates the general characteristics of each level of action logic for leaders, with their associated strengths and weaknesses.

## Table C – The Stages of Development – The Dominant Action Logics of Corporate Leadership

| | |
|---|---|
| **Magician/** Alchemist | **Characteristics:** Generates social; transformations. Integrates material, spiritual and societal transformation. <br> **Leadership Strengths:** Good at leading society-wide transformations. |
| **Strategist** | **Characteristics:** Generates organisational and personal transformations. Exercises the power of mutual inquiry; vigilance and vulnerability for both the short and long term. **Leadership Strengths:** Effective as a transformational leader within large contexts such as organisations. |
| **Individualist** | **Characteristics:** Interweaves competing personal and company action logics. Creates unique structures to resolve gaps between strategy and performance <br> **Leadership Strengths:** Effective in venture and consultancy roles. |
| **Achiever/** **Expert** | **Characteristics:** Effectively achieves goals through teams; Juggles duties & market demands. **Leadership Strengths:** Well suited to managerial roles; action & goal orientated <br> **Characteristics:** Rules by logic and expertise. Seeks rational efficiency. **Leadership Strengths:** Good as an individual contributor. |
| **Diplomat** | **Characteristics:** Avoids overt conflict. Wants to belong; obeys group norms; rarely rocks the boat. <br> **Leadership Strengths:** Good as supportive glue within an office; helps bring people together' |
| **Opportunist** | **Characteristics:** Wins any way possible. Self-oriented; Manipulative; 'might makes right'. <br> **Leadership Strengths:** Good in emergencies and in sales opportunities |

## The Human Positioning System

Each of the Action Logics/Developmental Levels/Value Systems described above can be likened to what philosopher Ken Wilber likes to call a "Kosmic Address". Just as we use a global positioning system (or "GPS") to find out where we are and to navigate to our next destination, so too does the human positioning system (or "HPS") work to help us establish where we are, and also, where others are, and what journey/s they are on too.

> **PRACTICAL TOOL - LeaderView and CultureView** instruments are used in the ThriveAbility Assessment, to assess the developmental "stage" of individual leaders and stakeholders. This is their "centre of gravity" in developmental terms, the place they are most comfortable and competent. Highly developed leaders can "upstretch" and "downstretch" to build rapport with other developmental levels, and motivate them according to their unique value system perception of incentives.

Clearly, knowing where people are at right now and where they might be going next is a very valuable way of building rapport, improving communication and influencing, all key tools required for effective leadership. In turn, strategy, innovation and ThriveAbility all need to be developed and implemented in ways that are relevant to people at different levels of development, with very different Kosmic Addresses.

## ThriveAble Innovation through Stratification and Alignment

> "Wrong-footing the old, fading order is a key part of our collective task, as is moving beyond either-or stereotypes to get a better sense of how, on a both-and basis, we can combine the best aspects of the old order with the very different characteristics of the new. <u>We must also get a far better grip on what it is that turns ordinary leaders – and people – into effective agents and champions of breakthrough change</u>"
> *John Elkington and Jochen Zeitz – The Breakthrough Challenge*

Once we are able to place ourselves and others on the human positioning system grid, we can begin to be much more effective in orchestrating the collective shifts needed to create a better future for ourselves, our organization and its stakeholders. Where are we, and where would we like to be? Put in terms that everyone can appreciate and feel motivated by.

Then, as John Elkington and Jochen Zeitz put it in the quote above, we will be able to get a far better grip on what it is that turns ordinary leaders – and people – into effective agents and champions of breakthrough change and transformation

The key to orchestrating such large-scale change, transformation and breakthroughs is a combination of two forces: *stratification* and *alignment*.

**Stratification** arises from the ability to distinguish between the different motivational flows in and around an organization, and to then ensure that the incentives and leadership in place to harness the energy in those motivational flows are appropriate to move an organization in a beneficial direction for its key stakeholders. This is what we would traditionally call the domains of *leadership and human resources/talent management*.

**Alignment** then describes the process by which strategy and innovation in an organization are aligned to both the longer-term interests of key stakeholders, and how the strengths of the organization are aligned with the opportunities in its competitive landscape, as well as ensuring resilience against threats that might penetrate organizational weaknesses. Stratification is like a lubricant that facilitates the flow of energy through the organization toward the strategic goals the organizational is able to pursue as a result of its alignment. This is what we would traditionally call the domains of *strategic management and innovation management*.

**Transformation** is usually a combination of many incremental innovations accompanied by a few breakthrough innovations, led and managed from within an existing organization or business ecosystem. Successful transformations tend to result from leadership that implicitly understands how to connect with the different incentives needed for different stakeholder groups (implicit stratification), and then is influential and powerful enough to drive change and innovation through the alignment of the organization, its key stakeholders and the challenges of its strategic landscape.

**Innovation** is a complex and multi-facetted phenomenon, which is why it is obligatory to make it as simple as possible in all of its dimensions if we are to get anywhere defining the difference between *sustainable* and *thriveable* innovation, and *incremental* and *breakthrough* innovation.

*ThriveAble innovation* offers us a new way to think about breakthroughs, moving beyond the old clichés and misunderstandings, and the mythic stories of heroic lone inventors shouting "Eureka" deep in the dark bowels of a laboratory somewhere in Corporate TransSylvania. Here we can fully appreciate the role of the six capitals and the ThriveAbility Equation in action, helping to create true future value for all of us.

## The Role of ThriveAble Innovation

"Success and sustainability are two sides of the same coin. Where the priorities of business and society align, everyone stands to gain. Better still, there are countless stories of entrepreneurial spirit and energies that help make the impossible possible".
*Sir Richard Branson*

Most fans of innovation know that there are many different kinds, from incremental improvements to existing technologies, products, services and business models, to radical breakthroughs (often known as "disruptive") which result in very new and different technologies, products, services and business models. In the end the incremental innovations usually end up being used to extend the lifespan of sunset industries, while breakthroughs generally tended to accelerate the sunset.

For example, we all know that the minicomputer disrupted the mainframe, and that the PC disrupted the minicomputer, and now there are very few mainframes left, no minicomputers and mainly glowing internet servers in data centres around the world and laptops/ tablets/ smartphones in the hands of a few billion smart users. Any firm that did not adapt to this saw its life cut short very swiftly. Even the mighty IBM almost died, and had to be resuscitated through radical surgery in the 1990's.

ThriveAble innovation takes an evolutionary view of socio-technical development to explain how a radical effect is a consequence of an _entire interdependent, multi-capital landscape_ rather than of the radical development of a specific innovation.

Radical innovations prompt significant subsequent technological and social developments and exhibit novelty and "architectural" innovation, i.e. rearranging the way design elements are put together in a system. Thus, radical innovations often serve as the foundation for new technological systems, industries or domains and are seen to involve significant conceptual breakthroughs, through either luck or genius. The much more common incremental innovations are perceived as mere improvements to existing technologies.

The term "disruptive innovation" is frequently overused. Clearly the term has sometimes become a cliché among those who don't understand. Decreasing returns from incremental innovation are understood to motivate a search for a new radical innovation to provide a platform for more incremental innovation. However, deeper study shows that the conceptual "distance" a radical breakthrough travels is far shorter than would initially appear.

On closer inspection, several innovations with undoubtedly radical effects comprise several small inventive steps that appear self-evident, even logical, to the developers. This conundrum appears to stem from conflating a radical effect with a radical development. What's more, this limited view of radical innovation views inventions as isolated from the broader currents of technological development.

ThriveAble innovation sees innovations as embedded in a _co-evolutionary socio-technical landscape_, where inventions develop in a socio-technical environment and become building blocks for further inventions. Although only inventions adopted for use can be called innovations, "inactive" inventions can also serve as building blocks. In this view, (almost) all steps to innovation are incremental, but the _system's self-organized criticality_ (SOC) allows spontaneous radical effects.

For example, the airplane was developed by the Wright brothers as a result of many small, individually unremarkable technological experiments in a logical progression, with no readily apparent novel, unique element, and conceptually distant from rival technologies, despite undoubtedly being developed incrementally. As a further contrast, the many unsuccessful contemporaries of the Wright Brothers attempted the "conceptual leap" strategy of testing complete aircraft designs and failed.

To further dissociate the development and effect of invention, there are cases of genuine, original thoughts, devised by lone geniuses, which languished in obscurity until a time when they represent the next, logical step. For example, Gregor Mendel's theory of trait inheritance was rejected until independent discovery of the theory well over a century later. It seems that truly radical conceptual breakthroughs may be dismissed until incremental development catches up to provide a contact that can support them.

Kasmire et al[60] propose that inventions and innovations are not independent introductions to a waiting world, but instead are interacting entities in the constantly shifting socio-technical landscape of a Complex Adaptive System (CAS). This landscape of past and present inventions is shaped by research programs, problems needing solutions, and the costs of energy, materials, parts and labour.

---

[60]  Many researchers have already begun to consider innovation as a CAS and SOC has been found to emerge in models of uniform technological development. For example: "How radical is a radical innovation? An outline for a computational approach", J. Kasmire, Janne M. Korhonen, Igor Nikolic, TU Delft Faculty of Technology, Policy and Management, Jaffalaan 5, 2628BX, Delft, The Netherlands, Aalto University School of Economics, Runeberginkatu 14-16, 00076 AALTO, Helsinki, Finland. Technoport RERC Research 2012

Every invention is an incremental step in a wander through the landscape, and every step taken distorts that landscape. The movements and resulting shifts create or destroy links along which materials, information or influence flow, ameliorate some problems and make others worse. These inventions compete with close neighbours for utility, advantage and popularity, but can also become building blocks for distant inventions, even if they never succeed as standalone inventions.

The statistical relations found between characteristics of inventors or development approaches and impact do not indicate a conceptual breakthrough in development, but reveal an attractor in the fitness landscape. As part of a CAS, the attractors are neither permanent nor independent so the characteristics linked to success will also shift and react to the rest of the system.

Even when all steps in the socio-technical landscape are incremental, some trigger big changes as a consequence of the capacity of CAS for emergent behaviours and self-organized criticality (SOC). Thus, some innovations result in spontaneous radical effects and returns while others do not, just as when roughly equivalent grains of sand added to a pile can either stick or precipitate an avalanche. And, just as avalanches, earthquakes, meteor strikes, cracks in pavement and many other phenomena follow power law distributions, so too do patent citations, scientific journal citations, and other measures of innovation impact. This strongly suggests that the frequency of major impact innovations varies as a power of the impact size of that innovation, meaning that the impact of an innovation has more to do with the impact (or lack thereof) of all the preceding and concurrent innovations in the socio-technical landscape than with the innovation itself.

## What If You Are an Incumbent?

How can industry leaders and other incumbents reinvent themselves in response to disruptive market shifts, technologies, or start-ups? Can a new business model quickly replace all the revenue an incumbent has lost to market upheaval? Only in rare instances, says an article in a recent issue of *Harvard Business Review*[61]. It appears that companies under assault need to pursue two distinct but parallel efforts: "Transformation A" should reposition the core business, adapting it to the altered environment. "Transformation B" should launch a separate, disruptive business that will be the source of future growth.

This dual approach allows the company to realize the most value from its current assets and advantages, while giving the new initiative the time it needs to grow. The dual transformations of three companies that were facing massive disruption: the Deseret News, which was losing advertising to online upstarts; Xerox, whose copier business had been eroded by Asian rivals; and Barnes & Noble, which was threatened by e-books.

---

[61] Two Routes to Resilience – Rebuild Your Core while you reinvent your business model. C. Gilbert, M. Eyring and RN Foster. HBR, 2012.

In each instance, a key to making the dual transformations work was the establishment of a "capabilities exchange," which allowed both efforts to share resources without interfering with the mission or operations of either.

## Making ThriveAble Innovation and Transformation Happen

So far we have explored how:

1. *Integrated thinking and leadership* for ThriveAbility are made possible through the Six Capitals Equation;
2. To *calculate True Future Value* so that it takes into account the 80% of the corporation's share price that is based on intangibles which are currently measured either badly or not at all, as well as the externalities of natural and social capital costs not factored into share price;
3. *Stratification and Alignment* can help Leaders drive ThriveAble Innovation;
4. *ThriveAble Innovation* occurs on a strategic landscape where the inter-dependencies are critical to the self-organising criticality of breakthroughs (tipping points);
5. To *Dual-Track ThriveAble Innovation* in Incumbents.

In Chapter 3 we explained the ThriveAbility Six Step Process, which begins with an organizational assessment and a strategic scan in order to carry out an alignment diagnosis that leads into the innovation process directly through the *Strategic Alignment Outlook.*

What we will now explore is how all of these methods can be integrated into the *Strategic Alignment Outlook* which blends the outcomes of Steps 1 ("Assess"), 2 ("*Scan*") and 3 ("*Align*") in the six step ThriveAbility process, providing valuable inputs and insights into Step 4 ("*Transform*"). You can refer to Diagram 14 in chapter 3 to refresh your memory on these six key steps.

In Step 1, *Assess*, the Sustainability, Organizational and Culture/leadership online assessments have highlighted the gaps, blockages, misalignments and drivers that will enable those gaps to be closed in and around the organization. This provides a baseline of areas that could benefit from change, innovation and/or transformation. Current human resources and leadership profiles, together with management and sustainability KPI's[62] would provide a baseline and information resource for these three online assessments.

In Step 2, *Scan*, we have understood the *Life Conditions* that frame the *Stakeholder Outcomes* that would provide them with the incentives to support or engage in an aspect of the innovation and transformation process. The *Innovation and Industry Challenge drivers* would also have been clarified through a quick research program that surveyed the competitive landscape and parallel innovations and inventions in other key players in the business

---

[62] KPI = Key Performance Indicator

ecosystem. Such a Scan would build on pre-existing, recent strategic analyses as well as some fresh forays into the field to ensure the current relevance of the information.

In Step 3, *Align*, the internal diagnosis provided in the Assess step, and the external diagnosis provided in the Scan step, are then compared and contrasted using the ThriveAbility Six Capitals Equation and an Innovation/Transformation potential filter. The result is a *Strategic Alignment Outlook*, that defines:

- ThriveAble Innovation Pathways, with matching
- Leadership and Organisational Development Pathways.

In Step 2, *Scan* data on the degree of thriving of key stakeholder groups, relative to preferred stakeholder outcomes, enables the organization and its leaders to engage meaningfully with each key stakeholder group, within a frame of reference that provides a degree of objectivity around the issues that are arising for each key stakeholder group. Such engagements are probably already occurring in most organizations, but lack any objective criteria by which desirable stakeholder outcomes can be linked to the innovation and transformation processes within the organization.

Organisational transformations and breakthroughs all take place within the context of very specific life conditions for the stakeholders of the organization. Customers, employees, suppliers, business partners and the communities they operate in will all have their developmental opportunities and journeys shaped by the life conditions they are operating in. One of the goals of ThriveAbility is to improve these life conditions through intelligent strategies and designs that deliver breakthroughs and accelerate human development in all key stakeholders groups. How can that be done effectively?

> **PRACTICAL TOOL - Desirable Life Conditions & Stakeholder Outcomes** – as part of the organization's engagement with stakeholders, different stakeholder groups are asked a module of questions which allows them to be assessed to what extent they are thriving, struggling or suffering (for example, those conducted by Gallup for its World Poll). This is a measurement of the "**initial state**" of the individual stakeholder, which is also then linked to their aspirations and frustrations with their engagement/collaboration with the Organization, leading to an exploration of *desirable stakeholder outcomes* that are also beneficial for the organization and can be incorporated in one or more ThriveAble Innovation Pathways.

In diagram 18, ThriveAble Innovation Pathways, a portfolio of possible breakthroughs and transformations is assembled during Step 3, *Align*, as part of the *Strategic Alignment Outlook*.

Understanding what motivates individuals at many levels in different kinds of stakeholder groups is key for ThriveAbility leaders to *identify what the right things to do are, and how to get those right things done well*. At its best, this approach builds on a fusion of the best innovation methods with an approach known as "Appreciative Enquiry", where one builds on what is already working in an around the organization, while encouraging an open, imaginative and appreciative mindset in the collaborative innovation process.

The ThriveAbility Innovation Pathways strategy co-creation process:

- Offers a wiser and more intelligent way to engage with the organization's key stakeholders in *collaborative strategy building*, in order to maximize the ThriveAbility of all stakeholders, thus ensuring the *long-term success of the organization* itself; Is capable of being translated into *real-options valuations* using the ThriveAbility Six Capitals Equation, where each of the strategic options (A, B and C in diagram 18 above), is capable of being ranked according to its *True Future Value;*
- Transcends traditional innovation methodologies that value only the value-added of the functional/utility value of the invention/innovation, rather than the *longer-term stakeholder experience enhancement* that is associated with True Future Value methods.

### DIAGRAM 18 - ThriveAble Innovation Pathways, the Core of the Strategic Alignment Outlook

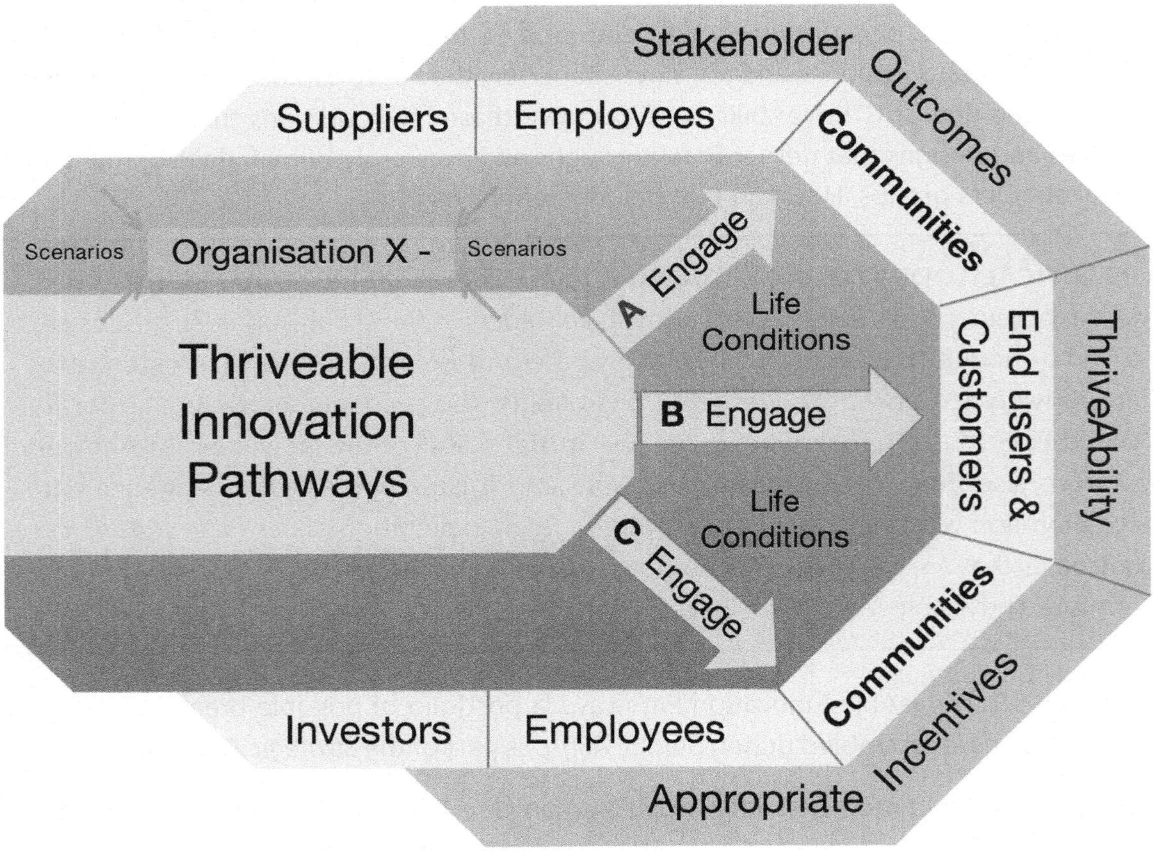

## Translating Fresh Strategic Perspectives into ThriveAble Outcomes

To close this chapter, we will end with a few key reminders about the way in which strategic perspectives, developmental levels and managerial style preferences interact to shape the ThriveAble Innovation Process:

- **Strategic Perspectives** – some strategies are based on partial perspectives grounded in lower levels of development, and others are based on more inclusive/whole systems perspectives grounded in higher levels of development. Whether or not a strategy/policy is adaptive and leads to stakeholder thriving or maladaptive and leads to stakeholder suffering will depend to what extent it is aligned with the life conditions and stage of development of the organization and its stakeholders.

- **Developmental Levels** – top management, employees and select samples of external stakeholders are assessed to establish their "centre of gravity" according to widely accepted developmental surveys (for example, the LeaderView and CultureView instruments). This is a measurement of the developmental "**stage**" of the individual stakeholder;

- **Managerial Style Preferences** – leaders and managers exhibit strong preferences for different approaches to the changes needed to bring about thriving. For example, some prefer incremental change, while others prefer breakthroughs and transformational approaches. These preferences exert a strong influence on the success of the initiatives and projects they lead and manage.

The interactions mentioned above are illustrated in Diagram 19 below. In this diagram we can see that strategic perspectives that guide the top management team in an organization in setting their priorities and those of the organization, will only be capable of successful implementation if the appropriate incentives are in place relative to the value systems of those responsible for implementation. (As illustrated in the "Value System/ Action Logic box in the centre of diagram 19).

In turn, even if the appropriate incentives are in place, having the right managers in the right places to bring the innovation hotspots alive is critical, as illustrated in the bottom-most box. Managers who are risk averse and prefer incremental change will be innovation killers if place in the wrong roles. Imaginative managers with a preference for transformative (second-order) change are critical to ensuring that innovations are shepherded through the stage-gates of the new product/service/experience development process. An ability to engage and build rapport with key stakeholders at each stage of this process will also be essential.

There are two very different kinds of interactions between strategic perspectives, management style preferences and value systems with the organization's stakeholders:

- **Inside Out** - dynamics are characteristic of an organization that seeks to shape its stakeholders and its environment, a leader and innovator- and such "shapers/ innovators" need to pay very careful attention to outside-in feedback once they have developed an offer in the ThriveAble Innovation Pathway (though not too early, as otherwise they will be trapped by incremental improvement minded customers and other stakeholders). Organizations that focus largely on shaping their environment and marketplace will also tend to focus more on innovations and opportunities in their strategies;

- **Outside In** - dynamics are characteristic of "adaptor" and "reactor" organization types who tend to follow the market (late-followers), though adaptors tend to have faster response times than reactors, who are at most risk of becoming "Disappearors". There is really not much that one can do with an organization full of incremental-change minds, except allow them to get on and fine-tune their organization, products and services to their heart's content.

  They may stay alive in a simple stable environment, but if the environment starts moving faster and becomes complex and dynamic, it is only a matter of time before a shaper or disruptor will ensure their extinction Organizations that focus largely on adapting to or reacting to their environment and marketplace will tend to focus more on risk aversion and resilience.

Moving beyond sustainability to ThriveAbility requires us to be able to measure and align several key ingredients at the organisational level including:

- **Stage on the ThriveAbility Journey** – what stage the organization is currently at on the ThriveAbility Journey, and what direction it is travelling in;

- **Innovation Portfolio and Pathways** – how both incremental and breakthrough changes and transformations can deliver the shifts required to move the organization from one level on the ThriveAbility Journey to the next;

- **Strategic Alignment** – how well aligned the organization is with reference to its strategic direction, leadership team, cultural centre of gravity and its natural capital context gap opportunities; Recent research shows that values alignment is key to successful organisational sustainability initiatives in three ways[63]:

  - The design and implementation of such initiatives must be rooted in an understanding of—and tailored response to vastly different stakeholder values.

  - Leaders must understand different types of values and tailor all aspects of sustainability projects accordingly.

  - Components of the assessment, design, implementation, evaluation, and all communications should align the values of all key stakeholders.

---

[63]  Barrett Brown, Phd Thesis, Conscious Leadership For Sustainability: How Leaders With a Late-Stage Action Logic Design and Engage In Sustainability Initiatives, Fielding Graduate University, 2011

- **ThriveAbility Dashboard** - the ways in which the allocation of funds to investments could enhance the thriving of key stakeholders in and around the organization, from employees to customers to suppliers and business partners.

**DIAGRAM 19 – Incremental vs Transformative Managerial Preferences:
Risks and Resilience vs Innovations and Opportunities**

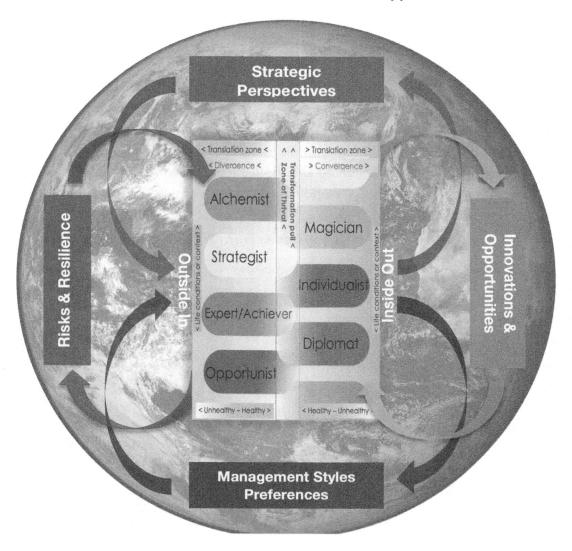

We can now also more clearly see how the evolution of the values of individuals, families, teams, organisations, communities and nations aligns with the different stages of evolution of the ThriveAbility Journey, as mapped out in Table A as extended below. The important point to note is that different coping mechanisms (the value systems) are appropriate at different points in the ThriveAbility Journey, and may indeed be driving the mindsets and worldviews that generate an opportunistic approach to denial/compliance, for example. Further along on the journey we can see how individualist, "green" value systems and coping mechanisms are the key driver in the sustainability movement, but also a limiting way of seeing the world which can lock-in existing practices and thinking and prevent the breakthroughs needed which do not come from their own way of seeing the world.

As we progress on the ThriveAbility Journey, we can also see how critical it is to have mindsets and values that are able to embrace world-centric levels of complexity while also being able to think systemically and holistically from a big picture perspective. In order to move through from sustaining to resilience to thriving as the main focus of our efforts, we need to be able to see that others have different ways of looking at and understanding the world, and we need to be able to meet them where they are at and not expect them all simply to "trust us" or believe in the one-right "corporate way". This is a key aspect of the skills of a strategist within and between organisations.

For full-scale organisational and social transformations, magicians and alchemists are required in the leadership teams. This is because they have the depth of trans-disciplinary experience and vision to see how things will/might unfold over longer time-frames at larger scales in human systems, and know how to frame and motivate key options and decision processes that ensure buy-in from the widest stakeholder base for the greatest benefit for all life.

### Table A [extended] – Value systems: From Suffering to Thriving

| | Suffering | Improving | Sustaining | Resilience | Thriving |
|---|---|---|---|---|---|
| **Desire** | Survive! | Comply! | Repair! | Recalibrate! | Thrive! |
| **Define** | Continue to live or exist, especially in spite of danger or hardship | Experiment with ways to improve CSR performance | A system that maintains its own viability by using techniques that allow for continual reuse | Achieving new balance by optimizing performance within broader ecological and social systems | For all life to develop vigorously, prosper, and flourish within planetary boundaries |
| | | Doing less bad | Meet thresholds | Net Positive | ThriveAble |
| **Response** | React | Mitigate | Balance | Adapt | Innovate & Breakthrough |
| **Focus** | Basic needs | Incremental improvements without limits and demand on social and environmental resources | Mitigate damage, sacrifice, austerity, obligation, externalities | Network structure of complex flow systems. Natural & Human Eco-system mapping | Key leverage points in global systems that align the Six Capitals for ThriveAbility |
| **Value System** | Red/Amber [Opportunists] | Orange/ [Diplomats/Experts/ Achiever] | Green [Individualist] | Green/Teal [Strategists] | Teal/Turquoise [Magicians & Alchemists] |

Let us now turn to some examples of real-world shapers who are showing the way in which breakthroughs can help create a more ThriveAble world, and who have already taken their organisations a long way on the ThriveAbility Journey.

# 5. Leading from the Perspective of ThriveAbility

*"Aim to do the apparently impossible"*
*First Leadership Principle of the B-Team*

As the words of the famous song say: "Dream the impossible dream[1]." It is always difficult to imagine what currently appears to be impossible- and it is always easy to ridicule people who do dream of the impossible. But most progress appears to come from people who do, denying the naysayers and ignoring the cynics.

A century ago, experts of the day proclaimed heavier than air flying machines would "never take off", that a rocket "would never leave the earth's atmosphere", that locomotives will never "travel twice as fast as stagecoaches", that the automobile has "practically reached the limits of its development", and that "the coming of the wireless era will make war impossible"[2]. More recently other experts have predicted that "there is no chance that the iPhone is going to get any significant market share", and that there is "no reason for any individual to have a computer in his home".

Visionaries who are also effective at getting the right things done in creating paths toward their vision are essential to our species and its survival and thrival.

Today it seems quite impossible that the world will avert the certain disaster of a four-degree warmer world. Approaching the 21st United Nations Climate Change Conference in Paris in December 2015[64], whose aim is: "a binding and universal agreement on climate, from all the nations of the world", one would have to be an inveterate optimist to believe that such a deal can be pulled off, and even if it could, that it would actually be binding enough to limit warming to two degrees.

Cynics would also argue that large corporations will be the least likely to change their ways given that they have few short to medium term incentives to do so. We beg to differ, as would the following executives and sustainability thought leaders[65]:

- "The C-suite should be a team of sustainability champions that understands both the challenges and opportunities...The number one CSO should be the CEO" – *Guilherme Leal, Natura co-founder and Board member;*
- "We should strive for a situation where the board as a whole, and not just a separate CSR or CSO officers feels responsible, and where decision making tools like the environmental profit and loss and social profit and loss approaches are reflected into rule-based integrated reporting systems. In this world of integrated thinking, the CFO

---

[64] The overarching goal of the Convention is to reduce greenhouse gas emissions to limit the global temperature increase to 2 degrees Celsius above pre-industrial levels.

[65] John Elkington and Jochen Zeitz, The Breakthrough Challenge, Jossey-Bass, 2014

becomes responsible for all forms of capital, not just financial capital" – *Peter Bakker, President of the World Council for Sustainable Business Development (WBCSD);*

- "A key challenge has been convincing business leaders that sustainability issues are not fads, and that to be successful long term, these issues need to be central to their strategies....it has been rewarding to see business leaders develop a growing awareness that developing products that make our customers more sustainable is a great growth strategy" – *Linda Fisher, Vice President and CSO at E.I. DuPont Nemours and Company.*

To hear these, and similar statements coming from the mouths of mainstream business leaders is indeed refreshing, and a cause for real hope. But there is a great deal more work to be done, and many more bold dreams to be dreamed.

So, what exactly does the role of a "ThriveAbility Leader" entail, and why is it crucial? Let us begin with some exemplars of the current generation of sustainability leaders who embody one or more of the Six ThriveAbility Principles.

## What Does Being a "ThriveAbility Leader" Look Like?

There are many thousands of high profile leaders doing amazing things right now, who would qualify as prototypical "ThriveAbility Leaders" They have arrived at this distinction as "naturals" rather than having completed a ThriveAbility Leadership curriculum, and there is a great deal we can learn from each of them and their example.

The goal of this ThriveAbility Leadership Guide is to enable you and your colleagues to embody the qualities that these "naturals" already have and demonstrate the capabilities that these "naturals" already do, doing what you do. These naturals are all result-producing visionaries, who are not only inspiring others to become more ThriveAble, but also catalysing the change and breakthroughs needed in and around their own organizations and movements to deliver ThriveAble outcomes.

Let's take a closer look at some of the leaders who are "naturals" at ThriveAbility Leadership. Some started out as "green champions" early on in life (the **Activists/Advisors),** while others underwent a green conversion in their businesses or started a green/cleantech business (the **Entrepreneurs**), and the final category brought sustainability into the centre of their organization's strategy (the **Intrapreneurs).**

They are all, of course, part of much larger teams and organizations, as well as part of on going stories about how they achieved what they have, so we have included some of their colleagues as appropriate.

Although there are hundreds of thousands of talented individuals making a real difference out there today, here are the 50 we have selected based on their impact, influence and thought leadership: 17 Activists/Advisors, 17 Entrepreneurs and 16 Intrapreneurs. True exemplars of

ThriveAbility Leaders, who deserve our recognition and celebration for their achievements and the inspiration they offer to us and future generations.

| Activists/Advisors |
|---|
| 1. Peter **Bakker**, Former CEO at TNT and President WBCSD |
| 2. Janine **Benyus**, Biomimicry 3.8 |
| 3. Michael **Braungart** and Bill **McDonough**. Cradle-to-Cradle |
| 4. John **Elkington**, Founder of SustainAbility and Volans |
| 5. Gil Philip **Friend**, Chief Sustainability Officer for the City of Palo Alto, California |
| 6. John B. **Fullerton**, Founder and President of Capital Institute |
| 7. Al **Gore**, Former US Vice-President |
| 8. Paul **Hawken,** Founder Natural Capital Institute and WiserEarth |
| 9. Hazel **Henderson**, Founder of Ethical Markets Media |
| 10. Ban **Ki-Moon**, UN Secretary-General |
| 11. James **Lovelock**, UK Scientist |
| 12. Amory **Lovins**, Rocky Mountain Institute |
| 13. Hunter **Lovins**, Founder Natural Capital Solutions |
| 14. Kumi **Naidoo**, Executive Director Greenpeace International |
| 15. Jeremy **Rifkin**, Author and Advisor |
| 16. Jeff **Skoll**, Founder Skoll Foundation and Global Zero |
| 17. Dr. Wayne **Visser**, Director of Kaleidoscope Futures, Founder of CSR International |

| Entrepreneurs |
|---|
| 1. Ray **Anderson**, Founder of Interface |
| 2. David **Blood**, Generation Investment Management |
| 3. Sir Richard **Branson**, Founder of the Virgin Group |
| 4. Sergei **Brin and** Larry **Page**, Co-founders of Google |
| 5. Robin **Chase**, transportation entrepreneur, co-founder of Zipcar, Veniam, Buzzcar |
| 6. Sir Ian **Cheshire**, Founder of the Kingfisher Group & Richard Gillies, CSO |
| 7. Fadi **Ghandour**, Visionary and CEO of Aramex |
| 8. Guilherme **Leal**, Natura co-founder and Board member |
| 9. Richard **Mattison**, CEO of TruCost& Alastair MacGregor Chief Operating Officer |
| 10. Rob **Michalak**, Global Director of Social Mission of Ben & Jerry's |
| 11. Elon **Musk**, Founder of Tesla |
| 12. Gunter **Pauli**, Founder of ZERI and Ecover |
| 13. Thomas **Rau** and Sabine Oberhuber, Founders of Turntoo |
| 14. KoAnn Vikoren **Skrzyniarz**, Founder of Sustainable Brands and Sustainable Life Media |
| 15. Allen **White**, Co-Founder and Former CEO of GRI, (Global Reporting Initiative), Founder and Co-chair of Global Initiative for Sustainability Ratings |
| 16. Andrew **Winston**, Founder of Winston Eco-Strategies, Author |
| 17. Zhang **Yue**, Founder and Chairman of the Broad Group |

| **Intrapreneurs** |
|---|
| 1. Mike **Barry**, CSO at Marks & Spenser & Adam Elman, Global Head Of Delivery For Plan A |
| 2. Niall **Dunne**, CSO at the BT Group |
| 3. Linda **Fisher,** Vice President and CSO at E.I. DuPont Nemours and Company & Paul Tebo, DuPont "Hero of Zero" |
| 4. Mark **Gough,** former CSO at The Crown Estate & John Lelliott Finance Director |
| 5. Steve **Howard**, CSO at IKEA Group |
| 6. Lisa **Jackson**, Apple's Vice President of Environmental Initiatives |
| 7. Hannah **Jones,** Nike Inc's Vice President of Sustainable Business and Innovation & Santiago Gowland, Managing Director, Sustainable Business & Innovation |
| 8. Gail **Kelly**, Former CEO at Westpac |
| 9. Paul **Polman**, CEO of Unilever |
| 10. Nick **Robins**, Head of UNEP Initiative on Sustainable Finance |
| 11. Emma **Stewart**, Head of Sustainability Solutions at Autodesk |
| 12. Dave **Stangis**, CSO at Campbells |
| 13. Susanne **Stormer**, CSO at Novo Nordisk |
| 14. Kathrin **Winkler**, CSO at EMC Corporation |
| 15. Steve **Waygood,** Head of Sustainability Research & Engagement of Aviva Investors |
| 16. Jochen **Zeitz,** Director and Chairman of Sustainability Committee at Kering, formerly CEO of Puma |

## Activists/Advisors[3]

### Peter Bakker, Former CEO at TNT and President of WBCSD

Under the leadership of Mr Bakker, TNT became a leader in Corporate Responsibility in a partnership with the UN World Food Program, together with CO2 reduction targets from its Planet Me initiative resulting in leading positions in the Dow Jones Sustainability Index over the years. Peter then went on to become the President of the World Business Council for Sustainable Development, where he has already made his mark in terms of moving the Vision 2050 program toward high leverage actions through the Action 2020 program he conceived.

The Action2020 program of the WBCSD has identified priority areas where business can lead, developing solutions that will have significant impact against key challenges by 2020. WBCSD is pleased to contribute its work to the Global Opportunity Report, helping more companies to identify opportunities and develop solutions at scale that will help to drive the momentum of the required transformation.

### Janine Benyus, Biomimicry 3.8

Janine Benyus is a biologist, innovation consultant, and author of six books, including Biomimicry: Innovation Inspired by Nature. In Biomimicry, she describes an emerging discipline that emulates nature's designs and processes (e.g., solar cells that mimic leaves) to create a healthier, more sustainable planet.

Janine co-founded the world's first bio-inspired consultancy, bringing nature's sustainable designs to 250+ clients including Boeing, Colgate-Palmolive, Nike, General Electric, Herman Miller, HOK architects, IDEO, Interface, Natura, Procter and Gamble, Levi's, Kohler, and General Mills.

She also co-founded the Biomimicry Institute, dedicated to making biology a natural part of the design process. The Institute hosts annual global biomimicry design challenges on sustainability problems, mobilizing tens of thousands of people through the Global Biomimicry Network to solve those challenges, and providing practitioners with the world's most comprehensive biomimicry inspiration database, AskNature, to use as a starting place.

### Michael Braungart and Bill McDonough. Cradle to Cradle

Cradle to Cradle[66]® design defines a framework for designing products and industrial processes that turn materials into nutrients by enabling the formation of cyclical material flow systems. Products optimized for biological cycles are termed biological nutrients (e.g. plant-based and biodegradable materials) and are intended for safe return to the environment as nutrients for living things. Products optimized for the technical cycle are termed technical

---

[66]  It should be noted that biological nutrients are not only functioning as nutrients for living things; the most important aim of these biological cycles (spheres) is to regenerate healthy top soil.

nutrients (e.g. metals and some polymers) and are intended to circulate in closed-loop industrial cycles.

William McDonough is a globally recognized leader in sustainable growth. He works as an architect, advisor, thought leader and designer at scales from the global to the molecular.

Professor Dr. Michael Braungart is a distinguished scientist with a background in chemistry and process engineering. His leadership and vision of ecoeffective design has inspired change throughout academia, NGOs, and industries worldwide. Since 2009 Prof. Dr. Braungart has held the Academic Chair 'Cradle to Cradle for Innovation and Quality' at Rotterdam School of Management, Erasmus University, the Netherlands.

"Conventional environmental approaches focus on what not to do", they write, adding that this is "a kind of guilt management for our collective sins". But instead of making something that's 20% better, or 10% less harmful, what if we designed products and processes that were 100% good?"

## John Elkington, Founder of SustainAbility and Volans

John Elkington is a writer, thought-leader and strategist, a serial entrepreneur and known as an 'advisor from the future', working with large corporations, particularly at C-Suite level, as well as the finance & investment community, industry bodies, intrapreneurs, media, academia, government, innovators and entrepreneurs across the globe.

John has been described by Business Week as "a dean of the corporate responsibility movement for three decades." In 1987 he founded SustainAbility, a think tank and consultancy that works with businesses through markets in the pursuit of economic, social and environmental sustainability. He originated the term 'Triple Bottom Line'.

John's day job, as Co-Founder & Executive Chairman of Volans (a consultancy & think-tank which launched in April 2008 and was certified as a B Corp in March 2013) is to help corporates, investors, innovators and other leaders to drive transformational change.

## Gil Philip Friend, Chief Sustainability Officer for the City of Palo Alto, California.

Gil was founder, chair, and until December 2013, CEO of Natural Logic Inc, helping companies design, implement and measure profitable sustainability strategies. He is widely considered one of the founders of the sustainability movement, and was named an inaugural member of the Sustainability Hall of Fame (along with Ray Anderson, Amory Lovins, Karl-Henrik Robert and Bob Willard) by the International Society of Sustainability Professionals, acknowledging "those people that have contributed the most to the emerging field of sustainability," and "one of the 10 most influential sustainability voices in America" by The Guardian.

Gil became CSO of Palo Alto in December 2013. His leadership has inspired many, and he has instituted some of the most innovative programs in the field, including the first sustainability business dashboards nearly 20 years ago. Gil's experience and connections are instrumental in making Palo Alto not only the greenest city in America, but also a major contributor to advancing world-class sustainability strategies that link to the San Francisco Bay region and beyond.

## Al Gore, Former US Vice-President

Former Vice President Al Gore is co-founder and chairman of Generation Investment Management. He is a senior partner at Kleiner Perkins Caufield & Byers, and a member of Apple Inc.'s board of directors. Gore spends the majority of his time as chairman of The Climate Reality Project, a non-profit devoted to solving the climate crisis.

On December 10, 2007, Gore accepted a Nobel Prize for work on global warming. In accepting the prize, he urged the world's biggest carbon emitters, China and the U.S., to "make the boldest moves, or stand accountable before history for their failure to act." Gore shared the prize with the Intergovernmental Panel on Climate Change (IPCC) for sounding the alarm over global warming and spreading awareness on how to counteract it.

He also starred in the 2006 documentary An Inconvenient Truth, which won an Academy Award for Best Documentary in 2007 and wrote the book An Inconvenient Truth: The Planetary Emergency of Global Warming and What We Can Do About It, which won a Grammy Award for Best Spoken Word Album in 2009.

## Paul Hawken

Paul Hawken is an environmentalist, entrepreneur, journalist, and author. He dedicated his life to sustainability and changing the relationship between business and the environment. His practice has included starting and running ecological businesses, writing and teaching about the impact of commerce on living systems, and consulting with governments and corporations on economic development, industrial ecology, and environmental policy.

Paul is founder of the Natural Capital Institute, which created Wiser Earth, an open source networking platform that links NGOs, foundations, business, government, social entrepreneurs, students, organizers, academics, activists, scientists, and citizens concerned about the environment and social justice.

In 1995 Hawken was hired by Interface, Inc. as part of a twelve-member group of outside consultants responsible to help make Interface the world's leading company in industrial ecology within the next ten years. The team as a whole helped move the company to a closed-loop manufacturing process so that product and waste is returned and remanufactured into new product. He conceived, wrote and co- designed the Interface Sustainability Report, which has won numerous awards and praise throughout the world.

## Ban Ki-Moon, UN Secretary-General

Ban Ki-moon is the eighth Secretary-General of the United Nations. His priorities have been to mobilize world leaders around a set of new global challenges, from climate change and economic upheaval to pandemics and increasing pressures involving food, energy and water. He has sought to be a bridge-builder, to give voice to the world's poorest and most vulnerable people, and to strengthen the Organization itself.

One of the Secretary-General's first major initiatives was the 2007 Climate Change Summit, followed by extensive diplomatic efforts that have helped put the issue at the forefront of the global agenda. Ban continues to lead the global agenda on the reduction of greenhouse gases and the incorporation of sustainability targets into the Sustainable Development Goals that will be formalised in Paris in late 2015.

## James Lovelock, UK Scientist

James Lovelock is an independent scientist, environmentalist and futurist. He is best known for proposing the Gaia hypothesis, which postulates that the biosphere is a self-regulating entity with the capacity to keep our planet healthy by controlling the interconnections of the chemical and physical environment. Lovelock manages to be both catastrophist and boundless optimist at the same time. He believes humanity will suffer crises that threaten the species, but will somehow pull through.

## Amory Lovins, Rocky Mountain Institute

Amory Lovins is a consultant, experimental physicist, Chairman/Chief Scientist of the Rocky Mountain Institute. Amory has been active at the nexus of energy, resources, economy, environment, development, and security in more than 50 countries for over 40 years. He is widely considered among the world's leading authorities on energy—especially its efficient use and sustainable supply—and a fertile innovator in integrative design and in superefficient buildings, factories, and vehicles.

Amory's work turned the energy challenge on its head by suggesting a radically different focus: providing the amount, type, scale and source of energy that would provide desired services in the cheapest way, as opposed to getting the most energy from any source at any price. He has demonstrated that properly structured, sustainable, least-cost energy and resource options can be beneficial both to the environment and to industry.

## Hunter Lovins, Founder Natural Capitalism Solutions

Hunter Lovins is an author and has promoted sustainable development for over 30 years. She is president of Natural Capitalism Solutions, and the Chief Insurgent of the Madrone Project. She teaches sustainable business management at Bainbridge Graduate Institute in Seattle, Washington and at Daniels College of Business, University of Denver. She was a founding professor at Presidio Graduate School's MBA in Sustainable Management program (2002-2010). She co-founded with her then-husband Amory Lovins the Rocky Mountain Institute (RMI) which she led for 20 years.

Natural Capitalism Solutions (NCS,) educates senior decision makers in the business case for a Regenerative Economy. NCS helps companies, communities and countries implement more sustainable practices profitably. Hunter believes that we have all the technologies we need to solve all of the planet's problems, in energy, in food, in manufacturing, in transportation- we just need to get people and companies to adopt them as rapidly as possible.

### Kumi Naidoo, Greenpeace International

Kumi Naidoo is a South African human rights activist and International Executive Director of Greenpeace. After battling apartheid in South Africa in the 1970s and 1980s, Naidoo led global campaigns to end poverty and protect human rights. Recently, he led the Global Call for Climate Action (Tcktcktck.org), which brings together environmental, aid, religious and human rights groups, labour unions, scientists and others and has organised mass demonstrations around climate negotiations.

He thinks, that corporations and governments put power and profit over people. One thing that works is civil disobedience and peaceful protest. Every act of rebellion adds up. The planet doesn't need saving, because if we warm up the planet to a point that humanity cannot exist, the planet will still be here. This challenge is about securing our children and grandchildren's future.

### Jeremy Rifkin, Author and Advisor

Jeremy Rifkin is an economic and social theorist, writer, public speaker, political advisor, and activist. Rifkin is president of the Foundation on Economic Trends and the bestselling author of 20 books about the impact of scientific and technological changes on the economy, the workforce, society, and the environment. Jeremy has been an advisor to the European Union for the past decade and also served as adviser to President Nicolas Sarkozy of France, Chancellor Angela Merkel of Germany, among many others during their respective European Council Presidencies, on issues related to the economy, climate change, and energy security.

Mr Rifkin is the principle architect of the European Union's Third Industrial Revolution long-term economic sustainability plan to address the challenges of the global economic crisis, energy security, and climate change. The goal of this plan is to transform the entire building infrastructure of Europe into a network of micro power plants—each building in the continent collecting solar off the roof, wind off the side of the building, geothermal heat from underneath the building, garbage converted to biomass inside the kitchen.

### Jeffrey Skoll, Founder Skoll Foundation and Global Zero

Jeffrey Skoll, a founding president of the American auction website eBay, is chairman of Participant Media, the Skoll Foundation and the Skoll Global Threats Fund. In 1999, he created the Skoll Foundation, which takes an entrepreneurial approach to philanthropy by investing in, connecting and celebrating the world's most promising social entrepreneurs in order to effect lasting, positive social change worldwide.

As founder of film production company Participant Media, he produces blockbusters that feature political or social messages, e.g. Think Syriana, An Inconvenient Truth, Lincoln, Fast Food Nation and The Fifth Estate. Participant offsets its offices and travel, and in 2004, Syriana was the world's first carbon-offset movie. Traditional studios are now also joining the sustainability band-wagon: Fox, Disney and Warners all have sustainability groups at their companies.

### Dr Wayne Visser, Director of the Think Tank Kaleidoscope Futures, Founder of CSR International

Dr Wayne Visser is Director of the Think-Tank and media company Kaleidoscope Futures, and describes himself as a professional idea-monger, storyteller and meme-weaver. His work as a strategy analyst, sustainability advisor, CSR expert, futurist and professional speaker has taken him to over 70 countries in the past 20 years to work with over 130 clients, ranging from companies like Coca-Cola, Dell, DHL and HSBC to international organisations like the United Nations Environment Programme (UNEP), the World Bank and Worldwide Fund for Nature (WWF).

Wayne is a prolific writer and global lecturer, believing that we learn the best by constantly challenging ourselves to research, teach and write. He is the author of 23 books.

Wayne sees his mission as helping to bring about transformative thinking and action in business and society. This begins with letting go an industrial system that has served us well, but is no longer fit for purpose; old styles of leadership and outdated models of business; high-impact lifestyles and selfish values; cherished ideologies that are causing destruction; and beliefs about ways to tackle problems that are failing to resolve crises. Reaching sustainable frontiers like "thrive-ability", therefore, "must begin with changing our collective minds—and only then will we change our collective behaviour."

## Entrepreneurs[4]

### Ray Anderson, Founder of Interface

The story is now legend: the "spear in the chest" epiphany Ray Anderson experienced when he first read Paul Hawkens' The Ecology of Commerce, seeking inspiration for a speech to an Interface task force on the company's environmental vision.

20 years and a sea change later, Interface, Inc., is nearly 75 per cent towards the vision of "Mission Zero," the journey no one would have imagined for the company or the petroleum-intensive industry of carpet manufacturing which has been forever changed by Anderson's vision. Mission Zero is the company's promise to eliminate any negative impact it may have on the environment, by the year 2020, through the redesign of processes and products, the pioneering of new technologies, and efforts to reduce or eliminate waste and harmful emissions while increasing the use of renewable materials and sources of energy.

Interface spends the rest of its days harvesting yester-year's carpets and other petrochemically derived products, and recycling them into new materials; and converting sunlight into energy; with zero scrap going to the landfill and zero emissions into the ecosystem. That's their vision.

### David Blood, Generation Investment Management

Generation Investment Management was founded in 2004 by Al Gore and David Blood and began investing client money in April 2005. Gore and Blood urge investors to pressure executive teams to divert cash flow away from capital expenditures on developing fossil fuels and toward more productive uses in the context of a transition to a low-carbon economy.

Sustainability cannot be approached in isolation; we have to integrate it into the investment process. David believes that sustainability means long-term economic, environmental, social and governance risks and opportunities—things that really impact a company's ability to sustain profitability and deliver longer-term returns.

### Sir Richard Branson, Founder of the Virgin Group

Ever since a Virgin Atlantic aircraft made history in 2008, becoming the first flight by a commercial airline to be powered partly by biofuel, Richard Branson has been eager to further advance Virgin's use of clean fuels. In 2013 Richard talked of his desire to have all Virgin airlines use only clean burning fuels by 2020, making air travel one of the cleanest sectors.

There are huge challenges facing advanced biofuels, but also huge opportunities. Virgin airlines and all their companies and partners are working hard to ensure the success of the most promising and sustainable technologies. They announced that the company's new biofuel plant near Beijing had secured the "gold standard" certification, confirming that the fuel does not negatively impact the food chain or contribute to deforestation, as is the case with some biofuels.

Sir Richard Branson and Jochen Zeitz have together launched a global not-for-profit organization called The B Team. Thery work alongside a global community of partners, advisors and supporters to deliver a new way of doing business that prioritizes people and planet along with profit – a 'Plan B' for businesses the world over.

## Sergei Brin and Larry Page, Co-founders of Google

As Google's core business continues to thrive, Google is making huge bets on new technology—ingestible nanoparticles, balloons that beam down broadband—that could define the future. Sergei and Larry are trying to help solve the world's energy and climate problems at Google's philanthropic arm Google.org, which invests in the alternative energy industry to find more diverse sources of renewable energy.

In October 2010, for example, they invested in a major offshore wind power development to assist the East coast power grid, which will eventually become one of about a dozen offshore wind farms proposed for the region. They introduced an artificially intelligent car that drives itself using video cameras and radar sensors. These safer vehicles are lighter and consume less fuel and energy.

Google's Hamina Data Centre is one of the most advanced data centres and the first of its kind in the world. The high-tech cooling system uses sea water from the Bay of Finland to dramatically reduces energy usage.

## Robin Chase, transportation entrepreneur, co-founder of Zipcar, Veniam, Buzzcar

Robin focuses her considerable energies on climate change, making better use of resources (sharing!), and innovation as engines for our future prosperity, together with mesh networking, which brings all of these ideas together. She is driven by a vision of a high integrity future, where we each care about the sources and consequences of our lifestyle, and where individuals and companies thrive in a mutually beneficial and delightfully efficient system, where opportunities to participate and engage abound.

Transportation generates 23% of the world's GHG emissions and personal vehicles generate 60-70% of that. Over 50% of the world's residents live in cities, and urbanisation is increasing rapidly. Cities are dramatically more energy efficient than rural areas. Robin is passionate about making living in cities economically and personally rewarding. Providing easy, sustainable, low-cost access to jobs, education, retail, and leisure activities is critical.

Robin is excited about the revolution enabled by shared and distributed systems. The rise of collaboratively built, financed, and consumed infrastructure and services such as Zipcar,

Lyft, or Uber are all made possible by individuals contributing their assets (their car) to meet other individuals' demand for mobility.

## Sir Ian Cheshire, Founder and Ex-Chairman of the Kingfisher Group

Sir Ian Cheshire led the charge as Founder of Kingfisher to making the group's ambition to become net positive. Kingfisher's recent sustainability report makes it clear how an approach such as ThriveAbility can be a win-win-win proposition - by taking a restorative approach, putting back more than Kingfisher takes out, creates positive change for people and the environment, and a stronger and more resilient business, which is better placed to compete, connect with customers and innovate. By thinking differently Kingfisher is unlocking its creativity to create even more value for all its stakeholders.

Kingfisher's business model is to maximise their cash generation in a responsible way, maximising sales and minimising costs while observing key behaviours – responsibility, honesty, passion, openness and adaptability. Their strategy for delivering business growth is known as Creating the Leader, and Net Positive is an integral part of this.

Sir Ian has now moved onto an advisory role to the UK government, and continues his passion for Net Positive, while the helm of Kingfisher Group has now been handed to a new CEO, Veronique Laury.

*Richard Gillies-Group Sustainability Director*

Richard has taken a very practical approach to making this vision a reality- Kingfisher launched a closed-loop calculator that will helps measure and improve the closed-loop credentials of all product ranges, while measuring their carbon footprint across the whole value chain to help target further reductions to negative impacts on natural and human capitals.

## Fadi Ghandour, Visionary and Founder of Aramex

Fadi Ghandour is the Founder and Vice Chairman of Aramex where he served for 30 years as the company's CEO. Aramex International is one of the leading logistics and transportation companies in the Middle East and South Asia, and the first company from the Arab world to go public on the NASDAQ stock exchange. The company now trades on the Dubai Financial Market.

The Arab world is undergoing a transformative leap, the private sector must seize the moment, recognize its vital role in the development of the region, tap into the huge reservoir of knowledge and experience and put vision and resources in action. Concerted and innovative actions are needed to create a sustainable future for the Arab world as an integral part of the rapid global developments toward a thriveable world.

## Guilherme Leal, Natura co-founder and Board member

Natura Cosmeticos has long been considered a leader in sustainability, known for materials and marketing innovations that aim to reflect its tagline of "well being/being well." They feel responsible for the environmental impact of their activities, from raw material extraction to logistics, processing, manufacturing and packaging. Natura Brazil is now recognised as the second most committed business to sustainable development in the world. (Corporate Knights Order - Global 100. This ranking is announced each year at the World Economic Forum in Davos.)

The company is currently working on Programa Amazonia, a plan to inaugurate its Ecoparque — a 1.7-million-square-meter closed-cycle industrial complex in the Amazon region. The company hopes to eliminate waste and guarantee a clean destination for bio products from Amazonian fruits, oils and berries that are used to produce its cosmetics. The plan also will involve the application of innovations from process and product research.

## Richard Mattison Founder and CEO TruCost

TruCost has been helping companies, investors, governments, academics and thought leaders to understand the economic consequences of natural capital dependency for over 12 years. They are re-pricing the risks associated with environmental issues and reflecting these against traditional financial metrics.

A business case needs to contain quantified data on the effect of a proposed project so it can be compared to other options. Natural capital valuation means the environmental benefits of projects, such as reduced greenhouse gas emissions and air pollution from constructing renewable energy generation, can be fully accounted for alongside financial benefits.

*Alastair MacGregor - Chief Operating Officer TruCost*

Alastair oversees TruCost's operations and Corporate Services business. He manages Trucost's partner network and has led several large bespoke projects including the Natural Capital Coalition's seminal study on natural capital accounting, 'Natural Capital at Risk: The Top 100 Externalities of Business'.

Natural capital accounting enables companies to measure and manage their environmental impacts in a more effective, business-like way. By putting a monetary value on pollution and resource use, companies can better understand and integrate sustainability into their businesses to improve efficiency, reduce risk and increase revenues.

## Rob Michalak, Global Director of Social Mission, Ben & Jerry's

Rob is the lead advocate at Ben & Jerry's to keep Ben & Jerry's Social Mission in balance with the company's Product and Economic Missions. Ben & Jerry's Social Mission seeks to achieve innovative ways that the business can use its many resources to create positive social change in the world and make progress on the company's sustainable corporate concept of "linked prosperity," whereby as the company prospers, its stakeholders prosper too.

In 1993, the company led the fight for the right to label its products rBGH-free, and more recently has publicly opposed cloned and GMO animals, such as salmon.

## Elon Musk, Founder of Tesla

Tesla is a pioneer in electric cars and electric powertrains. Their technology offers an efficient path to a sustainable energy future. Elon transformed the car industry with his innovations to use renewable batteries and power plants. Tesla CEO Elon Musk announced in 2014 that the company will allow its technology patents for use by anyone in good faith, in a bid to entice automobile manufacturers to speed up development of electric cars. Elon Musk was listed as one of Time's 100 people who most affected the world in 2010.

## Gunter Pauli, Founder of ZERI and Ecover

Gunter Pauli is a visionary leader and inventor of the term Blue Economy: the circular economy is a basic reflection on how we should cascade matter, nutrients and energy. We have to change the concept of our production and consumption from a linear input/output to a circular one where everything has a new life and whatever is not consumed in the process is taken up in another process. Gunter started with his frustration with the green economy, as one of the top pioneers in the early 1990s bringing green economy to the market. He built an ecological factory company [Ecover] to make a biodegradable product from renewable sources - and then he realised it still wasn't sustainable.

Gunter believes we must change our mentality. It can't be that doing less bad is good. Pollution is bad - so rather than pollute less we have to start doing things that will create a positive impact on society. Circular economy, cradle to cradle, natural step are great, but really are only interim stages on the way to a new business model.

What we have to do is to eliminate what should never have been in the circle. It is important that many components of the economy never enter the circular economy. So why have a circular economy based on trees and water when we can substitute it with minerals that use no water, and can be recycled forever? There are no limits to growth - but there are limits to growth with the current business model.

## Thomas Rau and Sabine Oberhuber, Turntoo

Turntoo is a Circular-Economy frontrunner offering solutions and consulting services founded by Architect Thomas Rau. Their vision is a world in which products are depots of raw materials. For example, Turntoo doesn't purchase light bulbs anymore, but buys illumination (a certain amount of lux/surface/year). This is in their view a truly disruptive type of innovation. It can change the economy, even our whole life.

Sabine is responsible for the Turntoo Foundation, which has the task of connecting research with the practical implementation of Turntoo and to engage in business education about circular business models. For her the circular economy is one of the most powerful schools of thought in order to realize an economy that is beneficial for business, people and the planet alike.

## KoAnn Vikoren Skrzyniarz, Founder of Sustainable Brands and Sustainable Life Media

Koann is the Founder and CEO of Sustainable Life Media and Sustainable Brands whose involvement with the intersection of environmental and human issues in business dates back to the mid-1980s when she launched international conferences on improving log utilization, reducing Waste Paper, and eliminating ozone-layer destroying chemicals (CFCs).

Throughout her career she has been engaged in testing the connection between purpose driven leadership and competitive bottom line performance. Since 2003, KoAnn has devoted her full attention to the emerging field of social and environmental sustainability, launching Sustainable Life Media in 2004. She has helped various media entrepreneurs and NGO's including Sierra Club and Greenbiz.com establish their own paths to effectiveness and economic sustainability. In 2005, she produced the First International Conference on Cradle to Cradle Design in Practice with Bill McDonough, Michael Braungart, Peter Senge and others. In 2006, she launched what has now become Sustainablebrands.com and in 2007, the widely respected Sustainable Brands Conference. The Sustainable Brands community has grown dramatically each year, and has become the premier international community of sustainable business innovators, with engaged community members represented from all continents.

## Allen White, Founder and Former CEO of GRI, (Global Reporting Initiative), Founder and Co-chair of Global Initiative for Sustainability Ratings

Allen is the Co-Founder and former CEO for the Global Reporting Initiative (GRI). He serves as Vice President and Senior Fellow for Tellus Institute, a Boston-based think tank providing research and action for a global civilization of sustainability, equity, and well-being. In 2004, he co-founded and is now Director of Corporation 2020, an initiative focused on designing future corporations to create and sustain social mission.

Allan talks about the start of GRI: "We had to take a big step forward. Number one, let's go global. Number two, let's move from purely environmental reporting to sustainability reporting and number three, let's do it through the process where everyone has a voice," so we took our chances. It was a big aspiration, a big dream."

In the late 1990s, corporate sustainability reporting was virtually unknown. Yet, in little more than a decade, it has evolved from the extraordinary to the exceptional to the expected., Years of practice have revealed a purpose is even deeper and more transformational. That purpose is the redefinition of corporate value and value creation. In the future, the valuation of a company can and must accord parity to all forms of capital. The planet's well-being and business prosperity alike are at stake. Sustainability reporting stands to play a leading role in this seminal transformation, thanks to the work of Allen and his colleagues.

## Andrew Winston, Founder of Winston Eco-Strategies, Author

Andrew is a globally recognized expert on how companies can navigate and profit from humanity's biggest challenges. Andrew's first book, *Green to Gold*, was the top-selling green business title of the last decade. His latest book, *The Big Pivot*, has been selected among the "Best Business Books of 2014" by *Strategy+Business* magazine. The book provides a practical roadmap to help leaders build resilient, thriving companies and communities in a volatile world.

As founder of Winston Eco-Strategies, Andrew's views on strategy have been sought after by many of the world's leading companies, including Boeing, HP, J&J, Kimberly-Clark, PepsiCo, PwC, and Unilever. Andrew's message is both entertaining and practically optimistic: the world's challenges are great, but business has the tools, resources, and creativity to create a sustainable world.

The leaders of our largest companies currently focus primarily on maximising short-term earnings, and then maybe tackling environmental and social challenges if there's time or if enough stakeholders are giving them grief. The big pivot logic reverses the norm: business needs to operate in ways that help solve the world's greatest challenges, as a precondition for existing as a business (or as a species), and then work backward, using capitalism, markets, and competition to find the most profitable ways to do it. The upside is huge, as multi-trillion-dollar markets (energy, transportation, buildings, consumer products, finance) are in play. But companies will need to embrace new principles and challenge orthodoxies.

## Zhang Yue, Founder and Chairman of the Broad Group

"Responsibility is more important than growth", runs one of the company mottos of China's BROAD Group. BROAD is a world leader in the manufacture of central air-conditioning systems that use diesel or natural gas instead of electricity to cool office buildings, shopping malls and factories. BROAD states that its non-electric air conditioning units are 200% more energy efficient and that $CO_2$ emissions are 4 times lower than traditional models.

BROAD prides itself on its green credentials and lists protecting the environment, energy conservation and reducing greenhouse gases among its key company goals.

Zhang Yue's dream is that his non-electric air conditioning can replace its electric counterpart, as non-electric air conditioning is more than twice as energy efficient as normal electric air conditioning. But his greater dream is that through implementing his Building Energy Efficiency Guidelines, he can substantially increase the energy efficiency level of buildings themselves, because buildings hold 80% of the world's energy saving potential.

## Intrapreneurs[5]

### Mike Barry, CSO of Marks & Spencer

Mike Barry is head of sustainable business at Marks & Spencer. He is part of the team that oversees Plan A, the eco and ethical programme with the ambition to make the company the world's most sustainable major retailer by 2015. He is also Chair of the World Environment Centre, following six years on the WWF programme committee.

Mike deals with issues as diverse as sustainable fish sourcing, chemicals in products, labour standards in factories, animal welfare, food miles, privacy and data protection, genetic modification, fair trade, wood sourcing, community investment, cotton sourcing and climate change.

His suggestion to drive sustainability that others could replicate as best practice is to listen to stakeholders; create external partnerships; lead change; create a business case; have a plan; get leadership from the top; be resilient, and the most important is to create a great team.

*Adam Elman, Global Head Of Delivery For Plan A at Marks & Spencer*

Adam is Global Head of Delivery for Plan A - Marks & Spencer's ground-breaking eco/ethical plan. He is responsible for driving and reporting on the delivery of Plan A across every part of the business, ensuring that appropriate controls are in place and working with colleagues to manage issues and realise opportunities. Adam also has responsibility for M&S Energy - the UK's eight largest provider of gas and electricity to homes across the country.

The experience of M&S is that every time they make their business more sustainable they also deliver business benefit, and in turn this has enabled them to learn further lessons that help unlock further benefit. This approach is now embedded within M&S' Financial Analysis process through bi-annual reviews.

### Niall Dunne, CSO at the BT Group

Niall is the Chief Sustainability Officer (CSO) of BT Group. He has spent the past decade leading sustainability practices in Saatchi & Saatchi and Accenture and has chaired a number of industry initiatives, including the Sustainable Consumption Project Board for the World Economic Forum in 2009. Niall believes that though sustainability may not be trendy, it should become integral to everyday behaviours. He is a passionate and enlightened advocate about the need for products to have low environmental impact, which is at the core of innovation and business growth.

29 companies -- including the likes of Google, BT, Unilever and Nestle -- have laid aside their competitive differences and joined forces with non-profits and millennials to grace the global sustainability stage with an initiative called Collectively -- a global digital platform

designed to connect people, inspire action and change, and 'make sustainable living the new normal'. According to Niall, while sustainability talks had previously centred on issues such as supply sides and deforestation, the question now turns to how to engage people at scale and collectively engage the capabilities and resources of companies toward a greener future.

## Linda Fisher, Vice President and CSO at E.I. DuPont Nemours and Company

Throughout its 214-year history, DuPont has drawn on its scientific expertise to create a continual course of innovative, science-based solutions for their customers, addressing growth markets where demand is driven by the need to ensure there is sufficient, nutritious and healthy food for people across the globe; to reduce our dependence on fossil fuels; and to protect people and the environment. Dupont's goal is for their stakeholders to keep engaging with them and keep helping them do what they can do, better.

Dupont has introduced a new Supplier Code of Conduct, which extends the commitments and expectations of their Core Values to the many thousands of people who provide the necessary supplies and materials to the company. Through this exciting transition and beyond, sustainability will remain central to their mission and key to DuPont's success.

*Paul Tebo, DuPont "Hero of Zero"*

Dr. Tebo had global responsibility for integrating safety, health and environmental excellence as a core business strategy, and for positioning and representing DuPont externally. He created and installed DuPont's "The Goal Is '0'" approach to environmental stewardship, and helped shape the DuPont commitment to "Sustainable Growth" including ambitious renewable energy and resource targets for 2010. He also created and managed DuPont's external global Biotechnology Advisory Panel.

## Mark Gough, former CSO of The Crown Estate

Mark was responsible for developing, delivering and driving innovative ways of embedding sustainability into the business - helping produce one of the first Integrated Reports and to develop a new approach to measure and value its Total Contributions. Mark is on the Natural Capital Committee (Landowners Group) and is a Sustainability Champion of the Scottish Public Sector Climate Leaders Forum (PSCLF).

The Crown Estate focused on reflecting all sustainability issues in a balanced way, but this created a homogenized approach where everything has the same value, which is just not true. One of the most important steps they took through working on an integrated thinking approach was to focus on what is material. For example already 98% of their waste is diverted from landfill, a great sustainability result from lots of hard work, but this is not material to their business, so you will not find it in their annual integrated report. It is after all integrated reporting and not just an integrated report so it should run through all of the communications.

*John Lelliott Finance Director*

John Lelliott has been with The Crown Estate for over 20 years. During this time, John's achievements include leading a review of The Crown Estate's governance framework which included implementing changes to the Boards and Committee structure as well as implementing a business change and efficiency project. John also has responsibility for championing The Crown Estate's move towards integrated reporting which, for the first time, was reflected in the annual report and accounts in 2013 and earned the coveted PwC Building Public Trust Award for 'Recognition in the Public Sector for Excellence in Reporting'.

## Steve Howard, Chief Sustainability Officer of IKEA Group

Steve Howard, founder and CEO of The Climate Group, is the chief sustainability officer (CSO) at IKEA. Steve's mission to take the complexity out of sustainability is evident in Ikea's new-look strategy. Its core goals are: make life at home more sustainable for customers; increase energy and resource independence; and improve life for the people and communities impacted by the company.

IKEA aims to have a positive impact on the world and be energy and resource independent. That means helping everyone in the value chain have a better quality of life. So the next decade's business is going to be shaped by who's really efficient, where they get sustainable raw materials from, and the way they make their products. And who can close the loop and fully recycle things, and who can dematerialize their offerings as much as possible.

IKEA make long-term business decisions. Most businesses don't. Steve looks far ahead, he is optimistic that we can solve all climate challenges and create a fantastic world, a world where we've aligned the environment, the economy and society.

## Lisa Jackson, Apple's Vice President of Environmental Initiatives

Lisa has spent her life dedicated to improving the quality of the environment, resulting in her becoming head of the Environmental Protection Agency under President Obama in 2008. She is also passionate about ensuring all stakeholders have a say in their local communities about issues that affect them, and a great champion of social justice for the less privileged in our world.

Steve Jobs' successor at Apple, Tim Cook, is also a passionate champion of the environment and social justice issues, and hired Lisa to oversee Apple's efforts to minimize its impact on the environment by addressing climate change through renewable energy and energy efficiency, using greener materials, and inventing new ways to conserve precious resources.

Apple has led the industry in powering all its data centres with 100 percent renewable energy and removing many harmful substances from its products.

Apple is going beyond the boundaries of what is required to challenge the boundaries of what's possible- Apple's computers run eight times more efficiently than the Energy Star standards recommend. Under the leadership of Tim and Lisa, this will be just the beginning of a tremendous shift in the way the consumer electronics industry becomes not only sustainable, but contributes to the ThriveAbility of all stakeholders.

## Hannah Jones, Nike Inc's Vice President of Sustainable Business and Innovation

Hannah Jones is Nike Inc's Vice President of sustainable business and innovation. She leads the team mandated with enabling the company to thrive in a future state sustainable economy through closed loop business models. Nike defines the sustainable economy as an economy where people, planet and profit are in balance. The SB&I teams role is to fuel and hothouse sustainable innovation, embed sustainability into the heart of the business model and mobilize key constituencies (employees, consumers, policy makers, civil society and other industry) to enable a rapid transition to a sustainable economy.

Hannah is a founding member of the business advisory council to the United Nations High Commissioner for Refugees (UNHCR), chairs the Sustainable Consumption initiative for the Consumer Industries grouping of the world economic forum and was named a Global Young Leader by the World Economic Forum in January of 2007.

*Santiago Gowland, Managing Director, Sustainable Business & Innovation*

Santiago is General Manager for Sustainable Business & Innovation (SB&I) at Nike Inc. He leads the Systems Innovation Function, which seeks to accelerate and scale innovation by catalysing external resources and new ways of collaboration. Within Systems Innovation Santiago is driving Nike's innovation external engagement agenda and developing network mobilization capabilities to catalyse knowledge, capital, creativity, and connectivity. Santiago leads the partnership with LAUNCH for Nike Inc. LAUNCH is a joined global initiative by Nike, NASA, US Department of State, and US AID. Its mission is to maximize human potential by transforming our existing human systems into new ones that are more sustainable, accessible, and empowering.

## Gail Kelly, Former CEO of Westpac Group

The most powerful woman in finance in Australia, Gail headed Westpac Group Australia's oldest and second largest bank with $651.4 billion in assets and more than 36,000 employees. She aimed for half of the bank's top managers to be women by 2017, the same year that it celebrates its 200th anniversary.

Westpac's vision is to be one of the most respected companies in the world: helping their people, their customers, and communities to prosper and grow. In the last two employee engagement surveys, 97 per cent of their people say 'yes, I understand how the work I do supports the vision of the company'.

## Paul Polman, CEO of Unilever

Unilever is the world's third-largest multinational consumer goods company, after Procter & Gamble and Nestlé. Its products are available in 190 countries. Unilever rigorously measures and reports its progress against three ambitious goals it aims to reach by 2020: helping more than a billion people across the globe improve their health and well-being; halving the environmental footprint of its products; and sourcing 100% of its agricultural raw materials sustainably while enhancing the livelihoods of those working across its supply chain.

The company has committed to doing all this while doubling the size of its business, to about $100 billion. (Unilever derives nearly 60% of its sales from emerging markets.) Paul is relentless about the need for business to serve society, rather than take from it—and his message appears to be getting through. He believes leadership is, first and foremost, about being a good human being, and that future generations will be purpose and values driven, and will only work for leaders that clearly understand this. Paul and his leadership team believe that it is vitally important to make people feel more comfortable working in situations where the win-win is not driven just by shareholders, but by all stakeholders.

## Nick Robins, Head of UNEP (United Nations Environmental Programme) initiative on Sustainable Finance, Former Head of HSBC`s Centre for Excellence in Climate Change

Nick has been at the forefront of sustainable finance initiatives since his time at HSBC where he pioneered research into the financial consequences of climate change risks, leading to a fundamental change in HSBC's lending and investment policies away from fossil-fuel based industries. In 2014 UNEP asked Nick to co-lead it's initiative looking into policy options for guiding the global financial system to invest in the transition to a green economy. While leading financial institutions increasingly appreciate the imperative of climate change, resource scarcity and other environmental challenges, the current financial 'rules of the game' are ill-suited to accelerate this transition from mono-capitalism to multi-capitalism.

Nick believes the UK could become a world leader in energy efficiency financing if it gets the green deal right, constructing a smooth conveyor belt between residential renovation and the bond portfolios of ISAs and pension funds. Extra action to promote low-carbon investment will also need to be matched by efforts to recognise the risks of high carbon assets in investment portfolios. Environmental costs need to be fully integrated into capital expenditure plans for new coal, oil and gas reserves if the threat of stranded assets is to be avoided as the low-carbon economy takes shape.

### Emma Stewart, Head of Sustainability Solutions at Autodesk

Autodesk is a world leader in 3D design software for entertainment, natural resources, manufacturing, engineering, construction, and civil infrastructure. Dr Stewart is Head of Sustainability Solutions at Autodesk, where she leads the design software company's efforts to make sustainable design easy, insightful, and cost-effective for its millions of engineering and design customers. In 2008, she founded its Sustainable Operations program, which was named best-in-class by the Carbon Disclosure Project. In 2009, Emma founded Autodesk's Sustainable Design Living Lab program, which uses Autodesk facilities as a testing ground for new software to rapidly green existing buildings. She co-developed Autodesk's C-FACT methodology (a Corporate Finance Approach to Climate-stabilizing Targets), an open-source, science-driven, business-friendly approach to greenhouse gas target-setting.

The term" smart" can, for Autodesk purposes, be broken down into an acronym, as: S: Sets science-based targets, M: Makes the comprehensive business case, A: Absorbs water, R: Retrofits energy hogs, T: Transports people, not cars.

### Dave Stangis, Vice President of Public Affairs and Corporate Responsibility of Campbell Soup Co., and President of the Campbell Soup Foundation

Dave Stangis is Vice President of Public Affairs and Corp. Responsibility, President of the Campbell Soup Foundation and Chief Sustainability Officer. Dave designs Campbell's overarching CSR, sustainability and community affairs strategy, including its efforts to drive environmental sustainability and make a measureable impact on the health of young people in Campbell communities. Working closely with other senior leaders, he is advancing Campbell's operational and communication strategies in these areas and oversees the development of CSR and sustainability goals, policies and programs for Campbell's.

Dave believes that incremental goals don't drive real change - they simply help focus a little bit of attention. It's just doing the same thing a little bit differently or a little bit better. The goals that seem impossible are the ones that force behaviour change and force people to ask themselves new questions. And it drives a ripple effect all through the company. More and more companies are applying this this "future-driven/backcasting" approach being led by pioneers such as Dave.

### Susanne Stormer, Vice President Corporate Sustainability of Novo Nordisk

Novo Nordisk is a global healthcare company with nearly 90 years of leadership in diabetes care and a leader in haemostatic management, growth hormone therapy and hormone replacement therapy. Susanne sets the strategic direction for Novo Nordisk as a sustainability leader and is responsible for the integration of the company's financial and sustainability reporting. She developed Novo Nordisk's employee volunteer program "Take Action!" where employees are offered the opportunity to engage in activities with a social purpose related to the business, such as working in diabetes clinics or in schools teaching children about nutrition.

The Novo Nordisk Way is central to innovations in the company's structure, business proposition, communications and reporting. Susanne found her niche bridging the divide between the companies she was representing and their stakeholders. While her role has evolved to be about managing sustainably, her core role still revolves around getting communication right. The biggest challenge in that regard is the diversity of languages spoken around the sustainability table, and Susanne's speciality is creating a common understanding of the role of business in contributing to sustainability.

As a part of this work, Novo Nordisk participates in the UN Global Compact LEAD platform that works towards the implementation of the "Blueprint for Corporate Sustainability Leadership", a comprehensive roadmap for businesses towards achieving greater sustainability.

## Kathrin Winkler, Chief Sustainability Officer, EMC Corporation

EMC is a global company that enables organizations, in every industry and sector, to transform their operations and deliver Information Technology as a service. EMC's storage hardware solutions promote data recovery, improve cloud computing, and help IT departments to manage, protect and analyse information in a more agile and cost-efficient way. EMC has committed to improving its operations and becoming more transparent through setting ambitious environmental impact goals and consistently reporting on its progress.

Transforming corporate mindsets about sustainability has been both a personal and professional journey for Kathrin Winkler, Senior Vice President and Chief Sustainability Officer for EMC Corporation. Winkler provides the vision, strategy and leadership for EMC's global sustainability initiatives with a mission to integrate sustainability into every aspect of corporate culture, business strategy, and day-to-day decision-making. At EMC they really mean what they say, demonstrating a very high level of integrity in walking their talk.

## Steve Waygood, Chief Responsible Investment Officer at Aviva Investors

Aviva Investors is part of Aviva plc., one of the UK's largest insurance services providers and one of the leading providers of life and general insurance in Europe. Thanks to Steve and his colleagues leadership, Aviva Investors has embedded sustainability practices into its own operations. Steve's primary focus is on remedying the flawed methodologies that are currently used to value corporate assets and profitability, and the role both policymakers and the private sector need to play in addressing those flaws.

Aviva Investors played a prominent role in helping to establish the Sustainable Stock Exchange (SSE) in 2009 in partnership with the United Nations. The SSE promotes sustainable capital markets and also explores how stock exchanges can work together with investors, regulators and companies on environmental, social and corporate governance issues, encouraging long-term approaches to investment.

At Aviva sustainability issues are routinely important when valuing companies for their clients' portfolios. That's why Aviva is a long-standing champion of the idea that companies should be more transparent about their sustainability performance. However, it is often very difficult to source accurate performance data with over 75% of companies currently reporting no quantitative data on sustainability performance. Steve is leading the charge to change all that.

### Jochen Zeitz, Director and Chairman of Sustainability Committee at Kering, formerly CEO of Puma

Kering (previously PPR) is a French luxury goods holding company for luxury, sport & lifestyle brands distributed in 120 countries. Jochen Zeitz is the Director and Chairman of the board's sustainable development committee following his successes as CEO of the Sport & Lifestyle division and Chief Sustainability Officer (CSO) of Kering since 2010. Prior to this, Zeitz served 18 years as Chairman and CEO at Puma. He is a member of The Economics of Ecosystems and Biodiversity (TEEB) Advisory Board, and a co-founder and co-chair with Sir Richard Branson of The B Team. He also demonstrates his commitment to sustainability and global environmental protection with his Zeitz Foundation for Intercultural Ecosphere Safety.

Jochen was instrumental in turning Puma into an open-source design playground. Everyone said they were crazy, but their vision was that if you want to change the industry and do something completely new and innovate, research is a bad tool because all you will get fed back is perception today and not tomorrow. What is needed is a clear vision of a very different future, a visionary role Jochen plays in whatever arena he decides to contribute his formidable talents.

## A Salute!

We salute these ThriveAbility Leaders, and look forward to helping many other leaders and managers to follow their brilliant and courageous examples, through the application of the ThriveAbility Approach in organizations, and the development of the ThriveAbility Index for financial markets. It is high time future leaders become capable of generating true future value, and we hope that your journey through these pages has encouraged you to explore your own journey as a ThriveAbility Leader, and how you might enable one or more organizations that matter to you, to take the next step on its own ThriveAbility Journey.

We will now pull everything we have explored in this "Leader's Guide to ThriveAbility" together into a single, over-arching model in Chapter 6, so that you can not only share this exciting story with others, but also find ways to apply ThriveAbility thinking and processes in your own life and career.

# 6. Why There is Hope – Toward a Planetary Delta

In this book we have explored how measuring true, inclusive value becomes possible in every key decision made by individuals, organizations and investors based on a set of principles and metrics embodied in a new discipline we call "ThriveAbility", and how this can transform the way capital and capitalism function, while enabling both corporate transformation and "governance /regulation for good", rather than just "less bad", possible.

ThriveAbility has been designed from two very different yet complementary perspectives:

- An **"Outside – In"** model where change in the system is driven by factors outside of an organization and usually outside its direct control (the *governance /regulation for good" approach*), and
- An **"Inside – Out'** model where change in the system is driven by factors largely internal to and within the control of an organization and its leadership team (the *"corporate transformation"* approach).

In the first five chapters of this "Leader's Guide to ThriveAbility", we have assembled all of the necessary ingredients for both models, and in this chapter we will take you through each model and its key features as built into the ThriveAbility "System". We will then present you with a "Grand Finale" diagram of the marriage of the two virtuous cycles into a single, coherent system that *"plugs and plays"* with existing organizational methods for strategy, innovation, resource allocation and transformation.

At this point we also need to reiterate that we are standing on the already broad shoulders of giants in the fields of leadership, sustainability, biology, climate science and psychology, so that we can see further and deliver the breakthroughs needed for our survival and thrival as a species.

Our critique of existing models and ways of doing things is done solely with the intent of creating even better models, in the humble acknowledgement, based on empirical evidence, that 90% of what is being done in the name of sustainability today is applying the older, "less bad" approaches, while only 10% of practice is currently heading in the direction of a ThriveAble world. And encouraging that good/better practice is the entire purpose of this book, and the ThriveAbility Foundation.

Let us begin with a brief recap of two of the core ingredients of ThriveAbility: incentives and motivation, to better appreciate the need for both **"Outside – In"** and **"Inside – Out'** approaches.

## Of Carrots and Sticks – What Motivates Us

The history of human beings has been dominated by the stick, rather than the carrot. The "upside-down thinking" that lies at the heart of ThriveAbility is designed to make the carrot more important than the stick, if we are to survive and thrive as a species on a thriving planet. That is a pretty big carrot....though, as we shall see, neither can we throw away the stick yet either. We shall also see that in the right circumstances, intrinsic motivation is going to get us a lot further than just extrinsic (carrot and stick) motivation on its own.

Think of just about any moral, religious or legal code- full of sticks. "Thou shalt not....", "It is an offense to ...", "Punishable by....". Even our educational systems are generally stick-oriented, where authority figures highlight the negative consequences of not getting a good education. "You will not get a good job unless you...", "If you fail this subject....", "Do that once more and I will...", and so on.

We've all been there. And we can all probably remember a few remarkable exceptions to this rule of the stick in the form of an encouraging parent, an inspiring teacher/professor, a good/wise cop, a friendly neighbour, mentor, boss or coach. These are people who knew the power of the carrot, which works to motivate us through rewards in the future for doing the right thing, and for doing things right, now and in the future. Such leaders offered us "carrots" to motivate us, and if they were particularly inspiring, may also have helped shape our own, inner, intrinsic motivation based on the enjoyment we derive from doing a specific activity or creating something.

There are good historical reasons for the stick being our species' favourite tool when it comes to enforcing desired behaviours and beliefs- it is relatively simple to use, and requires little relationship beyond a "power over" another based on physical dominance. Sticks are the path of least resistance for those who are confident of their superiority, and ignorant of the longer-term consequences of their mind-set and actions.

In 1960, Douglas McGregor published "The Human Side of Enterprise" where he outlined a shift in management styles from the stick-based "Theory X", to the carrot based "Theory Y". Theory X applies to individuals whom are reluctant to work and need to be urged to work in most cases and are more inclined to work for extrinsic rewards, and as such, an **authoritarian style** needs to be adapted in order to keep these individuals in line.

Carrot-centric Theory Y, on the other hand, applies to individuals who have a high level of autonomy within a workplace. In their case, the authoritarian Theory X style is ineffective, as these individuals have a high degree of self-direction, crave intrinsic rewards, and show an unwavering commitment towards achieving a given objective. A participative style is much more suited to these individuals as more participation means that these individuals can easily satisfy their intrinsic needs of self-respect and achievement.

Theory X "assumes that people are lazy, dislike and shun work, have to be driven and need both carrot and stick . . . and have to be looked after." Theory Y, on the other hand, "assumes that people have a psychological need to work and want achievement and responsibility."

It appears that McGregor preferred Theory Y. "Yet things are far less simple than McGregor's followers would make us—and themselves—believe," management guru Peter Drucker observed in *Management: Tasks, Responsibilities, Practices*.

For one thing, most of us prefer the "security of order and direction," at least to some extent, and that cannot come purely from internal drive. For another, Drucker pointed out, "ordinary, everyday experience teaches us that the same people react quite differently to different circumstances."

He added, "Or at the very least, *there are different human natures which behave differently under different conditions.*" This is why ThriveAbility applies a "stratified" approach to leadership, management and human behaviour in general, as explained in much great detail in chapter four and the appendices. Diagram 20 below offers a peak into just how different incentives and disincentives ("Hot" and "Cold" buttons, respectively), can look from different levels of perspective.

**DIAGRAM 20 – Carrots and Sticks Viewed from Different Developmental Perspectives: Stratified Leadership Tips on Hot and Cold Buttons from each Perspective**

| Stage | LIKES: HOT BUTTONS | DISLIKES: COLD BUTTONS |
|---|---|---|
| **Magician** | – Passion for planetary concerns<br>– Likes to see everything at once<br>– Recognizes ego as most serious threat to development<br>– Thinks in holographic mosaics<br>– Respect for all life, implicit order in universe<br>– Understands mega systems, social relations, evolution, business and need to preserve planet earth for future generations<br>– Likes freedom to re-frame and completely disrupt existing paradigms | – Resents disturbance of 'other worldly' bubble while tuned into everyday systems transcending anything practical<br>– Intolerant of and condescending of those not tuned into their deeper connection with the Kosmos<br>– Being confronted with dogmatic or linear thinking<br>– Dislikes 'silver bullet' advocacy intensely |
| **Strategist** | – Have to see and work with big picture<br>– Values what is natural likes voluntary simplicity<br>– Focuses on competency, responsibility and freedom of choice.<br>– Likes info and knowledge based decision making<br>– Capable of fearless creative problem solving<br>– Understands chaos & flows are natural & flexibility key<br>– Enjoys magnificence of existence | – Being boxed trapped in plus trapped in the detail<br>– Rejects conformity and authoritarian structure<br>– Especially rigid structures based on role or rank<br>– Detest opinionated fact free arguments and belief systems<br>– No patience with whingers, complainers |
| **Individualist** | – Create a sense of belonging, sharing, harmony;<br>– Show sensitivity to human issues, Nature, and others;<br>– Call for an expansion of awareness, self understanding, and liberation of the oppressed;<br>– Use symbols of equity, humanity, and bonding;<br>– Use gentle language and Nature imagery;<br>– Build trust, openness, exploration for growth;<br>– Present real people and authentic emotional displays;<br>– Encourage participation, sharing, consensus, teamwork, community involvement. | – Assault the group's goals and ideals;<br>– Try to get centralized control;<br>– Reject the collective for individual accountability;<br>– Deny affect and feelings;<br>– Degrade quality of life or environment;<br>– Rely on "hard facts" and exclude people factors;<br>– Act elitist. |
| **Achiever/ Expert** | – Appeal to competitive advantage and leverage;<br>– Draw upon success, progress, and status motivations;<br>– Inspire to face the challenge;<br>– Call for bigger, better, newer, faster, more popular;<br>– Cite experts; use scientific data, calculated risks, proven experience;<br>– Show increased profit, productivity, quality, results;<br>– Demonstrate as best option, strategy;<br>– Show as way to pre-empt government intervention. | – Put down profit or entrepreneurship;<br>– Talk about collectivization;<br>– Challenge compulsive drives;<br>– Deny rewards for good performance;<br>– Force sameness;<br>– Trap with rules and procedures;<br>– Seem inflexible or ordinary;<br>– Treat as one of the herd. |
| **Blue** | – Invoke duty, honour, country;<br>– Use images of discipline and obedience to higher authority;<br>– Call for good citizenship, stewardship, self sacrifice for a higher cause;<br>– Appeal to traditions, laws, order, and being prepared;<br>– Draw upon propriety and responsibilities;<br>– Show how behaviour will insure future rewards, require delayed gratification, assuage guilt. | – Attack religion, country, heritage, or standards;<br>– Desecrate symbols or Holy Books;<br>– Put down the One True-Way;<br>– Violate chain of command;<br>– Disregard rules and directives;<br>– Appear unfair or sleazy;<br>– Use profanity. |
| **Opportunist** | – Demonstrate "What's in it for me, now?";<br>– Offer "Immediate gratification if ...";<br>– Challenge and appeal to machismo/strength;<br>– Point out heroic status and legendary potential;<br>– Be flashy, unambiguous;<br>– Be reality-based, and strong;<br>– Use Simple language;<br>– Use fiery images/graphics;<br>– Appeal to narcissistic tendencies. | – Challenge power or courage;<br>– Shame or put down person! group;<br>– Move onto turf;<br>– Be derisive and laugh;<br>– Taunt as an outsider;<br>– Appear or talk weak;<br>– Make excuses. |

To become a ThriveAbility Leader, it is necessary to master the ability to "get" where people are coming from, at all levels, and be able to motivate them where they are at, rather than wishing they were "at your level". The latter simply leads to frustration, miscommunication and poor results.

We also need to remember that leadership is situational, and that great leaders always offer what is needed in a situation by adapting themselves and their leadership style. ThriveAbility leaders will, in addition, be able to sense what behaviours will lead to the most thriveable outcome in any situation.

If leaders are too far ahead of those they are leading in a particular situation, then they risk being "out of touch", while if they are at the same developmental level as their teams, then they will build good rapport but may not offer the vision or direction setting required to move the organization or team to the next level.

For more detailed explanations of how to tune your leadership style for ThriveAbility in any situation, go to Diagram 17 in chapter four and also Appendices B and C.

We will now explore how different kinds of incentives influence ThriveAbility, and what you should be aware of as a leader to be able to spot what Thriving and ThriveAbility look like in any given situation, before we go on to see how this is operationalized in the ThriveAbility Models and program. For our grand finale, we will present what might be called a "Unified ThriveAbility System", which summarises this entire book in a single diagram, while also providing a handy reference to every single other model used in the Leader's Guide to ThriveAbility via its two parts, the Outside – In and Inside – Out models.

The unified ThriveAbility system can also be thought of as an operating system, which is open source, and which has common interfaces to all the other key parts of the worlds of organizations, business, technology, strategy, sustainability and the sciences of the Anthropocene. In this way the new ways of thinking, leading and organizing recommended in these pages can become firmly embedded at a global scale, as the next level of "good practice" everywhere.

## How Extrinsic and Intrinsic Incentives Influence ThriveAbility

> "Those three things - autonomy, complexity and a connection between effort and reward - are, most people agree, the three qualities that work has to have if it is to be satisfying. It is not how much money we make that ultimately makes us happy between nine and five. It's whether our work fulfils us."
> *Malcolm Gladwell, Outliers: The Story of Success*

At the beginning of this book we emphasised that ThriveAbility is based on an *understanding of incentives*, and how they motivate different people with different value systems in different situations. The most common incentive is a reward. Rewards can be tangible or intangible, and are presented generally after the occurrence of the action or behaviour that one is trying to correct or cause to happen again. This is done by associating positive meaning with the desired behaviour and or action, rather than simply expecting people to be "good".

Motivation comes from two sources: oneself (*intrinsic*), and other people (*extrinsic*). A number of studies have demonstrated that offering excessive external rewards for an already internally rewarding behaviour can actually lead to a reduction in intrinsic motivation, a phenomenon known as the over-justification effect[67].

Most of us are not happy about extreme extrinsic rewards such as compensation schemes and bonuses that are out of line with longer-term outcomes, especially given the increasingly wide gap between what some top executives earn and what most of us earn. That feeling is exacerbated when we keep hearing how the top one per cent has managed to do increasingly well, with special tax breaks and special investment opportunities while many of us are experiencing flattened incomes or worse. The inherent unfairness and the uncertainty we feel about the economy, driven home by what we and/or friends are experiencing, moves money and other extrinsic rewards closer to the top of our minds. Fair enough.

Two of the popular writers on this topic, Daniel Pink and Malcolm Gladwell, emphasize the *power of intrinsic rewards* to motivate us. Pink[68] suggests that intrinsic rewards have a stronger and more beneficial effect on us than extrinsic benefits- he asserts that the secret to high performance and satisfaction in today's world is the deeply human need to direct our own lives, to learn and create new things, and to do better by ourselves and the world. Along the way, he points out companies that are enlisting such new approaches to motivation. Gladwell stresses the importance of autonomy, complexity and a connection between effort and reward together with continual practice in creating mastery.

From the perspective of leadership for ThriveAbility, it is key that the ultimate and most powerful incentive appears to be the desire to "Thrive", rather than simply survive. This desire to thrive is expressed at all value system levels, in very different terms, as is made clear in earlier chapters. What Daniel Seligman points out in "Flourish", is that the generic features of the most powerful incentives include those he lists as "PERMA":

- Positive Psychology
- Engagement
- Relationships
- Meaning, and
- Accomplishment.

---

[67] The over justification effect occurs when an external incentive decreases a person's intrinsic motivation to perform a behaviour or participate in an activity. Researchers have found that when extrinsic rewards (such as money and prizes) are given for actions that people already find intrinsically rewarding, they will become less internally motivated to pursue those activities in the future. Why does the over justification effect occur? According to one theory, people tend to pay more attention to these external rewards rather than their own enjoyment of the activity. As a result, people think that their participation in the activity is the result of the external rewards rather than their own internal appreciation of the behaviour. Another possible explanation is that people sometimes view external reinforcement as a coercive force. Since they feel like they are being "bribed" into performing the behaviour, they assume that they are doing it only for this external reinforcement.

[68] Daniel H. Pink's Drive: The Surprising Truth About What Motivates Us. Canongate Books, 2011

The way in which the Gallup Organization measures thriving, builds on this model and also injects some powerful global statistics into framing what suffering, struggling and thriving mean across 180 different countries, using 20 standard questions and the World Poll model.

## Motivation to Thrive and Incentives to do so Sustainably

The desire to thrive appears to be universal across all life forms. Given a choice, most well-adjusted beings take the option they believe will enhance not only their survival but also their thriving. In the past few years, the link between sustainability and happiness has been highlighted by many[6].

To take just one example, in which the Gallup Healthways Well-Being Index was used – in a recent study[69] researchers found that cities with strong sustainable development practices and policies self-report higher levels of happiness. In fact, sustainable practices, such as community gardens, green spaces, green homes, and sustainable transportation, have all been shown to increase happiness. Sustainable design can also enhance and strengthen social networks—and the importance of that can't be overstated.

The most important psychological effect of the city is the way in which it moderates our relationships with other people. Connected people sleep better at night, are more able to tackle adversity, live longer and report being happier. [70]

We also know that a direct concern for sustainability tends to be expressed differently at different levels of adult development, from a great deal of research into how values shape the cultures and wellbeing of different parts of cities[71].

The future measurements for the wealth of cities and nations will definitely include the enhancement of human, social and natural capital for the least manufactured capital footprint, through the most effective allocation of financial and intellectual capital. Social learning drives this socially innovative process together with complex systemic thinking associated with the advanced leadership mindsets we explored in chapter 4, notably the strategist and alchemist levels of leadership.

What would the world look like if we were to elect civic[72] and national leaders who understood the importance of this kind of governance and regulation for the future of our species and all life on earth? Very different, one suspects. And alongside such developments, what would our

---

[69]  http://link.springer.com/article/10.1007/s10668-013-9499-0 published in the journal *Environment, Development and Sustainability,*

[70]  Charles Montgomery, Happy City: Transforming Our Lives Through Urban Design. MacMillan, 2013.

[71]  See the research of Dr Marilyn Hamilton at http://www.integralcity.com/ and her book "**Integral City: Evolutionary Intelligences for the Human Hive** – New Society Publishers, 2008. 12 chapters exploring the contexting, individual, collective, strategic and evolutionary intelligences of the city.

[72]  The approach of the former mayor of New York City, Michael Bloomberg, is an interesting example of this kind of stewardship.

world look like if we applied the principles of ThriveAbility to our leadership and organizations and markets? What if the CEO's of the 80 000 global corporations got up every morning, looked in the mirror at themselves, and said:

"Today I am going to add more true value to create a thriveable future for our organization and its stakeholders?"

Let us now turn to our two models of ThriveAble transition to see how both extrinsic and intrinsic rewards, with *more carrots than sticks*, can help accelerate and scale what is already working, while also delivering much needed breakthroughs across key industries.

## The Outside – In Model – The "Regulation for Good" Approach

In this model, change in the system is driven by factors outside of an organization and usually outside its direct control (the "governance /regulation for good" approach). Transitions and transformations are driven not only by the desire to be "less bad" according to the regulations, but also to aspire to be "good enough" or even "best" in a given category.

In diagram 20 below we set out the process by which an organization can be incentivized to transform itself from "less bad" to "thriveable". The one thing we know about organizations is that they are a lot like supertankers – they take a very long time to change direction in any profound way. This is due not only to the sheer scale and complexity of their operations, but also the time it takes the leadership teams and stakeholders to shift their mindsets sufficiently to support the changes and transformations required to go from "less bad" to "thriveable".

For budding ThriveAbility Leaders, the Outside-In and Inside-Out diagrams provide a convenient summary of the contents of this book, as well as a guide to action and implementation. Let us start with the Outside-In model shown in diagram 21 below.

Four kinds of activity are demonstrated in diagram 21 – from *bottom to top* they are:

- *The ThriveAbility Index Generator, Six Capitals Equation and Innovation Pathways* – the three key components of the *ThriveAbility Assessment* are shown here in the *ThriveAbility Index Generator*, together with the "Delta", or shift that becomes possible through the alignment that arises during the assessment process. This is followed to the right by the *Six Capitals Equation*, the use of which informs the work done to map and prioritize the Innovation Pathways that will drive the Delta shifts that help an organization to map its progression along the ThriveAbility Journey; *(See Chapter 2)*

- *The Five Stages of the ThriveAbility Journey* – as we highlighted in chapters 1 and 2 of this Leaders Guide to ThriveAbility, 90% of organizations are today stuck in Stage One, the "denial/compliance" stage of the ThriveAbility Journey. Another 7% or so are moving through Stage Two, the "Less Bad" stage, with a variety of Corporate Social responsibility and "Green Branding" initiatives, where one or more products or parts of the organization are striving to become more sustainable. *(See Chapter 1, Diagram 3)*

A spearhead of several hundred highly ambitious organizations are moving from Stage Two to Stage Three, where some of the leaders in this group, such as InterfaceFlor, are close to becoming genuinely sustainable with programs such as "Mission Zero"[73], while also thinking hard about what lies beyond sustainability[74], (including exploring the ThriveAbility program).

In Stage Four, there is also a small advance guard of other organizations who are exploring how they might become "Net Positive" as we outlined earlier in chapter 1. The leaders of these organizations make it clear that Net Positive is a longer-term goal, and will take some time to reach, though we can hope that with the support of the ThriveAbility program such a journey might be accelerated.

Finally, Stage 5 may still represent a dream for any large organization, yet there are many wonderful examples of regenerative initiatives in the world of sustainable development and start-ups, which would take another book to describe. Such initiatives offer great hope that such thriveable innovations can be scaled as well as blended into existing corporate innovation pathways through the ThriveAbility program.

- *The four phases of the ThriveAbility program and the Six Step process* – finally, on the top row, we can see how the ThriveAbility Index is constructed through the six-step process, represented by the circles with the shaded parts that get "filled-in" with metrics and data based on the principles outlined in this book.

  - **Enabling** - comprising the ThriveAbility Assessments and Innovation Pathways mapping;
  - **Activation** - comprising the benchmarking of corporations within specific industries against each other regarding their "current state" and their desired "future states";
  - **Indexing** - developing the fundamental components of the ThriveAbiity Index within the ten Sustainable Accounting Standards Board industry classifications;
  - **Thriving** – launching the full ThriveAbility Index with linkages into stock and bond market indices as well as the lending portfolios of banks and the investment

---

[73] For example, zero carbon emissions (=100% renewable energy), zero waste, zero polluted water, zero accidents, and so on. Interface founder Ray Anderson often likened achieving sustainability to climbing a mountain higher than Mt. Everest. With this in mind, a path was laid out designed to achieve sustainability on seven ambitious fronts, to reach Interface's Mission Zero goal by 2020. For more details see http://www.interfaceflor.fr/web/sustainability/mission_zero/seven_fronts

[74] The new CEO of InterfaceFlor, Rob Boogaard, is already thinking hard with his leadership team how to prepare the organization for a Stage Four future http://www.floorinsite.com/interface-emea-appoints-rob-boogaard-as-ceo/

appraisal methods of funds managers and longer-term investors. *(See Chapter 3, Diagram 15)*

Here at the ThriveAbility Foundation, our collective experience working within and advising corporations tells us that a four year timeframe for major change or transformation is the minimum time period in which we can expect a system as large and complex as a global corporation to demonstrate a serious shift from one stage in the ThriveAbiity Journey to the next. Hence we have shown a hypothetical time-frame for four steps of the ThriveAbility program from 2015 – 2018. In turn, the ThriveAbility Index takes into account the current initiatives being undertaken by many different parties in the formulation and implementation of the Sustainable Development Goals, the work being done to complete a new global agreement on climate change, and the implementation of the Sustainable Stock Markets initiative, amongst other initiatives that could lead to sustainable bond markets and thriveable bank lending policies[75].

So, to summarize, the Outside-In model relies on extrinsic motivators with a weighting toward "carrots", while ensuring that both carrots ("Regulation for Good" through the ThriveAbility Index") and sticks ("Regulation as Usual" which enforces the law and industry standards with legal consequences through the regulatory bodies we have today), are used in appropriate ways based on what works best for different categories of "player" in each industry motivationally. This ensures both a "push" pressure from regulation, as well as a "pull" drive that can create the cultures and organizations that will strive for ThriveAbility rather than simply meet "Less Bad" standards and be awarded higher ratings for being "less bad". In order to ensure a thriving world in the 21st century, we need leading organizations in every industry to tangibly demonstrate the benefits of striving for good.

---

[75] The Sustainable Stock Exchanges (SSE) initiative is a peer-to-peer learning platform for exploring how exchanges, in collaboration with investors, regulators, and companies, can enhance corporate transparency – and ultimately performance – on ESG (environmental, social and corporate governance) issues and encourage sustainable investment. http://www.sseinitiative.org/

## DIAGRAM 21 – The ThriveAbility Index and the "Regulation for Good" Approach

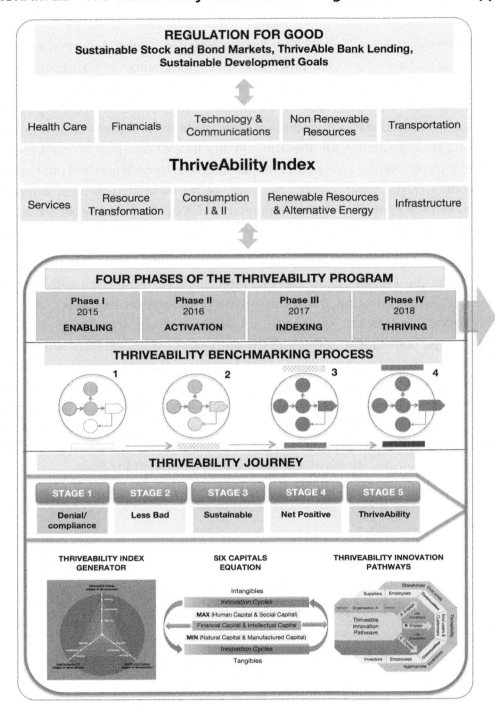

Luckily, as our 50 ThriveAbility Leaders highlighted in chapter five demonstrate, there are already hundreds of organizations striving for good who are already on the ThriveAbility Journey. What would it take to get the majority of global corporations to emulate them? The answer to this question invokes the second, Inside-Out ThriveAbility model.

## The Inside – Out Model – The "Corporate Transformation Approach"

In this model, change in the system is driven by factors largely internal to and within the control of an organization and its leadership team (the "corporate transformation" approach). In diagram 22 below we illustrate how the transformation of corporations based on a global public good approach to transformation i.e. an open source model, could create a virtuous cycle that enables organizations to accelerate their own change and transformation processes as a key part of their strategy, business and product design and innovation activities.

Of course in practice the incentives of both outside-in and inside-out approaches combine to create a whirlwind of beneficial change if correctly aligned, and such change is always to the advantage of the change agents, entrepreneurs, intrapreneurs and innovators who can shift the value equation in their favour and create sustainable competitive advantage. The beauty of using "true value" as the ultimate metric in both outside-in and inside-out approaches is that it produces a win-win-win for all stakeholders, and all capitals.

There are seven key components in the corporate transformation model that are all explained in detail in chapters 1 to 4, so if you need more detail on any of them you can go directly to that part of the book. Here we are more concerned with the overview and interconnections between these components, and how they create a virtuous cycle.

# DIAGRAM 22 – The ThriveAbility Program and the "Corporate Transformation" Approach

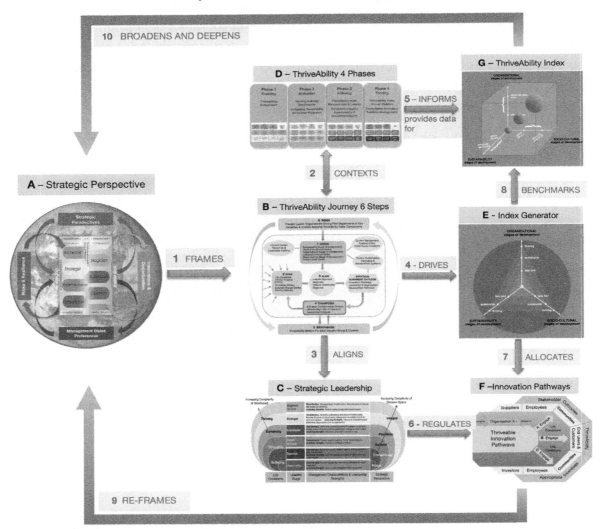

## And So the Story Begins…How Do Corporations and Industries Transform?

If we were to "tell the story" of how the inside-out model works, here is what it would look like. Remember that this story takes place over a period of three to four years, and also endures for many decades, even lifetimes beyond that in some cases. It might seem complex, but in reality it offers an incredibly effective way to tackle sustainability, innovation, stakeholder engagement, strategy and leadership in a single, highly economical way. This is the simplicity the other side of complexity, or what we call "*Simplexity*".

Please refer to *Diagram 22* above to follow the transformative tale of global corporations and small to medium sized organizations, "from A to G".

**A. Strategic Perspective** All things begin with the perspective from which one views the world, even corporate change, transformation and innovation. The **Strategic Perspective** tool enables leaders to appreciate the different mindsets and values that animate the strategic situation their firm and its stakeholders are in, and helps generate new insights into what is possible based on what is naturally "next" for those stakeholders. It also helps them discern how an incremental approach to guarding against vulnerabilities in the organization ("*risks and resilience*") requires a very different mindset to the transformative change mindset needed to imagine and profit from the "*innovations and opportunities*" that will create the organization's strengths and unique capabilities for the future. Very different management style preferences will be needed for incremental versus transformative leadership in different parts of the organization, and this is one of the key things leaders will have to pay attention to.

This strategic perspective **FRAMES** the six steps of the ThriveAbility Journey, in the sense that it both enables and constrains what becomes possible next.

**B. The Six Steps of the ThriveAbility Journey** then provide a ready-made process for strategy, transformation and innovation that is designed to work well with almost every existing approach in these areas. The distinctive feature of this journey is, however, that the assessment tools and alignment process are designed to identify *innovation pathways* that will generate *true value*, not just value-added with externalities. In addition, the metrics and data generated as a part of this journey are *benchmarked* with industry and generic peers, as an input into the creation of the ThriveAbility Index. This benchmarking forms part of a continuous improvement and organizational learning loop, and is also the *key link to the Outside-In process*.

The six steps of the ThriveAbility Journey then enable three key things- it:

- **CONTEXTS** the four phases of the *ThriveAbility program* as it unfolds, ensuring that a critical mass of organizations is moving through each phase to trigger the next;
- **DRIVES** the *ThriveAbility Index Generator*, which is a global database managed by the Foundation as a global public good that generates the statistics used in the Index and also as an input into the Innovation Pathways;

- **ALIGNS** the priorities for the organization's *Strategic Leadership* approach using a stratified set of lenses capable of seeing deeply into which incentives motivate which stakeholders on the journey toward true value.

**C. The Strategic Leadership Framework** translates the outputs from the Six Step process into a blueprint for leadership development and innovation priorities, building on the alignments emerging from the Six Step process

The priorities that emerge from that then **REGULATE** the scope and scale of the *Innovation Pathways.*

**D. The Four Phases of the ThriveAbility Program** are essential to ensure that the *Enabling, Activation, Indexing* and *Thriving* phases have at least four organizations per industry group to create meaningful benchmarks that can evolve into Index components. The program is run as a global public good by the ThriveAbility Foundation to co-create the ThriveAbility Index.

This program **INFORMS** the ThriveAbiity Index co-creation process, and ensures that the global database managed by the Foundation is well populated and able to generate the statistics used in the Index and also act as a meaningful input into the Innovation Pathways in each organization.

**E. The ThriveAbility Index Generator** maps the unique ways in which each organization can close the sustainability, organizational and leadership/culture gaps in its own activities and industry. The effective allocation of funds by capital markets to organizations that deliver thriveable innovation by harnessing their intellectual and financial capital to this end would then be much more likely, and the trillions needed to ensure we close the sustainability and sustainable development gaps much better targeted by corporate capital allocation processes, investors, banks and fund managers.

This, the progress that an organization is making on its ThriveAbility Journey as a result of the "Delta" generated through the six step process, serves to **ALLOCATE** all six capitals more effectively into the innovation pathways that will generate greatest competitive and stakeholder advantage and true value creation.

**F. The Innovation Pathways** tool offers a strategic way to prioritize the innovation portfolio in an organization according to the principles of true value and the six capitals. To make the transition from "less bad" through "sustainable" and "net positive" to "thriveable" involves identifying *robust innovation pathways* based on principles and metrics which clearly identify how to maximize the thriving of the organization's human and social capital for the least natural and manufactured capital footprint possible.

The successful outcomes from the Innovation Pathways then serve to **RE-FRAME** what is possible in the overall mindset of the organization, thereby expanding the horizons of the organization's Strategic perspective and focusing its efforts onto the 20% of efforts generating 80% of the true value.

**G. The ThriveAbility Index** eventually becomes a primary reference source for the allocation of capitals to an organization, and becomes incorporated into the Bloomberg and other data terminal systems used by financial decision makers around the world to make better long-term investment decisions.

As a result, this **BROADENS AND DEEPENS** the strategic perspectives of organizations everywhere, showing them what is possible and desirable, and what is not.

And then we all live happily ever after, or not, depending on how what we do in the next few decades manages to create the conditions for thriving for future generations. The choice is literally in our hands, and in your hands right now.

The marriage of the Outside-In and Inside-Out systems ultimately results in two reinforcing virtuous cycles which we believe are able to address the many challenges and opportunities of our new age, the Anthropocene, is they can be successfully embedded in leadership and managerial practices in a critical mass of organizations.

## The ThriveAbility Operating System – From Stranded Assets/Banks/Organizations to Integrated Capitals/investments/Business Ecosystems

When we pull together the Outside-In and Inside Out systems we find that the two reinforcing virtuous cycles integrate beautifully into a single cycle of on-going improvement and transformation from less bad organizations and economies to a thriveable world in which there is hope and new forms of prosperity for future generations.

Diagram 23 summarises this transformative cycle, and the logic of this entire Leader's Guide to ThriveAbility. We shall use this ThriveAbility Operating System or "TAOS" for short, as a handy map to the entire book.

### DIAGRAM 23 – The ThriveAbility Operating System

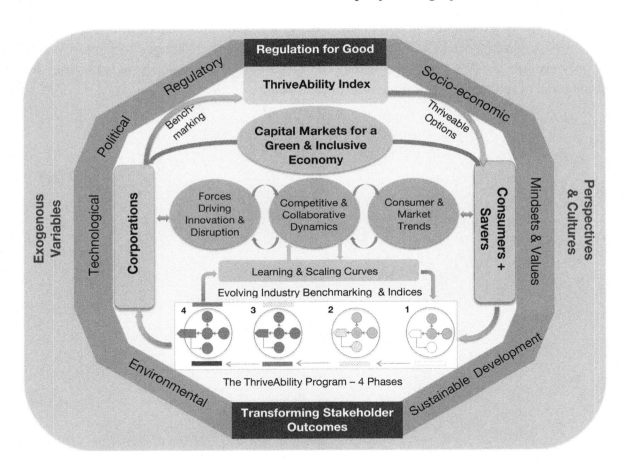

The TAOS map is built up layer by layer, from the outside toward the inside. Let us begin the explanation of this map with the *outer beige layer*- the human being and the unpredictable world we live in.

## Perspectives and Cultures – the Endogenous (Coming from within) Variables - PULL

On the *right hand side* we find that human beings create their worlds out of what social scientists like to call "native" *perspectives*, which are largely unconscious up until a certain stage of development. Such native perspectives through which we look at and attempt to understand the world, vary widely between *cultures*, and hence it is not surprising that we live on a planet which appears to be characterized by a mutual incomprehension between very different cultures in very different parts of the world, and this leads to much friction, tension and even war, from time to time. And much the same can be said of the world of organizations.

Luckily, in the past century we have developed a much more advanced understanding of what goes on in the interiors of human minds and hearts, and our cultures. These new insights are made actionable through *stratified leadership and organizational design methods that design incentives and pathways that motivate people at different levels of development in appropriate ways*, and form part of the ThriveAbility Cultural and Leadership Assessment.

Continuing on the *right hand side in the coral band inside the beige layer,* are some of the key products of perspectives and cultures: *mindsets and values* (at the individual and group levels), *socio-economic systems*, and our current *sustainable development* efforts. Each of these emerges unconsciously from our perspectives and cultures, until we reach a level of development at which we realize we can consciously choose to change our mindsets and values, and consequently design our socio-economic systems and sustainable development programs in ways which are more likely to succeed at enhancing thriving for a lower footprint.

The seven plus billion individuals alive today live their lives, do their work and choose their products, services and investments according to mostly unconscious criteria. Given that conscious evolution is a very slow process, the key to ThriveAbility on the right hand side of perspectives and cultures is to offer appropriate incentives to consumers and savers/investors to make thriveable choices. Economist and marketing people call this the "Demand" side of the economy, where consumers PULL what they need and want toward themselves.

### Exogenous Variables – Environmental, Technological, Political and Regulatory - PUSH

On the *left hand side in the coral band* we find the harder "exogenous" variables we have less direct control over as individuals, especially when we find ourselves in a situation where we have allowed ourselves to become vulnerable or powerless. Shocks and surprises are delivered by nature ("Environmental"), technological disruption ("Technological"), political swings and roundabouts ("political") and regulatory changes that are adverse or unexpected ("Regulatory").

In contrast, adept strategists are able to align such forces or spot synergistic trends that play to their strengths and create opportunities for true value creation, and ultimately, ThriveAbility.

Corporations and organizations of all kinds emerge as instruments of common cause and interests of many individuals, thereby amplifying the power of all stakeholders who are capable of driving the agenda forward in their own interests and from the perspective of their own values. This "scaling up" of different forms of social and technological control enables organizations and large corporations in particular, to play the games of oligopoly and monopoly. Luckily, there are always new players who innovate and/or disrupt the games played by those commanding the heights of the global economy.

Today _climate change is the most disruptive force on our planet_[76]. Following two decades in which advances in the digital economy, biogenetics, materials, green technologies and the science of human flourishing have been in the spotlight, business leaders in particular will find that the 21st century competitive challenges and opportunities are generated by the transition from a fossil-fuel powered, linear economy based on an eternal growth model to a circular economy powered by renewable energy, with an emphasis on green, inclusive growth.

Couple that with the generational shift in values driven by the Millennials who are now becoming influential in the workplace, and choosing to work mainly for socially responsible organizations, and you have a real firestorm of change coming for the 70 000 conventional global organizations who have not yet woken up fully to the implications of all of this for their business and organization. And amongst the other 10 000 global corporations moving from "less bad" to "sustainable" at varying speeds, there are at most a few hundred thought leading leadership teams who really "get" this to any extent.

## The Competitive and Collaborative Dynamics of Industries are Shifting Too

Let's shift our attention now to the _middle of diagram 23_ and explore some of the _industry dynamics_ that will accelerate both creative destruction and co-opetition at differential rates in different industries. Between the corporations on the left and the consumers and savers/investors on the right, we find that the competitive and collaborative dynamics of industries are shifting as well. One of the main drivers of this shift at the moment is the fact that most economic growth and demand is coming from consumers in developing countries. The other

---

[76]  Naomi Klein, This Changes Everything: Capitalism vs. The Climate, Allen Lane, 2014. Climate change, Klein argues, is a civilizational wake-up call, a powerful message delivered in the language of fires, floods, storms, and droughts. Confronting it is no longer about changing the light bulbs. It's about changing the world—before the world changes so drastically that no one is safe.Either we leap—or we sink. Though she identifies the prevailing type of capitalism as the culprit in the climate crisis, Klein doesn't outline anything like an alternative economic system, preferring instead to focus on particular local struggles against environmental damage and exploitation. In many ways this makes sense, but in a global environment of intensifying scarcities, giving priority to local needs is unlikely to be a recipe for harmony.

is the rapidly growing number of consumers who prefer green or sustainable brands[77] in the developed world (71% in the USA and 80% in Europe).

In other words, the PULL/Demand side of the global economy is driving product, service and business model innovation toward more sustainable, leaner/frugal, "bottom-of-the-pyramid" designs, while leading global businesses that are consumer facing have been developing their offerings in this direction. It also turns out that such offerings appeal to other consumers who are not interested in green/sustainable/ethical issues, simply because they are often superior and in some cases better value for money.

On the PUSH/Supply side of industry dynamics, organizations are joining forces in non-competitive areas to eliminate toxins from their suppliers, improve labour conditions, reduce the carbon and water footprints of supply chains and support local communities. They are also engaging together with NGO's and INGO's such as UN agencies in these activities. Such collaborative learning opportunities are increasingly common, and a source of new ideas and designs, as well as brand boosting if done well.

"Doing well by doing good" may just be a trendy slogan with great PR value for some, but many leading corporations are actually putting their money where there mouth is[78]. The ratings and rankings coming out of Bloomberg, Dow-Jones, Forbes, Newsweek, Robeco SAM, and many others contain similar lists of those in the Global 1000 who are making headway in terms of sustainability, and those who are not. Most of the "sustainability leaders" are in G7 countries, with a reasonable spread across the G20, as evidenced by the list of 75 companies in footnote 111 below.

The process of creative destruction driven by sustainability has been well documented in the past decade by thought leaders (including some of our own ThriveAbiity Leaders featured in chapter 5). Nimble innovators need to find early markets to "cross the chasm" from the few early adopters that want an electric car, or solar panels/a wind turbine on their roof, fair trade coffee and so on, to the mainstream mass markets. Firms in asset intensive industries, while having the fewest immediate incentives to "go green", paradoxically face the greatest threat if they ignore the challenge. Witness the current, highly successful anti-fossil fuel divestment campaign and the reality of "stranded assets" facing the oil, coal and natural gas industries,

---

[77]  http://www.environmentalleader.com/2013/04/03/71-of-consumers-think-green-when-purchasing/
http://ec.europa.eu/public_opinion/flash/fl_367_sum_en.pdf

[78]  For example, ABB, Accenture, Alcatel Lucent, Amex, Astra-Zeneca, Allianz, Autodesk, Aviva, Barclays, BASF, Bayer, Biogen, BMW, BNP Paribas, BT, Campbell's Soup, Carrefour, Cisco, Coca-Cola, Colgate-Palmolive, Danone, DuPont, EMC, Ford, Gap, General Electric, Google, GM, GSK, IBM, Hang Seng Bank, Hewlett Packard, IKEA, InterfaceFlor, Johnson & Johnson, Kingfisher, L'Oreal, M&S, Mattel, Microsoft, Natura, Nestle, Neste Oil, Nike, Nissan, Nokia, Novartis, Novo-Nordisk, Outoptec OYJ, Philips, P&G, Puma, Salesforce, Samsung, SAP, Scania, Siemens, Starbucks, Swiss Re, Tata, Telefonica, Unilever, Umicore, UPS, Veolia, Vinci, VISA, Vivendi, Vodafone, Volvo, Walmart, Westpac Banking, Whole Foods, Wipro. For more details see -http://mic.com/articles/81335/18-companies-that-are-doing-good-while-doing-well and http://www.forbes.com/sites/jacquelynsmith/2014/01/22/the-worlds-most-sustainable-companies-of-2014/

which will hopefully leave 75% of those toxic "assets" in the ground if we are to limit global warming to 2 degrees.

Retailers and firms in service industries are in a prime position to focus on disruption for ThriveAbility, because they are not wed to long-lived asset bases and can skip from one generation of products to the next rapidly while enhancing customer loyalty. IT, electronics, health care and consumer product firms are also well positioned to pursue hybrid strategies of both continuous improvement and creative destruction given their shorter life cycles and more rapid asset-turnover. When combined with the four billion consumers at the bottom of the pyramid, the opportunity to incubate the technologies, products, services and business models of the future is immense.

For those of you who remember watching the film: "A Beautiful Mind", about John Nash[79], one of the pioneers of game theory, the Nash-Cournot Equilibrium (otherwise known as the "Saddlepoint Solution") provides us with an appropriate analogy here. Game theory distinguishes between "Zero-Sum" and "Positive-Sum" games, inter alia. (Life is an "Infinite Sum" game, but that story is for another time and another book).

The words: "Zero-sum games" means exactly what they say: the sum of the winnings in the game is zero. For all the players in the game, if one or more of them wins, then someone else/ others have to lose. Much of the trading that occurs in the financial markets (for example the hundreds of trillions of US$ changing hands every day on the foreign exchange markets), is zero-sum by nature. Every day, some banks win, and some banks lose money on their foreign exchange trading portfolios, In fact, competition is so intense that even the most expert players can only "predict" market movements correctly 50.1% of the time. But that 0.1% of a few trillion US$ is very large sum of money indeed.

Sadly for the real economy, and taxpayers, in the past few decade banks have worked out how to shift a lot of the losses they make onto consumers and governments, by needing to be "bailed out" on a regular basis when they threaten to crash the economy. The derivatives and futures markets have also become a casino in which losses can be shifted into the future by clever instruments known as "swaps" and various kinds of "hedges" (hence the now infamous "hedge funds", who also like to be "bailed out" by the rest of us when they threaten to crash the economy).

Wars are another zero-sum game, and often end up "Lose-Lose" if fought destructively. Pure price competition between firms is also a "race to the bottom" where everyone can lose including the buyers if the firms competing purely on price go bankrupt and their goods and services can no longer be purchased. This is also one of the downsides of globalization, which tends to encourage manufacturing and routine service activities to be out-sourced to low wage developing economies in order to sell unsustainable products for lower prices simply so that the corporations involved can stay in business themselves. It is a pretty cut-throat

---

[79]  Nash was brilliantly portrayed by actor Russell Crowe in one of his finest performances.

world out there, and sadly the "competitive strategy" still taught at most business schools does not get much beyond teaching ambitious future executives how to play the games of oligopoly and monopoly.

In contrast, in decision theory a positive sum game is a 'win-win' situation where no one wins at someone else's expense, and the sum of winnings (positives) and losses (negatives) is positive. This becomes possible when the size of the pie is somehow enlarged so that there is more wealth to distribute between the parties than there was originally, or some other way is devised so everyone gets what they want or need. This can be done in a variety of ways. Extra funds might be obtained from new innovations allowing competitors to meet their budgets. Or it might be done with integrative bargaining, where different interests are negotiated to meet every sides' needs. The more different interests that are on the table for discussion, the more likely a positive sum solution can be worked out. This is known as "heterogeneity" in game theory and practice.

Most innovations have positive externalities[80], particularly where they result in *cooperative dynamic competition* in an industry. The Windows/Intel computing ecosystem is a good example of a way in which the creation of de facto standards enabling different software and devices to "plug and play" with each other, enabled a trillion dollar industry to emerge from "nowhere" between 1985 and 2005. Demand-side economies of scale are responsible for much of this value-added, much as is the case in global trade- everyone wins subject to that trade being fair and sustainable. The evolution of the internet from an obscure military/scientific/academic network in the early 1990's to a global cloud serving 7 billion mobile devices and several billion personal computers and organizational servers today is another good example of a wildly positive sum game[81].

Business is simultaneously both about competition and cooperation. It has ever been thus, and is reflected in the two best known works of the Scottish economist Adam Smith (**The Theory of Moral Sentiments,** published in 1759, which was essentially about governance, regulation and ethics, and followed by his much better known work, **The Wealth of Nations,** published in 1776, which focused on the way in which specialization and exchange/trade make a bigger pie possible through cooperation, and how competition then determines who gets the biggest shares of the pie).

---

[80] Thompson's model of Schumpeter's trustified firm uses an operational framework for identifying knowledge growth as the critical factor of Schumpeterian innovations. The spillover effects suggest that the total of innovation and R&D at the industry level can be considerable increased if a degree of co-operation or state subsidy is applied. See "Theory of Innovation: A New Paradigm of Growth" By Jati Sengupta

[81] Although as Jaron Lanier points out in "Who Owns the Future" (Allen-Lane, 2013), the effect of digital technologies can also be to concentrate wealth, reduce growth and challenge the livelihoods of an increasing number of people, one of the factors that is collapsing middle-class security and incomes. The de facto monopolies of the "Siren Servers" skew the way risk and reward are shared between those who can manage big data and those who do not have access to its pattern recognizing abilities.

"Co-opetition"[82] investigates the modern dynamics of how competition and cooperation combine to both make a bigger pie for everyone, while also ensuring that the system is made efficient and meritocratic through competition and regulation so that the pie is shared in a fair and humane way. Given the "bad news" about large organizations and their corrupt leaders we are fed every day, it is not surprising that most people view business as a "winner takes all" or "zero-sum" game. As the cynically classic Damon Runyon quote goes: "The race is not always to the swift nor the battle to the strong, but it pays to bet that way".

Under the right conditions, ThriveAbility in the networked economy can help us move away from these purely competitive plays to recognize cooperative relationships that leverage value created by those in the network. Cooperation, especially in networks, is defined as a form of organizational membership in a formalized multi-actor network that consists of autonomous organizations, and that has a particular joint goal for which certain resources need to be shared or co-developed. Heterogeneity in asset and information flows is needed to foster co-opetitive relationships, along with homogeneity in status to help build trust and relationship capital.

Cooperation in networks creates a bigger pie because organizations have access to each other's (frequently differing) resources, they can share costs and risks, and they can become more successful together. That is how Bill Gates of Microsoft and Andy Grove of Intel beat Apple in the 1990's, until Steve Jobs made his comeback and turned the tables on them using a similar strategy of co-opetition in the Apple universe. There are, however, also downsides to the concentration of key industry "choke" points in the hands of a few key strategic players, and regulators struggle to keep up with the fast moving dynamics of hi-tech industries. Only further disruptive innovation can really keep these industry giants on their toes, along with engaged stakeholders who can exercise countervailing power.

Competition - the other aspect of co-opetition - occurs after businesses have created value in the market and seek to allocate market share, price, cost and other finite benefits. Competition causes an organization to get a (bigger) piece of the pie: It generates economic efficiency through allocation of scarce resources and reduces transaction costs between partners, as well as enhances the drive for innovation and entrepreneurship. 'Co-opetition' occurs in a market situation in which cooperation and competition merge together to form a new kind of strategic interdependence between firms, giving rise to a co-opetitive system of value creation.

There is a duality in all relationships with respect to win-win and win-lose interactions: The success of most businesses is dependent on the success of others, yet they must compete to capture value created in the market and protect their own interests.

---

[82]  The concept of co-opetition was expanded upon by Adam Brandenburger and Barry Nalebuff, professors at the Harvard Business School and the Yale School of Management respectively. In their path-breaking book, titled Coopetition, 1996.

Since the 1996 publication of Co-opetition, Internet and mobile technologies have transformed business dynamics. A new paradigm has evolved where information, connectivity and time define how business is conducted. Information is richer in quality and quantity, promoting collaboration among players. Connectivity, in particular via the Internet, has also lowered barriers to entry and bred hyper-competition on a global scale. Furthermore, time is increasingly a critical, and scarce, resource. As instant access to data reduces information asymmetries, there is the heightened need for businesses to be able to detect changes in the market and respond quickly to address them.

The end result: highly competitive environments where rivals can emerge overnight from unexpected places, such as traditionally non-competing industries. These changing business dynamics make the collaborative value inherent in co-opetition more necessary than ever. Leveraging co-opetition to develop business strategy requires a thorough assessment of a company's network of players: customers, suppliers and competitors, as well as "complementors." Complementors are those companies that provide products and services that enhance the value of a firm's products or services. For example, software providers are complementors to hardware providers and vice versa.

A thriveable economy mandates the shift from industrial age, less bad "brick and mortar" strategic thinking to an emphasis on new alliances and a rethinking of traditional partnerships that can raise the game for all players and stakeholders. Alliances and partnerships can be formed with customers, suppliers, competitors and complementors in ways that increase value for all players. As companies in all industries develop strategies to leverage co-opetition in ways that are unique to their business environment, they will face similar questions:

- Who are the players in their network and how can they collaborate to maximize value?
- Which relationships are complementary in nature -- which companies can they work with that can add value to what they provide?
- Which players are competitors, and are there mutually beneficial ways to create value?

We are going to need a great deal of co-opetition and positive sum/win-win-win games to be played in the 21st century if we are going to make the breakthroughs needed to ensure the thriving of future generations. The ThriveAbility program design utilizes the dynamics of co-opetition wherever possible, encouraging industry working groups to out-compete those who are not farsighted enough to see its enormous long term advantages for everyone.

The co-operative and competitive parts or logics of a co-opetitive relationship are divided according to the closeness of an activity to the customer; the closer to the customer the more competition. The two logics of interaction inherent in a co-opetitive relationship are usually divided between different units within the participating organizations. The potential conflicts based on the two logics of interaction inherent in a co-opetitive relationship need to be controlled and co-ordinated by an intermediate organization that can set leading rules and regulations. For an excellent summary of how collaboration and leadership are growing in importance to create sustainable businesses, a recent survey by MIT Sloan Management Review, BCG and the UN Global Compact is a must-read. The research showed that:

"Corporate sustainability is moving steadily from the old model — comprised primarily of ad hoc or opportunistic efforts that often produced tense relationships with the public sector — towards strategic and transformational initiatives that engage multiple entities. The goals of these collaborations are many and include corporate benefits such as influencing standard-setting authorities, garnering access to resources and developing new markets.

Our research found that as sustainability issues become increasingly complex, global in nature and pivotal to success, companies are realizing that they can't make the necessary impact acting alone. The sentiment is nearly unanimous among managers: 90% of respondents agree that businesses need to collaborate to address the sustainability challenges they face.

The belief is echoed by a growing chorus of academic and nonprofit leaders and has spawned considerable research from organizations such as the Network for Business Sustainability and the Forum for the Future in conjunction with the business community. These organizations, and others, offer several suggestions about how to create effective sustainability collaborations.

Despite nearly unanimous consensus on the importance of sustainability collaborations, practice lags behind belief: Only 47% of businesses are engaging in sustainability-related partnerships. A majority (61%) of those assesses their collaborations as "quite" or "very" successful. Taken together, however, these responses indicate that less than 30% of all surveyed managers say their companies are engaged in successful sustainability partnerships."

This need to stimulate strategic co-opetition is one of the primary reasons we have structured the ThriveAbility Foundation and its programs as a "global public good", which works with other organizations with a similar character such as the GRI, the IIRC, UNGC and UN agencies and other Foundations dedicated to the common good rather than merely private gain.

## Capital Markets for a Green and Inclusive Economy

Hovering above the industry dynamics of creative destruction shown in diagram 23, we find a very fast-moving, complex evolving system known as the global capital markets. With over $300 trillion at its disposal, this global financial system has the power to completely transform the $75 trillion global economic system (or the "real economy"), if it desires to do so. How?

The supply of capital to all organizations and human systems lies at the heart of capitalism. What gets invested in happens, what doesn't get invested in, doesn't. Period. Money divested from fossil fuel goes into renewable energy. Money divested from other polluting and toxic industries goes into healthier alternatives. It is as simple and yet as complex as that.

As we saw in chapter three, the pathway to thriveable, regenerative capitalism is being primed by a fast-growing socially responsible, sustainable finance ecosystem. A US statistic just out today[83] shows that individual investors are looking for ways to make investing more sustainable - 71% of individual investors — defined as those "that actively trade stocks, mutual funds, bonds" — were interested in sustainable investing, though 54% believe choosing between sustainable investments and making financial gains is a trade-off.

Millennial investors are twice as likely to invest in companies or funds that target specific social or environmental outcomes. Furthermore, females are substantially more likely than males to factor sustainability into their investment decisions, being twice as likely to consider both rate of return and positive impact when making an investment. And 65% of individual investors believe that sustainable investing will become more prevalent in the next five years.

Dr Steve Waygood, one of the thought leaders in sustainable/green investing[84] and Chief Responsible Investment Officer of Aviva Investors, helped author a recent manifesto on sustainable capital markets that concluded that:

"We need policy-makers to ensure that the culture within financial services is one where each agent works to promote the interests of their client rather than their own".

In addition to this much needed shift in the culture of a sector badly in need of further reform, the manifesto made several detailed policy recommendations across four key areas, including ways in which the markets could be incentivized to **reward for long term success not failure**:

- **Investment consultants' fee structures** should be aligned with the long-term performance of the funds that they advise upon.
- **Fund manager bonuses** should be based both on an evaluation of the fund manager's long-term ability to generate investment returns as well as a view on how they are performing as stewards of capital.
- **Executives on stock exchanges** should also be rewarded for their work in ensuring that the companies that list on their exchanges are well governed and sustainable - and sanctioned when this work is poor.
- **Investment bank research** paid for from commission charges should not be banned but harnessed to encourage sustainable investment.
- **Fund managers** shouldbe required to allocate at least 5% of the research commission budget to ESG research from sell-side brokers, or explain why they have not done so. This would reward sell-side brokers for conducting this analysis, further building the small but influential market in this area.

---

[83]  According to a new survey conducted by the Morgan Stanley Institute for Sustainable Investing, Thanks to Robert Rubenstein at Triple Bottom Line Investing for this data.

http://cleantechnica.com/2015/03/06/71-percent-investors-interested-sustainable-investing

[84]  Also known as "SRI" – Socially Responsible Investing, or "ESG" – Environmental, Social and Governance" investing or "Ethical Investing".

- **Companies** should be required to report to the markets less frequently but on the wider set of issues including governance, sustainability and culture set out in the Non-Financial Reporting Directive. This would stop the obsessive drive for quarterly results that companies are strongly focused on. It would allow those companies to begin to think more long term in their outlook.

Further recommendations which would shift large sums of capital toward sustainable growth are also made that would encourage investment in long-term, sustainable infrastructure, better standards and labelling for investors, particularly for SME's and unlisted enterprises, joint private-public funding for green investments through the European Investment Bank, and re-orienting the debt purchases of the European Central Bank toward more sustainable investments, including green asset-backed securities. Such initiatives would all tie into EU member state governments developing national capital-raising plans informing the Commission how they intend to finance the delivery of a zero-carbon economy and meet, for example, the UN Sustainability Goals.

Some of the key dynamics and leverage points required to shift markets toward sustainable, even thriveable investment, appear in diagram 24 below.[85] "Regulation for good" rewards organizational transformation from perverse mono-capital incentives to thriveable multi-capital incentives. Sustainable stock exchanges, regulators, brokers, advisers and consultants are rewarded for selling thriveable investments to their clients.

---

[85] Our thanks to Dr Steve Waygood, Chief Responsible Investment Officer of Aviva Investors, for this enlightening diagram to which we have made some clarifying additions to make the links between the leverage points in financial markets and the ThriveAbility program and Six Capitals approach.

## DIAGRAM 24 – Global Capital Market Leverage Points for a Regenerative Inclusive Economy

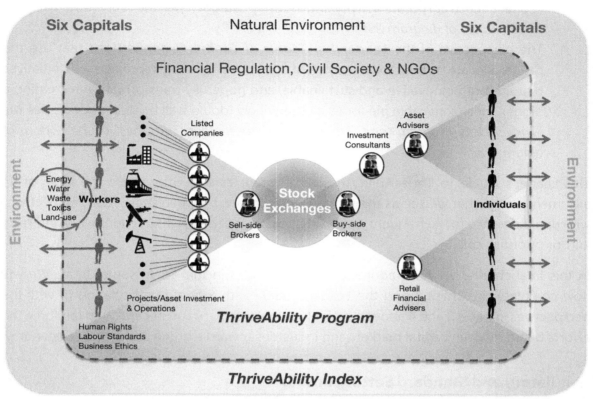

## How Long Will it Take for Global Regulatory Convergence toward a ThriveAble World?

The role of the ThriveAbility Index has been framed from four key perspectives to ensure that it can become embedded as rapidly as possible in existing reporting, rating and ranking systems and standards globally:

1. The perspective of the ***Global Capital Markets and the Reporting Systems*** they depend on that drive the allocation of capital to what are perceived to be "fitter" investments, depending upon the perspective of the investor type; *(see the "Capital Markets for a Green and Inclusive Economy" below "Regulation for Good" and the "ThriveAbility Index" near the top of diagram 23)*

2. The perspective of the ***Regulatory and Standard Setting Bodies*** at all levels that determine what "good" looks like, and what incentive systems are needed to punish the "bad", regulate for "less bad", and hopefully in the future, regulate and reward for "good" or thriveable; *(see "Regulation for Good" and the "ThriveAbility Index" near the top of diagram 23)*

3. The perspective of **Industries**, and the unique challenges each industry faces regarding its own limits to growth and how to allocate a fair and appropriate share of natural capital to each corporate activity and industry category. *(see the coopetitive dynamics in the middle of diagram 23)*

4. The perspective of the **_Leadership Teams of Global Organizations_** that use the capital allocate by the capital markets in one above, to invest in projects and initiatives that are both innovative and sustainable, and hopefully transformative in creating a bigger, more thriveable pie for us all- genuinely "doing well by doing good"; *(see the "ThriveAbility Program" and "Transforming Stakeholder Outcomes" at the bottom of diagram 23)*

This Leader's Guide to ThriveAbility has taken great care to interweave the logic of its argument using what we see as the virtuous interactions between these four perspectives, with due deference to the frequent clashes that characterize such interactions when interests and/or priorities collide.

In this final chapter we have addressed items 1 and 3 in this list in some detail. We will now complete this chapter and the Leader's Guide with a brief recapitulation of why the perspectives in items 2 and 4 above are highly complementary and necessary to reinforce the efforts being made in capital markets and industries toward a green and inclusive economy.

## Regulatory and Standard Setting Bodies

Regulatory and Standard Setting Bodies determine what "good" looks like, and what incentive systems are needed to punish the "bad", regulate for "less bad", and hopefully in the future, regulate and reward for "good" or thriveable. In an ideal world, they should offer a highest common factor synthesis of what good governance looks like, so that regulation becomes a force that acts like a rising tide that lifts all boats equally.

One of the more impressive reports to emerge from the regulatory world recently is from the UNEP Inquiry into the Design of a Sustainable Financial System – "Aligning the Financial System with Sustainable Development - Pathways to Scale", that concludes with:

**"2015 offers an opportunity to bring together the historically separate agendas of financial reform and sustainable development**. Within the UN system, critical policy milestones include the world disaster risk reduction conference, the Financing for Development conference, the finalization of the new Sustainable Development Goals and the completion of a new global agreement on climate change...

**The asset pools, tools and catalysts profiled in this report suggest some of the new and emerging ways of closing the asset and investment gap**. Considerable further work is needed to expand and evaluate the initial design options presented in this report. The continued rapid growth in 'green bonds' is not guaranteed, for example. But smart policy work now could ensure greater volumes of debt finance for the green economy at lower cost. Likewise, the extension of international banking standards to incorporate sustainability factors may have seemed unlikely just a year ago, but growing practice at the national level suggests that articulation of shared frameworks at the international level is a pragmatic option."

Although one would not want to pin our hopes for a thriving, green and inclusive world on a series of inter-governmental meetings alone, with all the political risks and not-so-subtle "mind-grenades" lurking beneath the rhetoric of compromise, perhaps this time world leaders will actually have both the courage and moral fortitude to do what is right by humanity, rather than their own narrow interests, which are also still sadly often simply the interests of many small elites in most countries on our planet.

Operating on the assumption that some progress can and must be achieved in these fora over the next few years, the role and voice of business and financial leaders will be crucial in providing the new thinking and mechanisms by which a more effective system of global governance can emerge to ensure that a global green inclusive economy becomes a reality.

In the meantime, the devil lies both in the detail as well as the forms of incentive and the ways in which regulation for good can encourage thriveable organizations and businesses that do not require as many developmental "band-aids" as we have today.

To put it simply, in a thriveable world, businesses and communities would be working together to enhance the thriving of all stakeholders, in contrast to today, where the negative "externalities" businesses and investors are allowed to get away with through ineffective regulation need to be corrected through sustainable development agendas. ThriveAbility aims at a world in which all development is inherently sustainable, and empowered by the win-win interactions between local communities/businesses, investors/lenders and global organizations. This is the ultimate goal of both the ThriveAbility Index and the ThriveAbility Program, to which we will now turn.

In *diagram 22* we outlined the seven key ingredients and ten interactions that provide a virtuous "inside-out" cycle of corporate transformation interwoven with the "outside-in" cycle of regulation for good covered above. In chapters two and three of this guide we offer a detailed explanation of each of the key ingredients of this "inside-out" cycle, while here we will offer a final overview.

From the perspective of the leadership teams of global organizations that use the capital allocated by the capital markets to invest in projects and initiatives that are both innovative and sustainable, the ThriveAbility program is a way of delivering transformative change that generates a bigger, more thriveable pie for us all, as shown at the bottom of *diagram 23* in "ThriveAbility Program" and "Transforming Stakeholder Outcomes".

The four phases of the ThriveAbility program are marked as four circles, each representing an organization working through the four phases of the process over a similar number of years. Four of the six steps in the ThriveAbility process are shown as 4 small circles within the larger organization circle, with progressively darker shading representing the increasing depth of data and application of the ThriveAbiity principles within the organization and its leadership, management and reporting processes.

The final two steps in the ThriveAbility process are shown below and above the organizational circle as rectangles, representing the industry benchmarking and index design and activation processes respectively, again with progressively darker shading representing the increasing depth of data and application of the ThriveAbiity principles within the four year period of the four phases.

The purpose of this transformation process is two-fold: firstly, to accelerate and scale the learning in the organization around moving to the next stage of the ThriveAbility Journey from where it started out; secondly, to generate the benchmarks, frameworks and ultimately the data which emerges from the application of the ThriveAbility principles to that organization and its industry peers. This transformation process forms a key driver in the great virtuous cycle that ThriveAbility is designed to catalyse and accelerate, which is why we will finish this analysis by starting with the Corporation as a first mover in a great virtuous cycle.

## The Great Virtuous Cycle

This entire Leader's Guide to ThriveAbility, and indeed all the work of the ThriveAbility Foundation, is predicated upon a simple observation: that for anything alive to develop or transform, it will need to go through different stages of development, with each stage built upon previous stages, and fuelling successive stages. If you grow up into a teenager who can drive fast, crash your car and end up in hospital in ICU on a ventilator you almost have to go back to the beginning to go through exactly the same stages of development to get to where you were before your accident.

Equally, if you are training for the Olympics, and you want to go from winning bronze medals to gold medals, you again have to transform your technique and approach to be a winner- not just keep on doing what you have always done, but harder. It is easy to see that individuals transform through several stages of development, and even adults can continue to grow and develop in different, more complex ways if the impulse is there. Yet some are "arrested" in their development, and remain the same until the day they die from when they leave high school. Strange, is it not, how different we all are?

Organizations, comprised as they are of human beings interacting with each other, nature, infrastructure and technologies, are complex evolving systems that also develop unique identities and capabilities, and go through identifiable stages of development. They must also transform to go from one stage of development to the next, and such a transformation must always be intentionally aligned and managed to ensure the whole system keeps on working for all it's stakeholders so that each organization can justify it's ongoing existence.

Global corporations are more complex than the average organization, as they must span and reconcile/bridge many cultures, values, life conditions, natural systems, technologies and often very different stakeholder needs in different places, yet all the while maintain a unity of purpose, reputation and process. They are also at present the uncontested masters of the commanding heights of the global economy – a figure worth remembering is that there are nearly 80 000 transnational companies in the world with $49 trillion of revenue, amounting to 65% of world GDP of $75 trillion[86]. And of those 19 out of 20 companies traded in the world's capital markets and two-thirds of global economic activity do not report according to any sustainability standards at all, while 75% of the 63 000 companies listed on a Bloomberg terminal do not report on a single item relating to environmental, social or governance performance. Incredible, but that is where we are today. Yet it is also worth remembering that just over two decades ago, no one did.

Whether we like it or not, just about everything we do today relies on the activities of a large corporation somewhere, somehow. Combined with their massive impacts on the environment, society and governments, we also need to consider that despite the laggards, there are also many admirable corporations leading the way today in term of sustainability and environmental, social and governance reform. Hence we believe that ThriveAbility, while it starts with each one of us, also needs to address the single most pressing challenge and opportunity- to transform global corporations from the 95 out of 100 who are in denial or just grudgingly complying with environmental, health and safety regulations, through to the 3 out of 100 more progressive corporations who are experimenting how to be "less bad", to the 1.9% out of 100 corporations focused on becoming minimally sustainable ("zero harm"), to the 0.1% aiming at becoming net positive.

Hence we begin with the corporation as a first mover in the great virtuous cycle that ThriveAbility seeks to help accelerate. The ThriveAbility program feeds transformation through implementable innovation pathways into and with the corporation at the bottom of Diagram 23, through the application of the ThriveAbility principles. That transformation process then feeds into a benchmarking process that helps facilitate the journey of each organization with feedback on how it is doing relative to both its industry and generic peers. Once a critical mass of organizations in an industry is reached, then the components of the ThriveAbility Index (a global public good), can then be assembled for current users of sustainability and ESG/SRI reporting information, at the top of *Diagram 23*, working in conjunction with other standards and regulatory organizations.

---

[86] 63 000 companies are listed on listed on stock exchanges according to Bloomberg, and 7 000 traded in over the counter or "grey" markets in the US alone. CreditRiskMonitor's estimate is 78 480 companies globally.

Just beneath the ThriveAbility Index we have a market transformation process known as "Capital Markets for a Green and Inclusive Economy" (CMGIE). The ThriveAbility Index is being developed in conjunction with thought leaders in global capital markets who are working with the high leverage points in the system to change the rules of the game for the benefit of thriveable organizations and markets. There is also a feedback from the corporation into global capital markets and consumers and savers, which works together with the feedback loop between the Index and consumers and savers/investors.

Following the arrows from the Index and the CMGIE down to consumers and savers/investors in Diagram 23, we find this creating many more thriveable, transparent and fairly priced options for savings and investments, so that the proverbial "man on the street" can make better choices about where to put their money to do well and do good.

Next, the shifts that this all brings about in consumer and retail financial markets and banking feed again into demand for investments in and loans to thriveable organizations on the lower right hand side arrow in this virtuous cycle. Not only that, but those more thriveable organizations will be driving a transformation in stakeholder outcomes as well, meaning their products, services and brand are likely to be much more popular and successful, combined with rising employee engagement and supplier loyalty.

And finally, the competitive and collaborative dynamics shown in the middle of Diagram 23, in conjunction with this virtuous cycle, will tend to accelerate the cycle. The *ThriveAbility Industry Working Groups* will be at the forefront of demonstrating what is possible in terms of healthy co-opetition within and between industries, NGO's and markets.

Now that is a real win-win-win, positive sum game!

## In Summary

Sustainability and Innovation are both reassuring and yet puzzling and frustrating in this time of ecological, economic and social crisis/opportunity:

- Reassuring because both are held out as the silver bullets for all our problems;
- Puzzling because despite their ubiquity, they are so little understood; and
- Frustrating because we know we need to go faster and deliver real breakthroughs in all industries as soon as possible, yet we currently appear to be stuck in molasses (or "treacle" if you are Anglo-Saxon), which may slowly turn to quicksand if we are not careful.

The good news is that the heartbeat of technological innovation and sustainability collaboration between organizations and NGO's has seldom beaten this fast; the bad news is that without concomitant organizational and socio-cultural innovation, driven by shifts in perspective from our "leaders", all life as we know it may be headed in unforeseeable, perhaps catastrophic directions.

I am hopeful for our species because we have faced and surmounted similar extinction threats throughout our short history- and because crisis is an evolutionary accelerator. As the most imperfectly adapted species on the planet, innovation has literally been the lifeblood of our progression from hunter gatherers in the Holocene to planetary shapers in the Anthropocene, driven by over 10 000 life-changing innovations in as many years. We created this situation, and we can change it, but we need to crack the "breakthrough challenge" that may be the only thing that stands between us and a thriving future.

What it means to be human is, once again, changing fundamentally. The maelstrom we are in is the birthplace of not only new ways of living and prospering, but also new forms of consciousness and collective intelligence. In epochal shifts such as the one we are in, such new forms show up everywhere we look, from the arts and sciences to governance and politics to technology and business.

One of the many paradoxes such shifts pose is that our conception of what the "good life" is, always precedes our ability to deliver that special paradise- the "snake" is always with us in new forms in every successive version of the garden of Eden. There does not appear to have been a generation whose progress was not also a source of new forms of trouble that then needed to be resolved by newer and better versions of paradise.

The first, largely European Renaissance gave us the power to eradicate much disease, discomfort, hunger and ignorance through innovations in science, technology, organizations, culture and governance, making us the most prolific top predator in our biosphere- and with the same wand, also gave us the power to eliminate much of life on earth as we know it, either deliberately through weapons of mass destruction, or inadvertently through our sheer numbers and over-consumption.

The second, more global Renaissance we may now be entering will hopefully not require the 21st century version of the Black Death (would that be Heat Death?), to trim our numbers back to a point where the transformative innovations we need can become a reality. One positive sign is the way in which the civic-minded Millennial "We" generation appears to be picking up the baton dropped by the idealistic but quirky baby-boomers who went from blaming the "system" for all our ills, to running a "Me" generation system with only minor tweaks to our outdated global economic engine and the thinking that created it, when both are in need of a major overhaul.

The centuries-old clash between the ecophile romantic-humanists and the technophile, progressive positivists is now being transcended by a concern for what works and can endure at scale, from the green shoots of the urban sharing economy to the industrial scale of the circular, regenerative economy; from the rapidly emerging experiments in collaborative, co-creative forms of organization and governance to the demonstration of the kinds of major transformation and breakthrough that are made possible through transformative, far-sighted leadership in hitherto conventional corporations; and from the secrecy, greed and hypocrisy characteristic of rule by small elites slowly giving way to new forms of transparency, accountability and regulation for good rather than just regulation for less bad.

The opportunity for breakthroughs is ripe for those leaders and organizations far-sighted enough to maximize the thriving of their stakeholders within a sustainable footprint, taking their employees, customers, suppliers and other business partners with them on a "ThriveAbility" journey.

There seems to be general agreement amongst thought leaders in sustainability: we need to shift the direction of the "Great Acceleration" from progress with undesirable negative consequences baked in, to accelerating holistic positive impacts with a rapidly diminishing need for trade-offs between the positive and negative consequences of our current model of economic growth. We need to move from the outdated strategies of the Holocene to the breakthroughs made possible in the age we are now entering, the Anthropocene, with gusto.

Today 80% of the wealth of nations, corporations and communities is intangible, embedded in human, social, and intellectual capital. These intangibles are now measurable for the first time, yet not presently included in mainstream business strategy and policy. The critical role of natural capital in enhancing our thriving is now also making its way into the income statements and balance sheets of the world. The metrics and data needed to define what is "good / regenerative" are slowly emerging.

The implications of these social, technological, ecological and economic shifts suggests a great number of opportunities including:

1. **Measuring true value** in ways that include the leverage effects of enhancing the thriving of human and social capitals for a smaller footprint;
2. **Accessing a different human motivational system** in the shift from the psychology of avoidance to the psychology of thriving;
3. **Identifying breakthrough innovations** that solve both social & ecological crises *and* create truly profitable business models and thriving communities (across all six capitals);
4. **Co-creating open metrics and data infrastructures** that measure true value creation and enable integrated decision-making and reporting;
5. **Reshaping capital markets** so that they incentivize true value creation across all six capitals for shareholders *and* stakeholders, in comparable ways that offer better value and accessibility to all classes of investor.

The big question regarding these five opportunities, naturally, is "How, exactly?" followed swiftly by: "What's in it for me?" Each of these is a mega-challenge, yet ironically, tackled together they may prove to be more easily soluble than taken individually.

We invite you to join us in this journey toward ThriveAbility. If you are an individual or small organization, please join our "Embedding ThriveAbility" community and discussions on

Facebook or Linked-In. If you are a medium to large sized organization you are invited to join one of our industry think-tanks or apply to complete the ThriveAbility Assessment, which is coming to a country or city near you soon, and being the ThriveAbility program.

The ThriveAbility Foundation also holds online think-tanks with thought leaders globally to address these five challenges/opportunities, enabling them to engage in one or more of the five topics according to their own interests and priorities.

Thank you for engaging with us – and for deciding to find out what it might mean to become a ThriveAbility Leader. We wish you well on your journey toward ThriveAbility.

# Appendix A -
## Modelling Systemic ThriveAbility –Where do we Begin?

In order to develop a ThriveAbility Index that provides a consistent basis for measurement across all sectors of the economy, across all nations and organizations, the first step is to build a ThriveAbility Model with clear inputs, outputs and internal dynamical equations that build on what is already known about the causal linkages between the key factors involved. Many models of the global economy and biosphere already exist, from the original Club of Rome model based on Jay Forrester's Systems Dynamics modelling, to scenario models developed by the Tellus Institute, Global Business Network and many others. The basic dynamics of most of these models are very similar:

1. **Population Growth Drives Consumption** - Increasing population (driven by better medical treatment and healthier living conditions), motivated by a desire for wealth, drives economic activity and resource consumption;

2. **Consumption Drives Pollution** - Resource consumption gives rise to waste products and pollution, which are also an important source of disease;

3. **Scarce Resources Drive War & Famine**, **Reducing Population** - Competition for scarce resources leads to famine and war, which together with pollution, drives up the death rate. Disease, famine and war have kept the human population small for millennia.

4. **Non-Renewable Industrial Processes Drive Population Growth** - Industrial scale manufacturing, construction and agriculture (driven by breakthroughs in knowledge and technology), began to generate surpluses which enabled improved healthcare, sewage and sanitation and the development of drugs and antibiotics, increasing the birth rate and reducing the death rate.

5. **Educating Women and Girls Reduces Population** - Current evidence demonstrates that the quickest way to reduce the birth rate is to educate women and provide them with better health care so that they need to give birth to fewer children.

6. **The Earth Regulates its Own Temperature** - The earth's atmosphere is held in a dynamic, stable non-equilibrium state because its geology, chemistry, weather and life form a single adaptive, self-organizing system which both maintains and is maintained by life.

7. **Rising Greenhouse Gases Increase Storms, Floods and Famines** - Unfortunately, current levels of pollution, including greenhouse gas emissions such as carbon dioxide and methane, have begun to destabilize the natural carbon sequestration process that converts atmospheric carbon dioxide into limestone and chalk seabed rocks through the carbon cycle, resulting in a rapid rise in greenhouse gas levels and global temperatures.

8. **Storms, Floods and Famines Drive Greater Resource Consumption & Reduce Population** - The additional heat energy trapped in the atmosphere and oceans by excess greenhouse gases is dissipated by storms, droughts and ice cap/glacier melting causing increased flooding and destruction of habitats requiring even more resources to be consumed to counter such storms, floods and famines.

9. **Deforestation Adds More Carbon Dioxide to the Atmosphere than All Cars and Trucks** - while deforestation is slowing, it currently adds 15% of the annual increase in carbon dioxide in the atmosphere. It also contributes to the sixth mass extinction of species on land and in the oceans.

10. **Renewable Technologies & Resources Reduce Pollution & Greenhouse Gases** - renewable energy, habitats and industrial processes reduce unsustainable consumption and the production of pollution and greenhouse gases. There is, however, a time lag in this reduction as carbon dioxide remains in the atmosphere for fifty or more years, and methane for an average of twelve years.

The challenges and solutions one can draw from all the scientific evidence and models as summarized in the ten points above are wide-ranging, and can now be stated with very high levels of confidence thanks to two decades of extremely thorough research and data from all parts of the world.

The climate change-driven ecological destruction that we are witnessing today — immeasurable loss of human life, plant and animal species caused by natural disasters such as floods, droughts, wildfires and heat waves, the disappearance of vast snow caps, glaciers and almost half of the Arctic — is the result of a mere 0.8°C rise in average temperature since 1800. We can only imagine what a further 1.2 to 3°C rise before 2100 will mean for the Earth's already vulnerable ecosystems and at-climate-risk communities. Hundreds of millions of people are already suffering the effects of climate change, particularly in some of the world's poorest areas such as Africa, India, Central and South America and across the Asia pacific region, where Australia is being hard hit. Some of the absolute top priorities from a policy perspective for governments, businesses, NGO's and charities include:

A. **Renewable Energy** - Increasing fossil fuel usage to meet the world's rising energy needs will lead to an increase of 184% in greenhouse gas emissions by 2030[87] based on current policy projections, leading to a global temperature increase of between 3 and 4 degrees centigrade by 2100. Limiting the global temperature increase to 2 degrees would be possible if we invested heavily in renewable energies such as solar, wind, biomass and biofuels as fast as possible, while reducing the consumption of fossil fuels as quickly as possible.

---

[87] From 37 Gt Co2eq in 1990 to 68 Gt Co2eq in 2030. http://climateactiontracker.org/assets/publications/publications/CAT_Trend_Report.pdf

B. **Resilient Habitats** - More than half of the world's population live in cities, and that is forecast to rise to 70% by 2050. Designing, building and retrofitting cities and habitats to consume less energy, provide more green spaces, enhance human flourishing using renewable energies, technologies and processes wherever possible for construction, transport, offices and housing is therefore critical. Supplies of food and water also need to be sourced renewably with the elimination of all pollution and waste by 2050, a goal the world's top 200 companies have already committed to as part of the World Business Council for Sustainable Development[88].

C. **Enlightened Enterprise** - The largest 2000 companies in the world account for 53% of global economic output[89], and probably an even greater percentage of pollution and greenhouse gases (considering that a few hundred of them are fossil fuel producers or mega-mining companies). The Global Reporting Initiative[90] has just over 4 000 members, including most of the world's 2 000 largest companies. Their goal is to reduce their negative footprint, which is a start, but the overall data set out in A and B above indicates that a large majority of these companies are making very little if any real progress in their overall impact reduction.

This is due to many reasons, one the most important being what we call the "Context Gap" – meaning that the sustainability goals companies are reporting on through GRI are self-referencing, and often not very transparent, meaning that companies can suit themselves as to what they focus on, rather than be guided by the larger scale goals needed to make the changes needed to avert widespread disaster in time.

The World Business Council for Sustainable Development's[91] Vision 2050 program sets out some "must haves" including:

- Incorporating the costs of externalities, starting with carbon, ecosystem services and water, into the structure of the marketplace;
- Doubling agricultural output without increasing the amount of land or water used;

---

[88]  See the WBCSD Report on Vision 2050- http://www.wbcsd.org/vision2050.aspx

[89]  $38 trillion in revenues divided by Global Gross Domestic Product of $72 trillion in 2013.

[90]  The Global Reporting Initiative (GRI) is a non-profit organization that promotes economic sustainability. It produces one of the world's most prevalent standards for sustainability reporting — also known as ecological footprint reporting, environmental social governance (ESG) reporting, triple bottom line (TBL) reporting, and corporate social responsibility (CSR) reporting. GRI seeks to make sustainability reporting by all organizations as routine as, and comparable to, financial reporting.

A sustainability report is an organizational report that gives information about economic, environmental, social and governance performance. GRI Guidelines are regarded to be widely used. More than 4,000 organizations from 60 countries use the Guidelines to produce their sustainability reports. (View the world's reporters at the GRI Sustainability Disclosure Database.) GRI Guidelines apply to corporate businesses, public agencies, smaller enterprises, NGOs, industry groups and others. For municipal governments, they have generally been subsumed by similar guidelines from the UN ICLEI.

[91]  See the WBCSD Report on Vision 2050- http://www.wbcsd.org/vision2050.aspx *Vision 2050*, with its best-case scenario for sustainability and pathways for reaching it, is a tool for thought leadership and a platform for beginning the dialogue that must take place to navigate the challenging years to come.

- Halting deforestation and increasing yields from planted forests;
- Halving carbon emissions worldwide (based on 2005 levels) by 2050 through a shift to low-carbon energy systems;
- Improved demand-side energy efficiency, and providing universal access to low-carbon mobility.

## Carrying Capacity

*Carrying capacity* stands for the total sum of resources and flows available to support life in abundance, without compromising the Earth's ability to regenerate and recover from damages. This is the fundamental boundary condition for all actions. For life to survive and thrive, the carrying capacity has to be greater than our lifestyle and creations.

The most fundamental aspects of carrying capacity are measured by the Stockholm Resilience Centre, in its Planetary Boundaries research. In 2009, a group of 28 internationally renowned scientists identified and quantified a set of <u>nine planetary boundaries</u> within which humanity can continue to develop and thrive for generations to come. Crossing these boundaries could generate abrupt or irreversible environmental changes. Respecting the boundaries reduces the risks to human society of crossing these thresholds. The nine planetary boundaries are, briefly:

- **Stratospheric ozone layer** - The stratospheric ozone layer in the atmosphere filters out ultraviolet (UV) radiation from the sun. If this layer decreases, increasing amounts of ultraviolet radiation will reach ground level. This can cause a higher incidence of skin cancer in humans as well as damage to terrestrial and marine biological systems. Fortunately, because of the actions taken as a result of the Montreal Protocol, we appear to be on the path that will allow us to stay within this boundary.

- **Biodiversity** - The Millennium Ecosystem Assessment of 2005 concluded that changes in biodiversity due to human activities were more rapid in the past 50 years than at any time in human history, increasing the risks of abrupt and irreversible changes to ecosystems. The drivers of change that cause this severe biodiversity loss and lead to changes in ecosystem services are either steady, showing no evidence of declining over time, or are increasing in intensity.

- **Chemicals dispersion** - Emissions of toxic compounds such as heavy metals, synthetic organic pollutants and radioactive materials, represent some of the key human-driven changes to the planetary environment. These compounds can persist in the environment for a very long time, and their effects are potentially irreversible. Even when the uptake and bio-accumulation of chemical pollution is at sub-lethal levels for organisms, the effects of reduced fertility and the potential of permanent genetic damage can have severe effects on ecosystems. For example, persistent organic compounds have caused dramatic reductions in bird populations and impaired reproduction and development in marine mammals.

- **Climate Change** - Recent evidence suggests that the Earth, now passing 400 ppmv $CO_2$ in the atmosphere, has already transgressed the planetary boundary and is approaching several Earth system thresholds. We have reached a point at which the loss of summer polar sea-ice is almost certainly irreversible. This is one example of a well-defined threshold above which rapid physical feedback mechanisms can drive the Earth system into a much warmer state with sea levels metres higher than present. The weakening or reversal of terrestrial carbon sinks, for example through the ongoing destruction of the world's rainforests, is another potential tipping point, where climate-carbon cycle feedbacks accelerate Earth's warming and intensify the climate impacts. A major question is how long we can remain over this boundary before large, irreversible changes become unavoidable.

- **Ocean acidification** - Around a quarter of the $CO_2$ humanity emitted into the atmosphere is ultimately dissolved in the oceans. Here it forms carbonic acid, altering ocean chemistry and decreasing the pH of the surface water. This increased acidity reduces the amount of available carbonate ions, an essential 'building block' used by many marine species for shell and skeleton formation. Beyond a threshold concentration, this rising acidity makes it hard for organisms such as corals and some shellfish and plankton species to grow and survive. Losses of these species would change the structure and dynamics of ocean ecosystems and could potentially lead to drastic reductions in fish stocks.

- **Freshwater consumption and the global hydrological cycle** - The freshwater cycle is strongly affected by climate change and its boundary is closely linked to the climate boundary, yet human pressure is now the dominant driving force determining the functioning and distribution of global freshwater systems. The consequences of human modification of water bodies include both global-scale river flow changes and shifts in vapour flows arising from land use change. These shifts in the hydrological system can be abrupt and irreversible. Water is becoming increasingly scarce - by 2050 about half a billion people are likely to be subject to water-stress, increasing the pressure to intervene in water systems.

- **Land system change** - Land is converted to human use all over the planet. Forests, wetlands and other vegetation types have primarily been converted to agricultural land. This land-use change is one driving force behind the serious reductions in biodiversity, and it has impacts on water flows and on the biogeochemical cycling of carbon, nitrogen and phosphorus and other important elements. While each incident of land cover change occurs on a local scale, the aggregated impacts can have consequences for Earth system processes on a global scale. A major challenge with setting a land use boundary is that it needs to reflect not just the absolute quantity of unconverted and converted land but also its function, quality and spatial distribution.

- **Nitrogen and phosphorus inputs to the biosphere and oceans -** The biogeochemical cycles of nitrogen and phosphorus have been radically changed by humans as a result of many industrial and agricultural processes. Nitrogen and phosphorus are both essential elements for plant growth, so fertilizer production and application is the main concern. Human activities now convert more atmospheric nitrogen into reactive forms than all of the Earth's terrestrial processes combined. Much of this new reactive nitrogen is emitted to the atmosphere in various forms rather than taken up by plants. When it is rained out, it pollutes waterways and coastal zones or accumulates in the terrestrial biosphere. Similarly, a relatively small proportion of phosphorus fertilizers applied to food production systems is taken up by plants; much of the phosphorus mobilized by humans also ends up in aquatic systems. These can become oxygen-starved as bacteria consume the blooms of algae that grow in response to the high nutrient supply. A significant fraction of the applied nitrogen and phosphorus makes its way to the sea, and can push marine and aquatic systems across ecological thresholds of their own. One regional-scale example of this effect is the decline in the shrimp catch in the Gulf of Mexico's 'dead zone' caused by fertilizer transported in rivers from the US Midwest.

- **Atmospheric aerosol loading -** An atmospheric aerosol planetary boundary was proposed primarily because of the influence of aerosols on Earth's climate system. Through their interaction with water vapour, aerosols play a critically important role in the hydrological cycle affecting cloud formation and global-scale and regional patterns of atmospheric circulation, such as the monsoon systems in tropical regions. They also have a direct effect on climate, by changing how much solar radiation is reflected or absorbed in the atmosphere. Humans change the aerosol loading by emitting atmospheric pollution (many pollutant gases condense into droplets and particles), and also through land-use change that increases the release of dust and smoke into the air. Shifts in climate regimes and monsoon systems have already been seen in highly polluted environments. A further reason for an aerosol boundary is that aerosols have adverse effects on many living organisms. Inhaling highly polluted air causes roughly 800,000 people to die prematurely each year.

A quick overview of the current state of these boundaries is given in the diagram below. As you can see, we are already dangerously into the "red" for climate change, biodiversity and the nitrogen cycle.

**DIAGRAM 25 - Estimates of how the different control variables for nine planetary boundaries have changed from 1950 to present. The green shaded polygon represents the safe operating space**

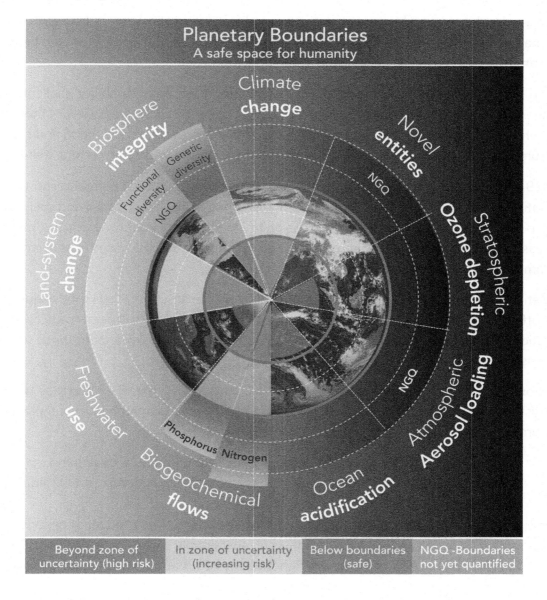

The WBCSD's Vision 2050 program has also defined a set of pathways to ensure we reduce our current "overshoot" of environmental and social boundaries, based on a specific set of industry analyses, as set out in the diagram below.

The result of extensive dialogues involving 200 companies spanning 20 countries, Vision 2050 has at its core the attributes of successful business planning: understand your current situation, identify the obstacles to success, and create a pathway to overcome those obstacles. The conclusion of this analysis is the need for a fundamental transformation of the way the world produces and consumes everything from energy to agricultural products. And in that shift, Vision 2050 identifies unprecedented opportunities for business – at least those that understand they can no longer operate in business-as-usual, autopilot mode.

Opportunities range from developing and maintaining low-carbon, zero-waste cities, to improving and managing biocapacity, ecosystems, lifestyles and livelihoods. In today's dollars, the market opportunities created by adapting to the new global reality for sustainable living are somewhere between $3-$10 trillion USD per year in 2050.

Vision 2050 is not only about economics, development and sustainability challenges for business. It suggests governments and civil society must create a different view of the future, one where, "economic growth has been decoupled from ecosystem destruction and material consumption and re-coupled with sustainable economic development and societal well-being."

With 9 billion people on the planet competing for a limited supply of natural resources, the definition of "living well" will also have to shift. Instead of a utopian dream, living well in 2050 means that all people have access to and the ability to afford education, healthcare, mobility, the basics of food, water, energy and shelter, and consumer goods. It also means living within the limits of the planet itself.

Sometimes the simplest questions are the hardest to answer. Vision 2050 asks those questions and offers a way to help businesses understand the pathways they will need to succeed. The question of where we will be in 2050 is well worth asking, for the rewards to those who get the answers right is unprecedented.

If Vision 2050 was to be successfully implemented by the WBCSD members and their business ecosystem partners and supply chains, we would reduce our current need for 1.5 planets of resources to 1.1 planets, which might also help us to:

- Ensure global warming does not exceed 2 degrees centigrade by helping...
- Reduce annual greenhouse gas emissions below 10 gigatonnes of $CO_2$ equivalent p.a. through shifts on both supply and demand sides
- Reduce waterstress, peak soil and overfishing effects while reducing air and water pollution & deforestation by incentivising sustainable supply chains & lifestyles
- Enhance the quality of life in and renewability of urban habitats, in particular in the world's 600 largest & fast growing cities
- Encourage entrepreneurs and community programs with positive social impacts in these cities through empowering, for-impact entrepreneurial activities

### DIAGRAM 26– Vision 2050 Pathways – The World Business Council for Sustainable Development

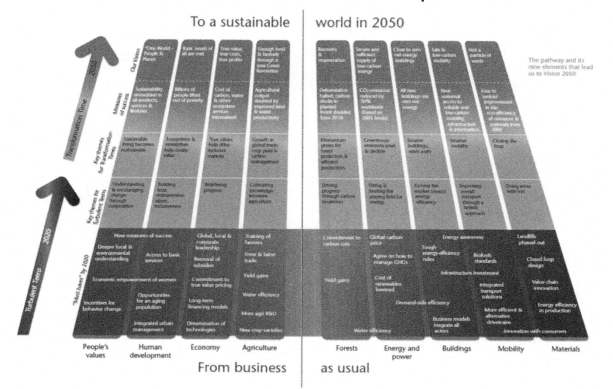

## Appendix B -
## The Human Journey – The Source of New Realms of Possibility

The *human journey* refers to our evolution as a species, and the way in which we evolve through several different stages to become world-centric adults who care about our planet. Each stage of development has its own "hot" and "cold" buttons and bottom lines, which can help motivate ThriveAbility Thinking. ThriveAbility draws upon the work of hundreds of complementary schools of psychology in defining a predictable set of developmental levels through which every human being passes on their way to adulthood, including more advanced stages of mature adult development that have only recently become the focus of detailed scientific research.

Both evolutionary and revolutionary processes drive the trajectory of human development. Evolution is slowly becoming a conscious collaborative process, driven by our hearts and minds, rather than a blind, unconscious and competitive struggle driven by unseen forces out of our control. The human species is maturing from a troublesome teenager to a more awake and progressive twenty-something, though our progress is measured in centuries rather than years.

The revolutionary aspect of our development lies in our ability to transform ourselves and our systems and technologies, making predictions into the future difficult if not impossible in most areas of life. Whether these transformations are political (from the fall of the Berlin Wall to the Arab Spring), technical (from a million songs on your iPod to cures for most major diseases), or social (think of the rise of social media and virtual communities in less than a decade), various aspects of our lives are undergoing radical transformations every decade. Imagine we find solutions to overpopulation (the global birth rate is already falling below UN estimates), and global warming/climate change in the next decade? What is hard to believe right now can become commonplace in a decade- that is the lesson of the last century.

So it is that we find the messy process of evolution delivering greater complexity and consciousness over the longer term, while being punctuated by radical breakthroughs or breakdowns from time to time. Within the general trend of "UP", we find both major progressions and major regressions, with the latter often acting as fuel for the former, embodied in the formula: "What does not grow, decays". In the human body we find the rate of cell growth and cell death sufficiently evenly balanced so that we do not notice that our entire body is renewed on average every seven years. In stable societies and civilizations, we also find a similar ratio of growth and decay in the population and the artefacts and infrastructure they live in.

What drives the evolution of human beings is the interplay between the growth and development of individuals, and their environment. Historically our environment dictated our life conditions, and it is only relatively recently (in the past few millennia), that we have been able to modify our environment to any significant extent. Scientists and historians are sufficiently impressed by our 21st century environment modifying abilities to name the geological age we are in the "Anthropocene"[92].

The interplay between our environment and ourselves is mirrored in us by the interplay between our exteriors and interiors- our bodies and our minds. From an individual perspective we are able to track three key developmental stages. In the first two stages, pre-personal and personal, we are operating out of the reptilian brain and the limbic system respectively.[7] The R-complex and limbic systems effectively correspond to System 0 (the core bodily functions), and System 1 (the intuitive, analog intelligence which has often been called "right-brained").

The bridge from the personal to the transpersonal phases of development is the neocortex, which in man constitutes two-thirds of our brain. A person without a neocortex is essentially a "vegetable" as they kindly put it in the medical business, while a mouse without a neocortex can function normally for all intensive purposes, so the development of the functions of the neocortex is crucial for humans to evolve into responsible, conscious, choice-making citizens in the highly complex world we have evolved over the past few thousand years.

We find System 2, the digital, procedural intelligence, emerging in this collaboration between System 0 and System 1, enabling us to program our actions and behaviours much more effectively, in the pursuit of specific goals, and in collaboration with others.

In the transpersonal phase of development the pre-frontal and frontal cortices become new control centres which enable individuals to activate System 3, the "strategic psychological helicopter", from which they are capable of getting an overview of the situation they are in and in which they are capable of being mindful and taking better decisions that benefit the greatest span of human beings while honouring the greatest depth in those individuals.

1. **Pre-personal Phase** - in our first decade or so of life we develop through the pre-personal phase. In the developed world this stage results in the emergence of a self that is distinct from our family, and in the developing world a self that is distinct from our tribe. Our heroes during this stage of development are powerful, often impulsive, egocentric and, of course, heroic. During the pre-personal phase we believe in Santa Claus, magical-mythic spirits, dragons, beasts, and powerful people. In ancient times these were archetypal

---

[92] Many scientists are now using the term and the Geological Society of America titled its 2011 annual meeting: Archean to Anthropocene: The past is the key to the future. The Anthropocene has no precise start date, but based on atmospheric evidence may be considered to start with the Industrial Revolution (late 18th century). Other scientists link it to earlier events, such as the rise of agriculture. Evidence of relative human impact such as the growing human influence on land use, ecosystems, biodiversity and species extinction is controversial, some scientists believe the human impact has significantly changed (or halted) the growth of biodiversity

gods and goddesses, while in the 21st century we find super-heroes and their archenemies embodied in books and film, from Harry Potter to Lord of the Rings to Batman. While we are developing our rational faculties during this phase, unconscious motivations and magical thinking often characterize our behaviour.

Dysfunction during these years can lead to issues arising throughout a lifetime. Challenging or primitive life conditions can also make it difficult for people to move beyond these developmental stages, and during times of war, famine, great hardship or personal difficulty, people often regress to these stages as mature adults. In such cases the family or the tribe is the ultimate shock absorber.

2. **Personal Phase** - At some point between being a child and becoming a teenager, we learn to be conscientious, responsible people, if all goes well, and experience a desire to conform to conventional norms and behaviours. With the emergence of our own conscious identity and rational mental faculties, we are now able to strike a balance between our intuitive (System 1) and reasoning thought (System 2) processes at a conscious level. We may even be experiencing some System 3 moments where we transcend ourselves and the situations we are in, gaining a helicopter perspective and perhaps even a "peak experience" with spiritual Aha! Moments.

Modern educational systems, modern organizations and institutions and some religions are powerful forces in helping to shape such conventional and rational mental processes. Those who have been shaped by such systems often reach the achievement and Affiliative levels by their mid-twenties and form the majority of the population in most developed societies. Modern "civil" society is based upon conscious mental processes being activated and used on a daily basis by most people.

3. **Transpersonal Phase** - In the transpersonal realm one transcends and integrates all other developmental levels, moving through the authentic integral level to the transcendent and unity levels of higher consciousness. According to recent research, hundreds of millions of people are now actively exploring these transpersonal levels worldwide, while at least 1% of the world's population is anchored at the transpersonal in their daily life.

This is the great leap psychologist Clare Graves was talking about in 1970 as he reviewed his latest research results with Abraham Maslow and the rest of the American Psychological Association members. Such post-modern stages of development are the basis upon which an integral, global civilization could be built in the 21st century. I say could because:

- the billions of conformist and achievement oriented power holders would have to be sufficiently attracted to the possibilities that they are able to let go of some of their narrow belief systems and vested interests to give the newer systems and structures room to grow;

- the hundreds of millions of affiliative, cultural creatives would need to become much more grounded and practical in their desire for transformation and demands for change, while also shedding the last remnants of their often narcissistic tendencies.

Diagram 27 below offers a simplified representation of the different pathways the evolution of human values can take. From an individual perspective we are able to track three key developmental stages. In the first-tier there are two stages, pre-personal and personal. Here we are operating out of the reptilian brain and the limbic system respectively.[8] The R-complex and limbic systems effectively correspond to System 0 (the core bodily functions), and System 1 (the intuitive, analogue intelligence which has often been incorrectly called "right-brained").

The bridge from the personal to the transpersonal phases of development is the neocortex, which in man constitutes two-thirds of our brain. The development of the functions of the neocortex is crucial for humans to evolve into responsible, conscious, choice-making citizens in the highly complex world we have evolved over the past few thousand years.

We find System 2, the digital, procedural intelligence, emerging in this collaboration between System 0 and System 1, enabling us to program our actions and behaviours much more effectively, in the pursuit of specific goals, and in collaboration with others.

This model simplifies the three main, overlapping models of human development currently used in a wide variety of organizations, psychology and philosophy textbooks. The names of the successive stages follow the classification system used by psychologist Jenny Wade and the colours used by Professor Don Beck, the co-creator of Spiral Dynamics.

The "Reactive" (or "beige") stage evolved about 100 000 years ago when our distinct sense of self began to emerge, and food, water, warmth, sex and safety were our top priorities. We used our very wide range of senses (far wider than the five main senses used today), instincts and habits to survive in the wilderness, and formed into small survival bands to perpetuate life, living off the land close to nature along with the other animals. The original Bushmen of the Kalahari Desert, aboriginal tribes on various continents including Australia and the remaining tribes of the rainforests in the Amazon, Borneo and elsewhere living in small bands of up around 30 people are typical of this stage of development, where the most highly developed part of the brain is the R-complex.

Around 50 000 years ago, a new stage of development began to emerge when we started to invent art, music and religion- in short, the beginnings of culture and metaphorical thinking that transformed our ability to communicate and coordinate ourselves in larger groups ranging up to 300 people. This new tribal form of existence placed a priority on the individual being a loyal group member, showing allegiance to the tribal chiefs, elders, ancestors and the clan.

**DIAGRAM 27– 9 Stages in the Evolution of Human Consciousness**

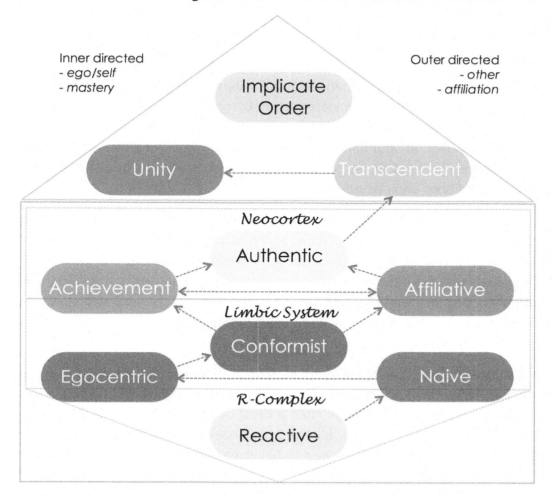

At this naïve (or "purple") stage of development, sacred objects, places, events and memories are paramount to making sense of the world. Observing the rites of passage, seasonal cycles and tribal customs are essential for tribal cohesion and bonding between its members. Spirit beings and mystical signs are paid close attention to, ensuring that individuals have a sense of belonging and safety in the face of an unpredictable and often cruel world. People at this stage of development are outer-directed towards others, and value their affiliation with the group above all else. The 400 or so original tribes of Europe and the 400 or so original tribes of Africa were all interconnected through a variety of familial and trading alliances, yet also engaged in warlike behaviour frequently when life conditions got tough or over-crowded.

About 10 000 years ago, the egocentric (or "red") stage of development began to emerge. Like the magical/naïve purple stage of development, this stage is a halfway house between the R-complex part of our brains and the limbic system, which processes emotions and stores a treasure house of memories. Unlike the magical/naïve purple stage, however, this egocentric red stage is driven by a focus on self and the mastery of power over others. Through our development of a variety of technologies 10 000 years ago, the world became at once a more settled and yet a more dangerous place as massive armies and empires began to be built for the first time, based on the surpluses generated through settled urban populations harnessing a variety of agricultural, building and military technologies, as well as elaborate social hierarchies.

The ancient Egyptians, Greeks, Persians, Mongols, Chinese and Romans are good examples of Empire builders who came to dominate parts of Europe and Asia for several hundred years at a time, only to be pushed back to their native territories as other more powerful Empires rose in their ascendant. In South and Central America the Aztec and Inca Empires also rose more recently and exhibited similar social structures and power dynamics, though with very different life conditions and cultural content.

Egocentric, "Red" stands tall, expects attention, demands respect and calls the shots, and attempts to dominate competitors by conquering or out-foxing them. Being what you are and having what you want, regardless of the consequences for others, is the primary goal of such individuals and cultures. The emphasis of life is to enjoy oneself to the fullest right now without guilt or remorse, and breaking free from any domination or constraints as required to fulfil immediate desires. Egocentric red is thus highly impulsive, generally opportunistic, and often unpredictable.

About 5 000 years ago, major religions began to arise and spread around the planet, beginning with Egyptian and Chinese religions. During the Axial Age which began around 3 000 BCE and ended around 700 CE, an intense burst of new religion creation began starting with Buddhist and Hindu traditions, followed by Judaism, Christianity and Islam. Over the course of these 6 000 years, a new way of being emerged cantered around a variety of belief systems encapsulated in "new stories", that gave life a meaning, direction and purpose with pre-determined outcomes. It must be stressed that not only are these religious belief systems- they also represent the emergence of new capacities in the human brain and being to recognize and participate in new forms of order that also have consequences for governance systems and culture, along with technological and scientific advances appropriate to that level of development.

Each religion has its founding leaders and/or gods, from Buddha and his three universal truths to the three principal gods of Hinduism- Shiva, Vishnu and Shakti, Moses and his God Yahweh, followed by the Hebraic Kings and Prophets and Jesus and Mohammed, both believed to be sons of God and god-like by Christians and Muslims respectively.

Such Conformist "True Blue" belief systems require a degree of sacrifice to their specific transcendent Cause, Truth or Righteous Pathway. There is a strong hierarchical order in which the powerful enforce a code of conduct based on eternal, absolute principles that, if followed and obeyed, produce stability now and guarantee future reward, whether in heaven or on earth. The impulsivity of the egocentric red way of being is now controlled through guilt and a desire to "do the right thing", where there is a place for everyone, and everyone is in their place (though not necessarily wildly happy about it). Laws, regulations and discipline build character and moral fibre, such that social and economic arrangements become more certain, predictable and enforceable.

The conformist stage of development is the last stage centred predominantly in the limbic system. Depending upon an individual's predisposition, the next stage of development can either be achievement or affiliation oriented. Some individuals might be balanced evenly between these developmental stages, though women tend to develop more strongly in the direction of affiliation, and men tend to develop more strongly in the direction of achievement.

The shift from the limbic system to the neocortex as the control centre that determines our priorities and creates our options and actions is a major advancement in human civilization. This was precisely the shift that occurred during the first European Renaissance starting in about 1500 in northern Italy. It has taken fully 500 years for the "Achiever" and "Affiliator" modes of consciousness to mature into fully-fledged ways of operating that form the centre of gravity of our modern and post-modern cultures in the developed world.

The Achievist ("Orange") level of development began to put down deep roots in European circles about 300 years ago. At its root this kind of consciousness is optimistic, risk-taking and stresses science, technology and competitiveness. It acknowledges that change and progress are built into the nature of things, and focuses on learning the secrets of nature and implementing the best solutions to hitherto difficult challenges. This modernist approach manipulates the earth's resources to create and spread abundance, without recognizing limits to growth. Achievist strategies are built around acting in one's own self-interest by playing the game to win- an approach Adam Smith would have applauded and which he set out clearly in his book "The Wealth of Nations" a few centuries ago.

It is no surprise, therefore, to learn that the Affiliative level of development exists in a strong tension with the Achievist level of development. This communitarian/egalitarian ("Green") mode of consciousness emerged slightly later than and often in reaction to aspects of the Achievist "orange" system. It can be seen in the better parts of the French Revolution, the American constitution, the early Quakers, the movement for the abolition of slavery, and various European philosophers of the eighteenth and nineteenth centuries. Where the Achievist level seeks to create wealth, the affiliative system is concerned with the equitable distribution of wealth, and is associated with Socialist and other liberal movements over the centuries.

The focus of green affiliators is on seeking peace within and without, co-creating caring in communities where feelings and sensitivity supersede cold rationality. One of the major contributions of "green" consciousness and movements it that it redresses the imbalances created by harsh blue TruthForce systems and often too greedy orange Achievist systems, helping heal old wounds and bringing reconciliation, truth and justice to the fore. The affiliative green system was at the forefront of the South African peace and reconciliation process after the harsh years of apartheid, enabling Nelson Mandela to be the "good guy" who took care of all South Africans, not just his own supporters.

The six levels of development from the Reactive Beige system through Magical Tribal Purple, Egocentric Red, Conformist Blue, Achievist Orange and Affiliative Green, are what is known as "First-Tier" systems. This is because they all share the common characteristic of believing that they are each "the only game in town". As one ascends from Beige through to Green, the higher levels systems take their own superiority for granted, as they are more complex and extend further in space and time than each of the previous levels. Blue TruthForce believes that if it could only evangelise everyone else effectively, then the "others" would sign up to their belief system or culture. Orange Achievists believe that everyone secretly wants progress above all else, and that people will do anything to get ahead. Green Affiliators believe that Orange Achievists are greedy and overbearing, and need to see the error of their ways, while those Blue Conformists are just so stuck in the mud and backward.

In reality, however, each value system is an adaptation to a specific niche, and in its own ways will be better or worse adapted depending upon specific life conditions prevailing in specific niches at certain points in time. The extent to which there is "dissonance" between people's values and their life conditions will determine to what extent their dissatisfaction with what no longer works for them will translate into action that leads them to evolve a more appropriate blend of values for their needs.

With the completion of the "Green Meme", human consciousness is poised for a quantum jump into "Second-Tier thinking." Clare Graves referred to this as a "momentous leap," where "a chasm of unbelievable depth of meaning is crossed." In essence, with second-tier consciousness, one can think both vertically and horizontally, using both hierarchies and heterarchies (both ranking and linking). One can therefore, for the first time, vividly grasp the entire spectrum of development, and thus see that each level is critical for the health of the overall Spiral. The Authentic, Integral, level of development is the starting point for this exciting journey, followed by the Transcendent and Unity stages of development. The latter two stages are not well mapped yet, as there are so few people in them at the moment.

Each wave of development transcends its predecessor, and yet it includes or embraces the best of and transcends/negates the worst of it in its own makeup. For example, a cell transcends but includes molecules, which transcend but include atoms. To say that a molecule goes beyond an atom is not to say that molecules hate atoms, but that they love them: they embrace them in their own makeup; they include them, they don't marginalize them. Each wave of existence is a fundamental ingredient of all subsequent waves, and thus each is to be cherished and embraced.

Moreover, each wave can itself be activated or reactivated as life circumstances warrant. In emergency situations, we can activate red power drives; in response to chaos, we might need to activate blue order; in looking for a new job, we might need orange achievement drives; in marriage and with friends, close green bonding. All of these value systems have something important to contribute.

But what none of the first-tier value systems can do, on their own, is fully appreciate the existence of the other value systems. Each of the first-tier value systems thinks that its worldview is the correct or best perspective. It reacts negatively if challenged. Blue order is very uncomfortable with both red impulsiveness and orange individualism. Orange individualism thinks blue order is for suckers and green egalitarianism is weak and woo-woo. Green egalitarianism cannot easily abide excellence and value rankings, big pictures, hierarchies, or anything that appears authoritarian and thus green reacts strongly to blue, orange, and anything post-green.

All of that begins to change with second-tier thinking. Because second-tier consciousness is fully aware of the interior stages of development--even if it cannot articulate them in a technical fashion--it steps back and grasps the big picture, and thus second-tier thinking appreciates the necessary role that all of the various value systems play. Second-tier awareness thinks in terms of the overall spiral of existence, and not merely in the terms of any one level.

Where the Green value system begins to grasp the numerous different systems and pluralistic contexts that exist in different cultures (which is why it is indeed the sensitive self, i.e., sensitive to the marginalization of others), second-tier thinking goes one step further. It looks for the rich contexts that link and join these pluralistic systems, and thus it takes these separate systems and begins to embrace, include, and integrate them into holistic spirals and integral meshworks. Second-tier thinking, in other words, is instrumental in moving from relativism to holism, or from pluralism to integralism.

## The Integral Stage of Development – MindShift and WorldShift

The European philosopher Jean Gebser and American philosopher Ken Wilber have written a great deal about what they call the integral stage of development- Wilber to the extent that he calls his life's work "Integral Philosophy". If Wilber and others such as Paul Ray, researcher and author of the "Cultural Creatives" are right, then roughly one hundred million plus individuals are engaged in a transition from first-tier ways of being and thinking, into second tier or "Integral" ways of being and thinking. What would that mean for the evolutionary trajectory of our species Homo sapiens, and what would that mean for ThriveAbility?

Wilber's Integral Theory places perspectives at the centre of his way of describing our world and Kosmos. Psychologist Don Beck has also explored this developmental level using colourful terminology for the first stages of integral development (which he calls "Yellow", and then "Turquoise" for the more holistic, planetary perspective). Wilber makes some grand claims for his integral approach- here is the introductory page on Amazon for his book "Integral Vision":

"Suppose we took everything that all the various world cultures have to tell us about human potential—about psychological, spiritual, and social growth—and identified the basic patterns that connect these pieces of knowledge. What if we attempted to create an all-inclusive map that touches the most important factors from all of the world's great traditions?

Ken Wilber's Integral Vision provides such a map. Using all the known systems and models of human growth—from the ancient sages to the latest breakthroughs in cognitive science—it distils their major components into five simple elements, and, moreover, ones that readers can verify in their own experience right now.

In any field of interest, such as business, law, science, psychology, health, art, or everyday living and learning—the Integral Vision ensures that we are utilizing the full range of resources for the situation, leading to a greater likelihood of success and fulfilment. With easily understood explanations, exercises, and familiar examples, The Integral Vision shows how we can accelerate growth and development to higher, wider, deeper ways of being, embodied in self, shared in community, and connected to the planet, which can literally help with everything from spiritual enlightenment to business success to personal relationships."

We do indeed live in an extraordinary age, where all of the world's knowledge and cultures, are available to each of us – something unprecedented in the history of our species. For the past few hundred thousand years a person was born into a culture that knew only of its own existence. For example, someone born in Africa, was raised as an African, married an African, and followed an African religion—often living in the same hut for their entire life, on a spot of land that their ancestors settled millennia ago. We have evolved out of Africa from isolated hunter-gatherer bands like the Bushmen, to the tribal settlements and farms of the Xhosa, to the ancient nations of Africa, to the conquering feudal empires of the Zulus and other warring tribes. In the past five hundred years we have also witnessed the emergence of international corporate states such as the Dutch East India Company to modern multinationals such as Unilever, and the other inhabitants of the global village including the United Nations and hundreds of thousands of NGO's and charities. We are now witnessing the next stage in our evolution toward an integral global village that seems to be humanity's destiny.

As Wilber puts it: "So it is that the leading edge of consciousness evolution stands today on the brink of an integral millennium—or at least the possibility of an integral millennium, where the sum total of extant human knowledge, wisdom, and technology is available to all. But there are several obstacles to that integral embrace, even in the most developed populations. Moreover, there is the more typical or average mode of consciousness, which is far from integral anything, and is in desperate need of its own tending. Both of those pressing issues (the integral vision as it relates to the most developed and the least developed populations) are related directly to the contents of this volume of the Collected Works."

# A Stratified Approach to Socio-Cultural Developmental Levels

## DIAGRAM 28 - Systems in Focus and Stages of Development

| Level of Complexity – Span & Depth of the System in Focus | Levels & Kinds of Responsibility & Accountability | Core Social Principle & Priority | Driving Forces of the System |
|---|---|---|---|
| Tribe & its Immediate Support Systems | TribeHolder | RitualAbility & Indigenous Wisdom | Rituals & Ways of the Elders |
| Empire & its Regional Support Systems | PowerHolder | ForceAbility & Respect | Physical & Charismatic Force |
| Belief System & its Socio-economic Support Systems | TruthHolder | BelieveAbility & Absolute Truth (Religious & Secular) | Dogma & Bureaucracy |
| Corporation & its Socio-economic Support Systems | ShareHolder | KnowAbility & Transparency | Science, Technology & Markets |
| Natural & Social Ecosystems both Locally & Globally | StakeHolder | SustainAbility & Community | Ecological/Systems Thinking & Movements |
| Holographic & Fractal Structures /Processes Transform Underlying Systems | ThriveHolder | ThriveAbility & Conscious Evolution | Integral Thinking & Global Collective Intelligence |

# Appendix C –
# How the Integral Model Ensures the ThriveAbility Approach is Complete & Easy to Apply

Throughout this book we have referred to the "integral model" as one of the bases for the ThriveAbility approach, and in this Appendix we provide a more detailed examination of how the integral model enabled us to develop a holistic approach to ThriveAbility. By using the integral model as a test-bed, we have ensured that all the key perspectives and components of human and natural systems are taken into account in our analysis, and during the ThriveAbility Journey.

The integral model or "operating system" (or "IOS" for short), is based on an analysis of our world and the kosmos which takes into account 5 key components: **quadrants**, **levels**, **lines**, **states**, and **types**. As you will see, all of these elements are *available in your own awareness right now*. These 5 elements are not merely theoretical concepts; they are aspects of your own experience, contours of your own consciousness, as you can easily verify for yourself.

### DIAGRAM 29 – The Integral Operating System

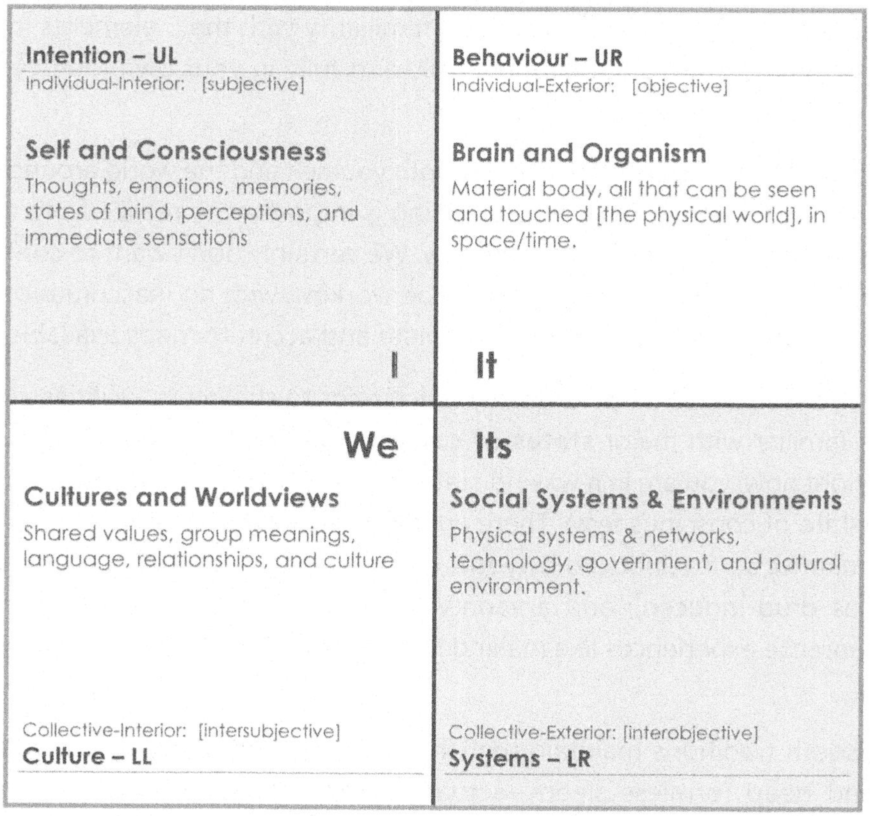

| Intention – UL | Behaviour – UR |
|---|---|
| Individual-Interior: [subjective] | Individual-Exterior: [objective] |
| **Self and Consciousness** | **Brain and Organism** |
| Thoughts, emotions, memories, states of mind, perceptions, and immediate sensations | Material body, all that can be seen and touched [the physical world], in space/time. |
| **I** | **It** |
| **We** | **Its** |
| **Cultures and Worldviews** | **Social Systems & Environments** |
| Shared values, group meanings, language, relationships, and culture | Physical systems & networks, technology, government, and natural environment. |
| Collective-Interior: [intersubjective] | Collective-Exterior: [interobjective] |
| **Culture – LL** | **Systems – LR** |

In an information network, an operating system is the infrastructure that allows various software programs to operate. The point is that, as you apply different "software" in each area of your life—from business, to work, play, or relationships—you need an operating system that offers the widest compatibility with all the key applications you may need.

An **IOS** can be used to help index any activity—from art to dance to business to psychology to politics to ecology. This indexing function is key – like an application programming interface (or "API" as it is known in the world of computing), it allows each of those domains to talk to the others. Using **IOS**, business has the terminology with which to communicate fully with ecology, which can communicate with art, which can communicate with law, which can communicate with poetry and education and medicine and spirituality. In the history of humankind, this has previously proven to be a major challenge.

When it comes to making the impossible possible as a ThriveAbility Leader, you will need a very accurate "GPS" to help guide you on your journey. If you are trying to fly over the Himalayas, the more accurate a map you have, the less likely you will crash, the more likely you will enjoy the journey and get to your destination. An Integral Approach insures that you are utilizing the full range of resources for any situation, with the greater likelihood of success.

Second, if you learn to spot these 5 elements in your own awareness—and because they are there in any event—then you can more easily appreciate them, exercise them, use them... and thereby vastly accelerate your own growth and development as a ThriveAbility Leader to higher, wider, deeper ways of being. A simple familiarity with the 5 elements in the Integral Model will help you orient yourself more easily and fully in your own journey through life and help your team and your organization too.

In short, the Integral Approach helps you see both yourself and the world around you in more comprehensive and effective ways. But one thing is important to realize from the start. The Integral Map is just a map. It is not the territory. We certainly don't want to confuse the map with the territory, but neither do we want to be working with an inaccurate or faulty map. The Integral Map is just one of the most complete and accurate maps available.

Let's start with states of consciousness, which refer to subjective realities. Everybody is familiar with major **states of consciousness**, such as waking, dreaming, and deep sleep. Right now, you are in a waking state of consciousness (or, if you are tired, perhaps a daydream state of consciousness). There are all sorts of different states of consciousness, including *meditative states* (induced by yoga, contemplation, meditation, and so on); *altered states* (such as drug-induced); and a variety of *peak experiences*, many of which can be triggered by intense experiences like making love, walking in nature, or listening to exquisite music.

The great wisdom traditions maintain that the 3 *natural states* of consciousness—waking, dreaming, and deep formless sleep—actually contain a treasure trove of wisdom and awakening.... if we know how to use them correctly. We all experience various sorts of states of consciousness, and these states often provide profound motivation, meaning, and drives, in both yourself and others. In any particular situation, states of consciousness may not be a very important factor, or they may be the determining factor, but no integral approach can afford to ignore them. Whenever you are using **IOS**, you will automatically be prompted to check and see if you are touching bases with these important subjective realities.

## STAGES OR LEVELS OF DEVELOPMENT

There's an interesting thing about states of consciousness: they come and they go. Even great peak experiences or altered states, no matter how profound, will come, stay a bit, then pass. No matter how wonderful their capacities, they are temporary.

Where states of consciousness are temporary, **stages of consciousness** are permanent. Stages represent the actual milestones of growth and development. Once you are at a stage, it is an enduring acquisition. For example, once a child develops through the linguistic stages of development, the child has permanent access to language. Language isn't present one minute and gone the next. The same thing happens with other types of growth. Once you stably reach a stage of growth and development, you can access the qualities of that stage—such as greater consciousness, more embracing love, higher ethical callings, greater intelligence and awareness—virtually any time you want. *Passing states* have been converted to *permanent traits*.

How many stages of development are there? Well, remember that in any map, the way you divide and represent the actual territory is somewhat arbitrary. For example, how many degrees are there between freezing and boiling water? If you use a Centigrade scale or "map," there are 100 degrees between freezing and boiling. But if you use a Fahrenheit scale, freezing is at 32 and boiling is at 212, so there are 180 degrees between them. Which is right? Both of them. It just depends upon how you want to slice that pie.

The same is true of stages. There are all sorts of ways to slice and dice development, and therefore there are all sorts of **stage conceptions**. All of them can be useful. In the chakra system, for example, there are 7 major stages or levels of consciousness. Jean Gebser, the famous anthropologist, uses 5: archaic, magic, mythic, rational, and integral. Certain Western psychological models have 8, 12, or more levels of development. Which is right? All of them; it just depends on what you want to keep track of in growth and development.

"**Stages** of development" are also referred to as "**waves** of development," the idea being that each stage represents a level of organization or a level of complexity. For example, in the sequence from atoms to molecules to cells to organisms, each of those stages of evolution involves a greater level of complexity. The word "level" is not meant in a rigid or exclusionary fashion, but simply to indicate that there are important emergent qualities that tend to come into being in a discrete or quantum-like fashion, and these developmental levels are important aspects of many natural phenomena.

The Integral Model works with around 8 to 10 stages or levels of values development. One stage conception often used is that of Spiral Dynamics Integral, founded by Don Beck based on the research of Clare Graves. Other stages of values development pioneered by Jane Loevinger and Susann Cook-Greuter; and orders of consciousness, researched by Robert Kegan are also useful. But there are many other useful stage conceptions available with the Integral Approach, and you can adopt any of them that are appropriate to your situation.

## A SIMPLE EXAMPLE

To show what is involved with levels or stages, let's use a very simple model possessing only 3 of them. If we look at moral development, for example, we find that an infant at birth has not yet been socialized into the culture's ethics and conventions; this is called the **pre-conventional stage**. It is also called **egocentric**, in that the infant's awareness is largely self-absorbed. But as the young child begins to learn its culture's rules and norms, it grows into the **conventional stage** of morals This stage is also called **ethnocentric**, in that it centres on the child's particular group, tribe, clan, or nation, and it therefore tends to exclude care for those not of one's group. But at the next major stage of moral development, the **post-conventional stage**, the individual's identity expands once again, this time to include a care and concern for all peoples, regardless of race, colour, sex, or creed, which is why this stage is also called **worldcentric**.

Thus, moral development tends to move from "me" (egocentric) to "us" (ethnocentric) to "all of us" (worldcentric)—a good example of the unfolding stages of consciousness.

Another way to picture these 3 stages is as **body**, **mind**, and **spirit**. Those words all have many valid meanings, but when used specifically to refer to stages, they mean:

Stage 1, which is dominated by my gross physical reality, is the "body" stage (using body in its typical meaning of gross body). Since you are identified merely with the separate bodily organism and its survival drives, this is also the "me" stage.

Stage 2 is the "mind" stage, where identity expands from the isolated gross body and starts to share relationships with many others, based perhaps on shared values, mutual interests, common ideals, or shared dreams. Because I can use the mind to take the role of others—to put myself in their shoes and feel what it is like to be them—my identity expands from "me" to "us" (the move from egocentric to ethnocentric).

With stage 3, my identity expands once again, this time from an identity with "us" to an identity with "all of us" (the move from ethnocentric to worldcentric). Here I begin to understand that, in addition to the wonderful diversity of humans and cultures, there are also similarities and shared commonalities. Discovering the commonwealth of all beings is the move from ethnocentric to worldcentric, and is "spiritual" in the sense of things common to all sentient beings.

That is one way to view the unfolding from body to mind to spirit, where each of them is considered as a stage, wave, or level of unfolding care and consciousness, moving from egocentric to ethnocentric to worldcentric.

We will be returning to stages of evolution and development, each time exploring them from a new angle. For now, all that is required is an understanding that by "stages" we mean progressive and permanent milestones along the evolutionary path of your own unfolding. Whether we talk stages of consciousness, stages of energy, stages of culture, stages of spiritual realization, stages of moral development, and so on, we are talking of these important and fundamental rungs in the unfolding of your higher, deeper, wider potentials.

Whenever you use **IOS**, you will automatically be prompted to check and see if you have included the important **stage aspects** of any situation, which will dramatically increase your likelihood of success, whether that success be measured in terms of personal transformation, social change, excellence in business, care for others, or simple satisfaction in life.

## LINES OF DEVELOPMENT

Have you ever noticed how unevenly developed virtually all of us are? Some people are highly developed in, say, logical thinking, but poorly developed in emotional feelings. Some people have highly advanced cognitive development (they're very smart) but poor moral development (they're mean and ruthless). Some people excel in emotional intelligence, but can't add 2 plus 2.

Howard Gardner made this concept fairly well-known using the idea of **multiple intelligences**. Human beings have a variety of intelligences, such as cognitive intelligence, emotional intelligence, musical intelligence, kinaesthetic intelligence, and so on. Most people excel in one or two of those, but do poorly in the others. This is not necessarily or even usually a bad thing; part of integral wisdom is finding where one excels and thus where one can best offer the world one's deepest gifts.

But this does mean that we need to be aware of our strengths (or the intelligences with which we can shine) as well as our weaknesses (where we do poorly or even pathologically). And this brings us to another of our 5 essential elements: our multiples intelligences or developmental lines. So far we have looked at **states** and **stages**; what are **lines** or multiple intelligences?

Various multiple intelligences include: cognitive, interpersonal, moral, emotional, and aesthetic. Why do we also call them **developmental lines**? Because those intelligences show growth and development. They unfold in progressive stages. What are those progressive stages? The stages we just outlined.

In other words, each multiple intelligence grows—or can grow—through the 3 major stages (or through any of the stages of any of the developmental models, whether 3 stages, 5 stages, 7 or more; remember, these are all like Centigrade and Fahrenheit). You can have cognitive development to stage 1, to stage 2, and to stage 3, for example.

Likewise with the other intelligences. Emotional development to stage 1 means that you have developed the capacity for emotions centring on "me," especially the emotions and drives of hunger, survival, and self-protection. If you continue to grow emotionally from stage 1 to stage 2—or from egocentric to ethnocentric—you will expand from "me" to "us," and begin to develop emotional commitments and attachments to loved ones, members of your family, close friends, perhaps your whole tribe or whole nation. If you grow into stage-3 emotions, you will develop the further capacity for a care and compassion that reaches beyond your own tribe or nation and attempts to include all human beings and even all sentient beings in a worldcentric care and compassion.

And remember, because these are stages, you have attained them in a permanent fashion. Before that happens, any of these capacities will be merely passing states: you will plug into some of them, if at all, in a temporary fashion—great peak experiences of expanded knowing and being, wondrous "aha!" experiences, profound altered glimpses into your own higher possibilities. But with practice, you will convert those states into stages, or permanent traits in the territory of you.

## THE PSYCHOGRAPH

There is a fairly easy way to represent these intelligences or multiple lines. In the graphic to the right, we have drawn a simple graph showing the 3 major stages (or **levels** of development) and five of the most important intelligences (or **lines** of development). **Through the major stages or levels of development, the various lines unfold.** The 3 levels or stages can apply to any developmental line—sexual, cognitive, spiritual, emotional, moral, and so on.

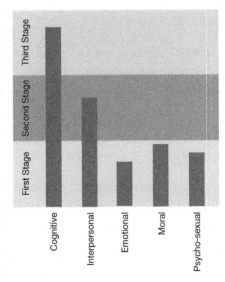

In the psychograph on the right, we have shown somebody who excels in cognitive development and is good at moral development, but does poorly in interpersonal intelligence and really poorly in emotional intelligence. Other individuals would, of course, have a different "psychograph."

The **psychograph** helps to spot where your greatest potentials are. You very likely already know what you excel in and what you don't. But part of the Integral Approach is learning to refine considerably this knowledge of your own contours, so that you can more confidently deal with both your own strengths and weaknesses as well as those of others.

The psychograph also helps us spot the ways that virtually all of us are unevenly developed, and thus helps prevent us from thinking that just because we are terrific in one area we must be terrific in all the others. In fact, usually the opposite. More than one leader, spiritual teacher, or politician has spectacularly crashed through lack of an understanding of these simple realities.

To be "integrally developed" does not mean that you have to excel in all the known intelligences, or that all of your lines have to be at level 3. But it does mean that you develop a very good sense of what your own psychograph is actually like, so that with a much more integral self-image you can plan your future development. For some people, this will indeed mean strengthening certain intelligences that are so weak they are causing problems. For others, this will mean clearing up a serious problem or pathology in one line (such as the emotional-sexual). And for others, simply recognizing where their strengths and weaknesses lie, and planning accordingly. Using an integral map, we can scope out our own psychographs with more assurance.

Thus, to be "**integrally informed**" does not mean you have to master all lines of development, just be aware of them. If you then chose to remedy any imbalance, that is part of Integral Transformative Practice, which actually helps to increase levels of development through an integrated approach.

Notice another very important point. In certain types of psychological and spiritual training, you can be introduced to a full spectrum of **states** of consciousness and bodily experiences right from the start—as a peak experience, meditative experience, shamanic state, altered state, and so on. The reason that this is possible is that the many of the major states of consciousness (such as waking-gross, dreaming-subtle, and formless-causal) are ever-present possibilities. So you can very quickly be introduced to many **higher states** of consciousness.

You cannot, however, be introduced to all the qualities of **higher stages** without actual growth and practice. You can have a peak experience of higher states, because many of them are ever-present. But you cannot have a peak experience of a higher stage, because stages unfold sequentially. Stages build upon their predecessors in very concrete ways, so they cannot be skipped: like atoms to molecules to cells to organisms, you can't go from atoms to cells and skip molecules. This is one of the many important differences between states and stages.

However, with repeated practice of contacting higher states, your own stages of development will tend to unfold in a much faster and easier way. There is, in fact, considerable experimental evidence demonstrating exactly that. The more you are plunged into authentic higher *states* of consciousness—such as meditative states—then the faster you will grow and develop through any of the *stages* of consciousness. It is as if higher-states training acts as a lubricant on the spiral of development, helping you to disidentify with a lower stage so that the next higher stage can emerge, until you can stably remain at higher levels of awareness on an ongoing basis, whereupon a passing state has become a permanent trait. These types of higher-states training, such as meditation, are a part of any integral approach to transformation.

The next component is easy: each of the previous components has a masculine and feminine type. There are two basic ideas here: one has to do with the idea of *types* themselves; and the other, with masculine and feminine as one example of types.

**Types** simply refers to items that can be present at virtually any stage or state. One common typology, for example, is the Myers-Briggs (whose main types are feeling, thinking, sensing, and intuiting). **You can be any of those types at virtually any stage of development**. These kind of "horizontal typologies" can be very useful, especially when combined with levels, lines, and states. To show what is involved, we can use "masculine" and "feminine."

Carol Gilligan, in her enormously influential book *In a Different Voice*, pointed out that both men and women tend to develop through 3 or 4 major levels or stages of moral development. Pointing to a great deal of research evidence, Gilligan noted that these 3 or 4 moral stages can be called *pre-conventional*, *conventional*, *post-conventional*, and *integrated*. These are actually quite similar to the 3 simple developmental stages we are using, this time applied to moral intelligence.

Gilligan found that stage 1 is a morality centred entirely on "me" (hence this pre-conventional stage or level is also called **egocentric**). Stage-2 moral development is centred on "us," so that my identity has expanded from just me to include other human beings of my group (hence this conventional stage is often called **ethnocentric**, traditional, or conformist). With stage-3 moral development, my identity expands once again, this time from "us" to "all of us," or all human beings (or even all sentient beings)—and hence this stage is often called **world-centric**. I now have care and compassion, not just for me (egocentric), and not just for my family, my tribe, or my nation (ethnocentric), but for all of humanity, for all men and women everywhere, regardless of race, colour, sex, or creed (world-centric). And if I develop even further, at stage-4 moral development, which Gilligan calls **integrated**, then....

Well, before we look at the important conclusion of Gilligan's work, let's first note her major contribution. Gilligan strongly agreed that women, like men, develop through those 3 or 4 major hierarchical stages of growth. Gilligan herself correctly refers to these stages as *hierarchical* because each stage has a *higher* capacity for care and compassion. But she said that women progress through those stages using a different type of logic—they develop "in a different voice."

Male logic, or a man's voice, tends to be based on terms of autonomy, justice, and rights; whereas women's logic or voice tends to be based on terms of relationship, care, and responsibility. Men tend toward agency; women tend toward communion. Men follow rules; women follow connections. Men look; women touch. Men tend toward individualism, women toward relationship. One of Gilligan's favourite stories: A little boy and girl are playing; the boy says, "Let's play pirates!" The girl says, "Let's play like we live next door to each other." Boy: "No, I want to play pirates!" "Okay, you play the pirate who lives next door."

Little boys don't like girls around when they are playing games like baseball, because the two voices clash badly, and often hilariously. Some boys are playing baseball, a kid takes his third strike and is out, so he starts to cry. The other boys stand unmoved until the kid stops crying; after all, a rule is a rule, and the rule is: three strikes and you're out. Gilligan points out that if a girl is around, she will usually say, "Ah, come on, give him another try!" The girl sees him crying and wants to help, wants to connect, wants to heal. This, however, drives the boys nuts, who are doing this game as an initiation into the world of rules and male logic. Gilligan says that the boys will therefore hurt feelings in order to save the rules; the girls will break the rules in order to save the feelings.

In a different voice. Both the girls and boys will develop through the 3 or 4 developmental stages of moral growth (egocentric to ethnocentric to worldcentric to integrated), but they will do so in a different voice, using a different logic. Gilligan specifically calls these hierarchical stages in women **selfish** (which is egocentric), **care** (which is ethnocentric), **universal care** (which is worldcentric), and **integrated**. Again, why are they hierarchical? Because each stage is a higher capacity for care and compassion. (Not all hierarchies are bad, and this a good example of why.)

So, integrated or stage 4—what is that? At the 4th and highest stage of moral development that we are aware of, the masculine and feminine voices in each of us tend to become integrated, according to Gilligan. This does not mean that a person at this stage starts to lose the distinctions between masculine and feminine, and hence become a kind of bland, androgynous, asexual being. In fact, masculine and feminine dimensions might become more intensified. But it does mean the individuals start to befriend both the masculine and feminine modes in themselves, even if they characteristically act predominantly from one or the other.

Have you ever seen a *caduceus* (the symbol of the medical profession)? It's a staff with two serpents crisscrossing it, and wings at the top of the staff (see fig. 2). The staff itself represents the central spinal column; where the serpents cross the staff represents the individual chakras moving up the spine from the lowest to the highest; and the two serpents themselves represent solar and lunar (or masculine and feminine) energies *at each of the chakras*.

That's the crucial point. The 7 chakras, which are simply a more complex version of the 3 simple levels or stages, represent 7 levels of consciousness and energy available to all human beings. (The first three chakras—food, sex, and power—are roughly stage 1; chakras four and five—relational heart and communication—are basically stage 2; and chakras six and seven—psychic and spiritual—are the epitome of stage 3). The important point here is that, according to the traditions, **each of those 7 levels has a masculine and feminine** aspect, type, or "voice." Neither masculine nor feminine is higher or better; they are two equivalent types at each of the levels of consciousness.

This means, for example, that with chakra 3 (the egocentric-power chakra), there is a masculine and feminine version of the same chakra: at that chakra-level, males tend toward power exercised autonomously ("My way or the highway!"), women tend toward power exercised communally or socially ("Do it this way or I won't talk to you"). And so on with the other major chakras, each of them having a solar and lunar, or masculine and feminine dimension; neither is more fundamental, neither can be ignored.

At the 7ᵗʰ chakra, however, notice that the masculine and feminine serpents both disappear into their ground or source. Masculine and feminine meet and unite at the crown—they literally become one. And that is what Gilligan found with her stage-4 moral development: the two voices in each person become integrated, so that there is a paradoxical union of autonomy and relationship, rights and responsibilities, agency and communion, wisdom and compassion, justice and mercy, masculine and feminine.

The important point is that whenever you use **IOS**, you are automatically checking any situation—in yourself, in others, in an organization, in a culture—and making sure that you include both the masculine and feminine types so as to be as comprehensive and inclusive as possible. If you believe that there are no major differences between masculine and feminine—or if you are suspicious of such differences—then that is fine, too, and you can treat them the same if you want. We are simply saying that, in either case, make sure you touch bases with both the masculine and feminine, however you view them.

But more than that, there are numerous other "horizontal typologies" that can be very helpful when part of a comprehensive **IOS**, and the Integral Approach draws on any or all of those typologies as appropriate. "Types" are as important as quadrants, levels, lines, and states.

There's an interesting thing about types. You can have healthy and unhealthy versions of them. To say that somebody is caught in an unhealthy type is not a way to judge them but to understand and communicate more clearly and effectively with them.

For example, if each stage of development has a masculine and feminine dimension, each of those can be healthy or unhealthy, which we sometimes call "sick boy, sick girl." This is simply another kind of horizontal typing, but one that can be extremely useful.

If the healthy masculine principle tends toward autonomy, strength, independence, and freedom, when that principle becomes unhealthy or pathological, all of those positive virtues either over- or under-fire. There is not just autonomy, but alienation; not just strength, but domination; not just independence, but morbid fear of relationship and commitment; not just a drive toward freedom, but a drive to destroy. The unhealthy masculine principle does not transcend in freedom, but dominates in fear.

If the healthy feminine principle tends toward flowing, relationship, care, and compassion, the unhealthy feminine flounders in each of those. Instead of being in relationship, she becomes lost in relationship. Instead of a healthy self in communion with others, she loses her self altogether and is dominated by the relationships she is in. Not a connection, but a fusion; not a flow state, but a panic state; not a communion, but a melt-down. The unhealthy feminine principle does not find fullness in connection, but chaos in fusion.

Using **IOS**, you will find ways to identify both the healthy and unhealthy masculine and feminine dimensions operating in yourself and in others. But the important point about this section is simple: various typologies have their usefulness in helping us to understand and communicate with others. And with any typology, there are healthy and unhealthy versions of a type. Pointing to an unhealthy type is not a way to judge people but a way to understand and communicate with them more clearly and effectively.

In this concluding section, we will briefly outline these patterns, all of which together are sometimes referred to as **A-Q-A-L**(pronounced *ah-qwal*), which is shorthand for "all quadrants, all levels, all lines, all states, all types"—and those are simply the components that we have already outlined (except the quadrants, which we will get to momentarily). **AQAL** is just another term for **IOS** or the **Integral Model**, but one that is often used to specifically designate this particular approach.

At the beginning of this introduction, we said that all 5 components of the Integral Model were items that are available to your awareness right now, and this is true of the quadrants as well.

Did you ever notice that major languages have what are called first-person, second-person, and third-person pronouns **First-person** means "the person who is speaking," so that includes pronouns like *I, me, mine* (in the singular), and *we, us, ours* (in the plural). **Second-person** means "the person who is spoken to," which includes pronouns like *you* and *yours*. **Third-person** means "the person or thing being spoken about," such as *he, him, she, her, they, them, it*, and *its*.

Thus, if I am speaking to you about my new car, "I" am first person, "you" are second person, and the new car (or "it") is third person. Now, if you and I are talking and communicating, we will indicate this by using, for example, the word "we," as in, "We understand each other." "We" is technically first-person plural, but if you and I are communicating, then your second person and my first person are part of this extraordinary "we." Thus second person is sometimes indicated as "you/we," or "thou/we," or sometimes just "we."

So we can therefore simplify first-, second-, and third-person as "**I**," "**we**," and "**it**."

That all seems trivial, doesn't it? Boring maybe? So let's try this. Instead of saying "we," "it," and "I," what if we said the **Good**, the **True**, and the **Beautiful**? And what if we said that the Good, the True, and the Beautiful are dimensions of your very own being at each and every level of growth and development? And that through an integral transformative practice, you can discover deeper and deeper dimensions of your own Goodness, your own Truth, and your own Beauty?

Hmm, definitely more interesting. The Good, the True, and the Beautiful are simply variations on first-, second-, and third-person pronouns found in all major languages, and they are found in all major languages because Truth, Goodness, and Beauty are very real dimensions of reality to which language has adapted. Third-person (or "it") refers to objective truth, which is best investigated by science. Second-person (or "you/we") refers to Goodness, or the ways that we—that you and I—treat each other, and whether we do so with decency, honesty, and respect. In other words, basic morality. And first-person deals with the "I," with self and self-expression, art and aesthetics, and the beauty that is in the eye (or the "I") of the beholder.

So the "I," "we," and "it" dimensions of experience really refer to: **art**, **morals**, and **science**. Or **self**, **culture**, and **nature**. Or the Beautiful, the Good, and the True.

And the point is that every event in the manifest world has all three of those dimensions. You can look at any event from the point of view of the "I" (or how I personally see and feel about the event); from the point of view of the "we" (how not just I but others see the event); and as an "it" (or the objective facts of the event).

Thus, an integrally informed path will therefore take all of those dimensions into account, and thus arrive at a more comprehensive and effective approach—in the "I" and the "we" and the "it"—or in self and culture and nature.

If you leave out science, or leave out art, or leave out morals, something is going to be missing, something will get broken. Self and culture and nature are liberated together or not at all. So fundamental are these dimensions of "I," "we," and "it" that we call them the four quadrants, and we make them a foundation of the integral framework or **IOS**. (We arrive at "four" quadrants by subdividing "it" into singular "it" and plural "its," as we will see.) A few diagrams will help clarify the basic points.

## How the Integral Model is Applied in ThriveAbility

In the diagram below, you will find an example of how the IOS is applied in applying ThriveAbility – from the individual thinking and being different, to their application of practices and tools that demonstrate the benefits of ThriveAbility, to the ways in which alignment and coherence are built up in organizations and cultures so that innovative ThriveAble Business Models and Systems end up scaling rapidly and become mainstream quickly.

**DIAGRAM 30: The Four "Quadrants" of the ThriveAbility Template[93]**

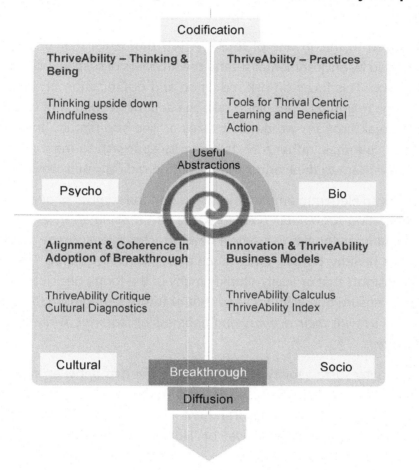

Here is a brief explanation of how ThriveAbility is applied in each of the four quadrants of the IOS, from a first person perspective.

---

[93]  Each of the four quadrants are described in greater detail below.

## 1. The "Psycho" (Psycho/Spiritual) Quadrant – ThriveAbility Thinking & Being

### o Thinking Upside Down

A few years ago I was preparing a speech on "Co-Creating a Viable Future- Vision 2050" for a conference. I sat there in my study wondering why, after half a century of major effort, environmentalists and practitioners of sustainability were still failing to close the gap between what we need for a viable future, and our current situation where we are using 1.5 planets worth of resources and heading for 3 degrees global warming. We must now deal with the challenges of accelerating climate change and the hard fact that sustainability 1.0 is not closing the gap fast enough for a viable future for mankind.

It suddenly occurred to me, in one of those "AHA!" moments, that the problem was the **equation** being used by environmentalists and practitioners of sustainability, with all its focus on impact reduction. This focus on risk reduction and optimization of the existing system fails to motivate the majority of people to take the actions needed, and to innovate in ways that deliver the breakthroughs we need. It takes a "one size fits all" approach to people, organizations and countries, rather than tailoring its approach to meet people where they are at and motivate them to think and behave in often radically new ways.

ThriveAbility offers an elegantly simple way of ensuring the survival of our species by finding new ways of integrating *sustainable breakthroughs* into *thriving lifestyles, organizations and communities*. The ultimate goal is to create a new attractor to encourage actions that enable life conditions for healthy human emergence and a thriving planet. ThriveAbility offers frameworks and insights that radically simplify many of the tough decisions we have to make on a daily basis to ensure our wellbeing and that of future generations. *In short, we learn to live lives that thrill us with their richness and lightness of footprint, while inspiring others to follow in our footsteps*

This "AHA!" about why sustainability was not closing the gap between what we need for a viable future and our current situation, led me to turn the traditional sustainability equation upside down. Instead of putting our Environmental Footprint on the top and our economic growth on the bottom, I put Human Thrival (or "Flourishing") on the top, and divided this by our Environmental Footprint. Rather than seeking footprint reduction only, while viewing our human activities as a "cost", I chose to focus on how we can create better lives, with smaller footprints, by being innovative and being collectively more intelligent and wise.

Thrival thus offers a motivational engine, while Impact Reduction generally only motivates "deep green" activists and consumers, while offering only a weak form of advantage for most businesses pursuing CSR and sustainability initiatives. The ThriveAbility model:

- offers a comparative integration of what we currently know, which then provides us with a base from which we can each begin to make better decisions immediately while accelerating our learning process with new and better information as we begin implementation, avoiding both analysis paralysis and suboptimal "shoot-from-the hip" decisions.

- places in perspective both the human and environmental trade-offs and synergies available in any situation, at any level of scale, from the personal to the global and all layers of complexity in between.

This then engenders a new way of thinking and being: "ThriveAbility Thinking", which goes beyond the currently most advanced thinking frameworks available, including some integral approaches, wellbeing psychology and advanced sustainability and innovation metrics – the latter being embedded in dozens of incompatible frameworks.

Most importantly, ThriveAbility Thinking enables us to get into our strategic psychological helicopter, transcend the situation and transform the outcomes possible in making often politically fraught, hard decisions.

The knowledge base for making better decisions through ThriveAbility Thinking is a continually expanding, global public good rooted in the communities of practice which comprise the ThriveAbility Consortium, a not-for-profit guardian of the principles and practices of Embedding ThriveAbility.

To Embed ThriveAbility in your life, family, community, organisation or nation, you will need to make ThriveAbility Thinking a habit, which is always able to answer the question:

*"In the current situation, what actions will yield the best outcomes for the greatest number while promoting the capacity of the group responsible for this decision to successfully implement this decision across a range of scenarios?"*

### o   Mindfulness and Mental Models

*Achieving sustainability is as much a challenge of **changing our mental models**, as it is a problem of **making flows of materials, energy and other resources eco-efficient**. Being mindful is the key to accelerated learning.*

Concentrated attention, reflective awareness, presence and reflective learning are all terms used to describe "mindfulness". From a ThriveAbility perspective, mindfulness is much more than a nonjudgmental present-centred form of awareness of one's experiences – it also brings to bear an "overview" perspective of one's choices and options in the moment, based on an intuitive understanding of how one's choices enhance the thrival of all life. As we grow and mature, so too do our values embrace ever wider spans of beings and worlds.

The consequences of such mindfulness result in the ability to make decisions and plan actions that will have the tendency to not only centre and deepen one's own present state in an experience of flourishing and wellbeing, but will also ensure that others and all living systems benefit from this state. There is a direct connection between the practice of mindfulness and the cultivation of morality

Learning in such a mindful state is also accelerated, enabling us to shift our "mental models" into more productive and beneficial patterns. The old cliché is that "Change = Learning and Learning = Change".

*Mindful Learning = Beneficial Change*

## 2. The "Bio" Quadrant (Biological/Behavioural) – ThriveAbility Practices & Doing

### o Tools for Thrival Centric Learning and Beneficial Change

Living well in ways that do not cost the earth is going to become a core skill for those of us transitioning from an unsustainable, linear economy, to a thriving, conscious economy. The big question is how to do this wisely and intelligently, as well as creatively and joyfully, rather than regressing back to more primitive and less satisfying lifestyles. Moving toward a Conscious Economy, means, amongst many other things, learning new skills and developing ourselves and others so that through our daily practices we are:

- transcending the materialism of modernity (growth for growth's sake), and getting more out of less while living a better quality of life;
- making choices based on a deeper understanding of the ingredients of thrival thereby enhancing our own wellbeing and that of our families, communities, cities, organizations and nations;
- embracing the full spectrum of human potential (developing oneself and others) by building on our own strengths and talents as well as those of others;
- enjoying the richness of diverse cultures, sharing common perspectives and reframing who we are within a global community (celebrating diversity);
- working for a planet that is increasingly alive, conscious & reaching for the stars (enjoying higher levels of consciousness and aliveness).

The tools and methods available for such practices are available in literally every corner of the world if we know where to look, and the ThriveAbility Consortium can recommend a dozen good places to start if you are interested. Just one example- Integral Life Practice (or "ILP"), blends physical, emotional, mental and spiritual practices that can be done on a daily basis in a busy schedule. Other more mundane but important practices such as recycling, buying sustainable products, eating healthy, local food, planting gardens and investing in sustainable businesses that promote ThriveAbility are also simple ways in which to begin to make a difference. Making all of this as fun and enjoyable as possible, along with healthy doses of music, art, dance and thriveable entertainment, is important too.

### 3. The Cultural Quadrant (Norms and Values) – Alignment and Coherence in Adoption of Breakthroughs

o **The ThriveAbility Critique**

One of the key differences between ThriveAbility and other approaches to ensuring a thriving human civilization on a thriving planet in the 21st century, is the fact that practitioners of ThriveAbility are not only self-aware but also conscious of the way they are thinking about specific issues moment to moment. In other words, ThriveAbility practitioners are aware of their own worldview in operation, and able to shift worldviews to find more appropriate ways of perceiving and thinking about a situation or challenge.

Depending upon one's sources, there are, at a very rough estimate, a few tens of millions of people alive today capable of such perspective shifting, and the number is growing daily. Such a shift in perspectives can yield a much more effective response to situations, challenges and opportunities, and in some cases, yield an outcome between ten to a hundred times more effective and ThriveAble. Some of the ingredients of the ThriveAbility Critique include:

a. **Perspective Awareness** - What is the thinking/worldview driving the way you are currently approaching a situation, challenge or opportunity?

b. **Options for Change** - what are the different ways in which one might approach changing the situation and moving toward a more ThriveAble outcome? (Including the eight possible kinds of change response inherent in the Gravesian change model)

c. **Creating Conditions for ThriveAble Change** - what would be the most appropriate methods, tools and technologies to support profound change in this situation? How can different worldviews and interests be "streamed" so that potential conflicts can be effectively managed? What is needed to ensure that the changes "stick", and that they do not fizzle out after the initial stimulus and enthusiasm wear off?

d. **Designing a Change/Transformation Process** - the ThriveAbility Critique is a useful first step in thinking through how a variety of visions can be translated into a design process to map out a change/transformation process. This needs to be done in conjunction with the tools for cultural diagnostics and alignment below.

o **Cultural Diagnostics and Alignment**

How can apparent conflicts and blockages in families, communities, organizations and nations be resolved during the change process? How can different visions of the future be aligned to create the synergies required in social systems at all scales? A variety of proven methods are available to help us move toward more ThriveAble outcomes:

a. **The Personal, Organizational and Social Alignment Wheels** - Over the past quarter of a century a variety of different action research programs have resulted in the development, testing and effective application of cultural alignment wheels at three different scales. These cultural alignment wheels have been proven to result in better strategic performance and more ThriveAble outcomes.

b. **Cultural Fit Factor** - using approaches developed from Gravesian roots with a thorough scaffolding of integral psychology, it is possible to assess where individuals and teams "fit" into a culture, at any scale. Although developed and tested mainly at an organizational level, the basic principles on which these tests are based enables them to be applied to much larger groups as a tool for the analysis of social cultural fields, and the resonance or dissonance being experienced by different individuals and groups within such social fields.

c. **ThriveAbility Inquiries** - much like appreciative enquiry before it, a ThriveAbility Inquiry not only examines what is already working within a social system, it also identifies the blockages to change and transformation. When used in conjunction with alignment wheels and cultural fit tools, a ThriveAbility Inquiry is a creative, dynamic process that both inspires the participants and also releases tremendous amounts of blocked energy that can be put to purposeful use in building the next stage of the system in focus.

## 4. The "Socio" Quadrant (socioeconomic systems) – Innovation and ThriveAble Business Models

○ **Breakthrough Innovations**

*Innovation is US* – We humans are alive today because our core strength is our ability to adapt and innovate to a constantly changing and often hostile world. Innovation is also evolution in action. Every stage of human development comprises a coherent and integrated way of making a living, exchanging and distributing value and dealing with shocks and surprises. The rate at which innovations are adopted is driven by the evolution of personal, cultural and social norms and habits, in the cultural quadrant we examined above.

At each level of human development, there are specific **Limits to Growth** and predictable **Crises** that need to be resolved through combinations of the tens of thousands of innovations that have been recorded since the dawn of humankind. **From Fire to Freud**, we overcome limits to knowledge and growth. Disruptive innovation drives breakthroughs based on removing artificial, often self-imposed constraints rather than more fundamental limits.

Each of these innovations is based on an **Original Idea** (UL), supported and scaled within a set of **Values and Needs** (LL) that create new opportunities and options for our species at each stage of development. Once they are adopted by the mainstream, such innovations are taken for granted and become "baked into" our civilization as an enabling layer of infrastructure, tools, habits and norms.

This in turn creates the crucibles in which new innovations can emerge to meet new life conditions. For example, the innovation of ThriveAbility builds on previous innovations in design, strategy, leadership, sustainability, integral philosophy, psychology and practices, and the art and science of disruptive innovation itself.

o **ThriveAble Business Modelling**

*Ideally, a "business model" is a way of conceptualising the design of a set of virtuous circles between human needs and the capabilities/possibilities of a supplier or network of suppliers, mediated through a set of fair exchanges.*

Socioeconomic innovations can be scientific, technological, product, process or business model based. We are all familiar with the way in which household products are continuously being improved, and increasingly often with sustainability in mind. For example, most manufacturers are now removing excess sugar, toxic substances and other harmful ingredients from their products, while also developing more eco-friendly packaging- they see this both as a moral necessity as well as a form of competitive advantage.

Equally, behind the scenes, many supply chains in many major industries, from food and beverages to retailing to energy to telecommunications, consumer electronics and transport, as well as building supplies, construction and engineering, are being revamped through process innovations to be more eco and energy efficient. Even the fashion industry is slowly becoming more eco-friendly, and pioneers in sustainable innovation from Interface Carpets to Puma and Nike sportswear and Unilever and P&G in foods and soaps are making major strides in reducing their footprints.

Such product and process innovations are an excellent starting point for the long journey ahead to attain what many are now calling "net positive impact" organizations. The opportunity for ThriveAbility practitioners is to accelerate these positive developments, especially through innovations at the level of business models and business ecosystems, where some truly major breakthroughs are now possible, in combination with the scientific and technological breakthroughs popping up everywhere in labs, social enterprises and "frugal innovators" in developing countries.

In particular, the cradle-to-cradle/circular economy and sharing economy business model approaches will all result in radical changes to the way we design, make, consumer and service products and services in the future, and offer tremendous opportunities for ThriveAble Business Modelling Breakthroughs.

ThriveAble business modelling can benefit from the use of software that enables innovation teams to experiment with the different components of a business model, and examine how the "wiring diagram" in a specific business, foundation or NGO can be modified in order to produce a new design that can be tested to see whether it is more ThriveAble than the previous version.

At the level of an entire business ecosystem, such ThriveAble Business Modelling can enable major synergies between different players across different industries to learn "new tricks" from each other, and to joint venture and partner to make the entire business ecosystem more ThriveAble.

### o   Applying ThriveAbility Calculus to Measure ThriveAble Outcomes

One of the greatest challenges faced by organizations of all kinds today in the rush toward sustainability and thrival, is the lack of holistic measuring systems enabling us to compare "apples with apples". Every organization, and every industry, tends to have its own set of protocols, benchmarks and measurement systems, which mean that attempts to compare progress toward ThriveAbility on a level playing field are difficult if not impossible.

From a consumer perspective, there are some apps that offer a degree of comparability between products on supermarket shelves (mainly in North America, such as "GoodGuide"), but at an organizational level the latest corporate reporting systems such as the Global Reporting Initiative are still struggling to get organizations to deal with material issues in their reporting systems, rather than simply choosing to measure what they can where the light is brightest. This is known as the "context gap", as while we have global metrics on critical ecosystem issues such as atmospheric greenhouse gases, ocean acidification, poverty, water, food supplies and so on, the organizational reporting systems are generally disconnected from such big picture metrics.

"ThriveAbility Calculus" has been developed to act as a starting point to resolve some of these reporting issues, and is designed to work in conjunction with the ThriveAbility Index currently in its early stages of development. ThriveAbility Calculus enables us to assign a ThriveAbility Factor to any organization or social system at a point in time, and then to enable us to track changes in that ThriveAbility Factor over time. The change between one measurement point and the next gives us the ThriveAbility Index of that organization or system at that point in time.

### o   The ThriveAbility Index and Dashboard

To apply ThriveAbility at all scales in any social system, from an individual to a planet, we have developed a Dashboard that illustrates the essence and five key ingredients of ThriveAbility Thinking and ThriveAbility Calculus. The application of the Dashboard is also possible on different levels, making it immediately useful to any user. The Dashboard shows that ThriveAbility has the potential to serve as 'the glue' between the hard, technical systems and the soft, human systems, when both work together synergetically.

ThriveAbility is a fractal concept that ranges across different scales of time and complexity – it is applicable from the level of individuals, families and communities right up to organizational, national and global levels.

**DIAGRAM 31: The ThriveAbility Dashboard – 5 Key Elements**

In table D below you will find a short description of each of the 5 key elements. What follows is a brief overview of how these elements interact in practice:

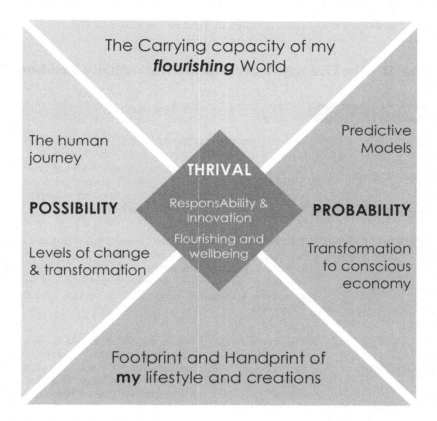

- *Vertical Dimension - The ThriveAbility Equation. -* Items 1 (*Carrying Capacity*) and 2 (*Lifestyles and Creations*) are the two key ingredients for the ThriveAbility Equation. To survive and thrive into the 22$^{nd}$ century, we humans will need to develop lifestyles and creations which have a smaller footprint than the carrying capacity of the parts of our biosphere and social systems they rely on for their sustenance and inputs.

- *Horizontal Dimension - Transformation to a Conscious Economy and Society –* Items 3 (*Human Development*) and 4 (*Predictive Modelling for Transformation to a Conscious Economy*) bring together two of the most powerful ingredients we know of to accelerate our shift toward a conscious, thriving economy: human potential and collective intelligence. Applying integral psychological models and methods to accelerate and improve the quality of human development, we are able to connect people up in synergistic ways that enable them to harness the latest data, models and insights into the pathways available to them to shift towards thriving lifestyles, organisations and a conscious economy based on ThriveAbility.

- *Centre - Thrival: ResponsAbility and Innovation -* Based on the first principles of ThriveAbility that "ThriveAbility starts with me", the central item 5 emphasizes that we each need to become role models of ThriveAbility Thinking and Doing, to ensure that the fantastic possibilities that exist in and around us are converted into probabilities that ensure our survival and thrival. Given that the next decades of the 21st century are likely to be full of shocks and surprises due to climate change and other stressors inherent on a planet of 9 billion people trying to make a living by 2050, the Ability to Respond to both the challenges and opportunities is the key message of the word "ResponsAbility".

### Table D – The Five Key Aspects of the ThriveAbility Dashboard

| Key Ingredient | Description |
| --- | --- |
| 1. Carrying Capacity | The *carrying capacity* stands for the total sum of resources and flows available to support life in abundance, without compromising the Earth's ability to regenerate and recover from damages. This is the fundamental boundary condition for all actions. For life to survive and thrive, the carrying capacity has to be greater than our lifestyle and creations. |
| 2. Lifestyles & Creations | The *lifestyles and creations* we bring into the world all depend on the carrying capacity of the planet for their aliveness and sustainability. Today humanity is already exceeding planetary boundaries, so we need to reinvent our way of living and accelerate sustainable innovation to create breakthroughs everywhere. |
| 3. Human Journey | The *human journey* refers to our evolution as a species, and the way in which we evolve through several different stages to become world-centric adults who care about our planet. Each stage of development has its own 'hot' and 'cold' buttons and bottom lines, which can help motivate ThriveAbility Thinking. |
| 4. Predictive Modelling | Ingredient four is *predictive modelling of transformation to a conscious economy*. This refers to new methods and tools that are developed through an integration of different models and frameworks to provide hands-on support to put the ThriveAbility ideas into practice. |
| 5. The Thrival Factor- ResponsAbility & Innovation | The *Thrival Factor* is the emergent indicator that is nurtured by all other ThriveAbility ingredients. It provides a simple measure of which pathways to thrival are likely to be most robust and which have most potential for catalysing flourishing and wellbeing. A high societal Thrival Factor will automatically lead to the development of systemic capabilities to respond and adapt to a changing and increasing complex environment. |

## Appendix D –
## Enhancing Stakeholder Outcomes

### Enhancing Stakeholder Outcomes– The Macro Perspective

Thrival is a composite measure of human and biosphere wellbeing together with measures of human progress and flourishing. The goal of human activity is to optimise Thrival for the maximum number of living creatures, with the least scarce resources.

Looking at the most recent findings from Gallup's World Poll[94], we find a strong correlation between the stage of development a country is at and its rating on the scale of thriving, struggling and suffering. In the diagrams below, we can see that Denmark, Iceland, Norway, Sweden and Finland (all countries in the "post-modern" centre of cultural gravity with a bias toward communal values) ranked first, second, third and fourth in terms of thriving in the world. At fifth and sixth, Canada and Australia are also in the "post-modern" centre of cultural gravity with a bias toward agentic (more individualistic) values.

### DIAGRAM 32 – The Link Between Thriving and Development – Most Thriving Nations

Balanced development contributes to thrival - for example, the top 7 thriving nations in 2013 were all 'post-modern' or 'modern' in their center of gravity, irrespective of their national cultural differences

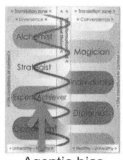

**Top 7 Thriving countries of the world**

| | | % |
|---|---|---|
| 1 | Denmark | 70 |
| 2 | Iceland | 70 |
| 3 | Norway | 70 |
| 4 | Sweden | 68 |
| 5 | Canada | 66 |
| 6 | Australia | 63 |
| 7 | Finland | 62 |

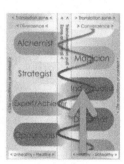

Agentic bias

Communal bias

On the other hand, as we look at the countries in which people are suffering the most, we find that they are without exception in largely agricultural, pre-modern societies that have become dysfunctional for various reasons. Topping the list is Afghanistan, which has an unenviable history of having been invaded or occupied for centuries, followed by Bulgaria and Armenia, where development has been blocked for a variety of reasons. Sadly these countries have

---

[94]  Gallup is one of the world's leading polling organisations. Their World Poll measures the state of mind of over 98% of the world's population in over 160 countries on an annual basis.

become victims of opportunists who are local Empire builders, who prey on the tribes and villages they hold under their sway.

Looking at Turkey and Egypt, both nations suffer from decades of stagnation for the middle classes and a failure to open up sufficient opportunities for the advancement of the poor, leading to fundamentalist groups and other extreme forces to be unleashed. The reaction from the modernist militaries in both countries has been forceful, while the political turmoil this has generated has not facilitated social and economic development for the masses.

Haiti has never recovered from centuries of French exploitation and a failure to develop beyond an opportunistic ruling class that impoverished the nation. Thanks to earth quakes and poor/no building standards, the country is now essentially run by NGO's. Cambodia has been run by a kleptocratic military junta until recently, and this has left most of the rural masses in poverty, and the country undeveloped.

**DIAGRAM 33 – The Link Between Thriving and Development – The Least Thriving Nations**

Underdeveloped/developmentally arrested nations suffer most- for example, the top 7 suffering nations in 2013 were all primarily agricultural

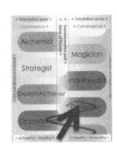

**Top 7 Suffering countries of the world**

|   |             | %  |
|---|-------------|----|
| 1 | Afghanistan | 55 |
| 2 | Bulgaria    | 41 |
| 3 | Armenia     | 36 |
| 4 | Turkey      | 35 |
| 5 | Egypt       | 34 |
| 6 | Haiti       | 32 |
| 7 | Cambodia    | 32 |

Red Burn-out

Blue Stagnation

One good example of how strongly diverging value systems can lead to completely different outcomes is the ongoing battle between "EcoPhiles" and "Technophiles".

## Finding the Synergy Zone between EcoPhiles and Technophiles

Extreme Ecophiles believe we can solve all our problems through rejecting modern lifestyles and "getting back to the basics". Their view is that for sustainable ecosystem services preservation is the top priority. Most 21st century green thinkers and activists are much more progressive in their views, however, and accept that business, government and NGO's/activists all need to collaborate to achieve a thriving future.

Technophiles believe we can solve all our problems through science and technology. Geoscientists and engineers, for example, share a major responsibility with many societal actors in setting the right example, particularly in searching for sustainable energy solutions. Such "geeks" genuinely believe that all we need is the right set of technologies to scale to solve our sustainability challenges.

The options for our ecological future can be visualized in a dilemma matrix which can help focus the debate on different scenarios and real synergies. Both views are needed, and we need to focus on the complementarities between them. ThriveAbility points us to the Synergy Zone between these clashing worldviews and gives us the means to get there in time.

For example life expectancy and happiness in Costa Rica exceed that of the USA with one-third of the footprint. It is possible to live sustainably, have economic growth and enjoy a degree of comfort in beautiful surroundings. Is it absolutely essential to have the latest technology and modern conveniences to live a good life and be happy?

# Appendix E -
# Research and Action Methodologies

"But in each of these discussions of some of the more important modes of human inquiry, we are not discussing them merely as an academic item of historical interest. We are driving towards a practical, hands-on, integral methodological pluralism, or what we are also calling an Integral Operating System (IOS), which specifically combines the very best of the time-tested modes of inquiry (from empiricism to phenomenology to hermeneutics to systems theory) in order to produce the most balanced and comprehensive approach to the Kosmos.
"IOS, when mastered, combines the strengths of all of the major types of human inquiry in order to produce an approach to any occasion that "touches all the bases," that refuses to leave some dimension untouched or ignored, that honours all of the important aspects of holons in all of the their richness and fullness.
IOS, as we said, is itself merely a third-person system of signifiers (i.e., it is nothing but a system of abstract ideas, symbols, and concepts, all of which are merely third-person symbols, not first-person or second-person realities).
"To repeat: IOS itself does not deliver first- or second-person realities, nor is it meant to; rather, it simply alerts the system to the fact that those realities exist, and urges the system to directly take them up. But that means that the person then has to actually engage in those other modes of inquiry, whether contemplative phenomenology, body work, intersubjective group processing, interobjective institutional organization, meditation, collaborative inquiry, and so on."
*Ken Wilber*

There are eight different types of research methodology that can be applied to make any human activity more effective. An overview of these eight types located in the eight "Zones" which arise in the application of the Integral Model to any situation are shown below in Diagram X.

How can we reliably know and understand such invisible, and "subjective" systems? Post-modernist philosophers and scientists distinguish between three main versions of the scientific method:

❖ *Empirical methods of enquiry* based on the five senses and our extensions thereof (from microscopes to satellites), to establish truths about the material world of exteriors, such as physics, chemistry, biology and so on. Here we establish ***propositional truths*** about an objective, external state of affairs, classically known as objective ***truth***;

❖ *Mental-phenomenological methods of enquiry* based on interior systems of meaning-making such as linguistics, mathematics, hermeneutics, logic and so on. Here we establish **cultural truths** about predictable truths in cultural contexts and spaces, classically known as **goodness**;

❖ *Transcendental methods of enquiry* based on traditions and practices such as contemplation, meditation, yoga and so on, whereby maps and models of the interior worlds and replicable processes for re-producing inner experiences are deduced and tested. Here we establish **interior or transcendental truths**, based upon the reliability of the interpretations, maps and models established by instructing and testing subjective states, classically perceived as **beauty.**

In our daily lives we encounter and use each of these kinds of truth frequently- for example, in going on a holiday we may rely on objective safety truth claims by airlines to ensure we arrive at our destination unharmed; we probably select our travel destination based on our inner perceptions of the goodness of the places and people at our destination (backed up by the perceptions of others on websites such as "Trip Advisor"); and we expect to be able to chill out and relax in the spa at our destination based on the predictable effects of therapeutic practices rooted in yoga, alternative medicine, meditation or simply closing one's eyes and taking several deep breaths of fresh air. A holiday is, in essence, a search for beauty and goodness at the right price to bring about a highly valued inner state we call relaxation or peace of mind.

## DIAGRAM 34 - Eight Types of Research Methodology Used in the Application of the ThriveAbility Approach

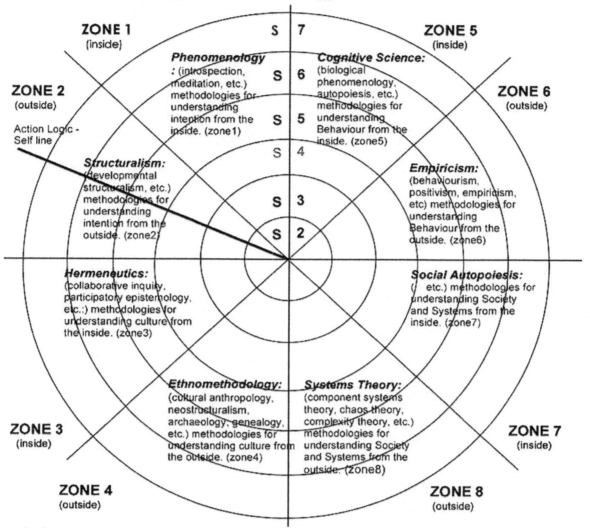

**Intention** - "What I experience"
"I" Subjective realities;
e.g. self and consciousness, states of mind, psychological development, mental models/ constructs, emotions, state of self, etc.

**Behaviour** - "What I do"
"It" Objective realities;
e.g. brain and organism, visible biological features, degree of activation of the various bodily systems, etc.

**ZONE 1**
(inside)

**ZONE 2**
(outside)

Action Logic - Self line

*Phenomenology:* (introspection, meditation, etc.) methodologies for understanding intention from the inside. (zone1)

*Structuralism:* (developmental structuralism, etc.) methodologies for understanding intention from the outside. (zone2)

**ZONE 5**
(inside)

**ZONE 6**
(outside)

*Cognitive Science:* (biological phenomenology, autopoiesis, etc.) methodologies for understanding Behaviour from the inside. (zone5)

*Empiricism:* (behaviourism, positivism, empiricism, etc) methodologies for understanding Behaviour from the outside. (zone6)

*Hermeneutics:* (collaborative inquiry, participatory epistemology, etc.:) methodologies for understanding culture from the inside. (zone3)

*Social Autopoiesis:* ( etc.) methodologies for understanding Society and Systems from the inside. (zone7)

*Ethnomethodology:* (cultural anthropology, neostructuralism, archaeology, genealogy, etc.) methodologies for understanding culture from the outside. (zone4)

*Systems Theory:* (component systems theory, chaos theory, complexity theory, etc.) methodologies for understanding Society and Systems from the outside. (zone8)

**ZONE 3**
(inside)

**ZONE 7**
(inside)

**ZONE 4**
(outside)

**ZONE 8**
(outside)

**Culture** - "What we experience"
"We" Intersubjective realities;
e.g. shared values, world views, webs of culture, communication, relationships, cultural norms and customs, etc.

**Society and Systems** - "What we do"
"Its" Interobjective realities;
e.g. social systems, environmental systems, visible societal structures, economic systems, political systems, etc.

## APPENDIX F –
## The UN Inclusive Wealth Report 2014 – Summary

For more than half a century nations have appraised their progress on the basis of how much they produce, consume, and invest, measured in U.S. dollars and aggregated into an easy-to-compare metric: gross domestic product (GDP). In the past few decades extensive research has demonstrated that:

- the declining resource base GDP growth is based on makes it unsustainable.
- human wellbeing is not accurately reflected in GDP, and
- GDP growth does not necessarily improve human wellbeing.

**Produced capital** (manufactured plus intellectual capital) is the capital type for which the most exhaustive (and reliable) data exists. This represents only about _18 per cent_ of the total wealth of nations.

It is salutary that corporate balance sheets globally reflect a similar ratio – only 20% of the value of listed corporations lies in their _tangible assets_ (natural, manufactured and financial capital) - the value of intangible assets (human, social and intellectual capital) accounts for the other 80%.

Yet such intangible assets are not included in corporate balance sheets, though leading investors rate intangible qualities such as the quality of leadership, strategy and ability to attract and retain talent amongst the top five factors when asked what measures really matter when they select stocks for their portfolios.

**DIAGRAM 35 - The Three-Capital Model of Wealth
Creation for Inclusive Wealth Accounting**

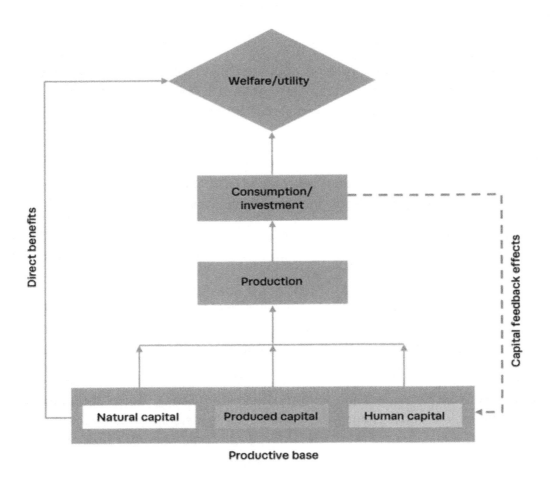

The remaining capital types, which together constitute 82 per cent of wealth (_54 per cent_ in **human capital** and _28 per cent_ in **natural capital**), are currently treated as, at best, satellite accounts in the System of National Accounts.

The Inclusive Wealth Report (IWR) is a biennial effort to evaluate the capacities of nations around the world to improve their citizens' wellbeing, and do so sustainably for the benefit of present and future generations. The report:

- provides a more comprehensive and accurate measure of human wealth, development, and progress;
- validates our suspicions that GDP is an inadequate measure for assessing long-term prosperity, and reveals education, health, and the environment as investments that will truly unleash the potential of young and interconnected populations around the world for development;

- promotes the *Inclusive Wealth Index* as a way of measuring progress toward the Sustainable Development Goals;
- recommends the *Inclusive Wealth Index* per capita as an indicator of human wellbeing used to assess nations' economic progress within the context of sustainable development;
- asserts that countries should expand the asset boundary of the present System of National Accounts (SNA), which currently captures only 18 per cent of a country's productive base, to include human and natural capital.

The IWR findings cover 140 countries over the time period between 1990 and 2010.Empirical evidence shows average positive growth in per capita inclusive wealth – and thus progress toward sustainable development – in 85 of the 140 countries evaluated (approximately 60 per cent). Gains in inclusive wealth were in general lesser than those in GDP and HDI: 124 of 140 nations (89 per cent) experienced gains in GDP, while 135 of 140 (96 per cent) showed improvement in HDI over the same period.

**Human capital** is the foremost contributor to growth rates in inclusive wealth in 100 out of 140 countries. In 28 countries **produced capital** was the primary contributor. On average, *human capital contributed 54 per cent of overall gains* in inclusive wealth, while *produced capital contributed 33 per cent* and *natural capital 13 per cent*.

Population growth and natural capital depreciation constitute the main driving forces of declining wealth per capita in the majority of countries. Population increased in 127 of 140 countries, while natural capital declined in 127 of 140 countries. Although both factors each negatively affect growth in wealth, changes in population were responsible for greater declines.

After adjusting for carbon damage, oil capital gains, and total factor productivity, the number of overall progressing countries drops from 85 to 58 of 140 counties (41 per cent). Results show that all three factors negatively affected inclusive wealth in most of countries; of the three, total factor productivity adjustments had the greatest negative effect.

Countries striving to improve their citizens' well-being in sustainable ways should reorient economic policy planning and evaluation away from targeting GDP growth as a primary objective toward incorporating inclusive wealth accounting as part of a sustainable development agenda. This includes investing in:

- **human capital** – in particular education – would generate higher returns for IW growth, as compared to investments in other capital asset groups, in countries with high rates of population growth;
- **natural capital**, in particular agricultural land and forest, can produce a twofold dividend: First, they can increase IW directly; second, they can improve agricultural resiliency and food security to accommodate anticipated population growth;

- **research and development** to increase total factor productivity, which decreased in 65 per cent of countries, can immediately contribute to growth in inclusive wealth in nearly every country.
- **renewable energy** which produce a triple dividend: First, they can increase IW directly by adding to natural and produced capital stocks; second, they improve energy security and reduce risk due to price fluctuations for oil-importing countries; third, they reduce global carbon emissions and thus carbon-related damages.

# Author's Acknowledgements

My own ThriveAbility journey would not have been possible without encouragement from and contributions by many people. What follows is a short list of those who have been more closely involved than most, including the participants of the Embedding ThriveAbility programs of 2013 and 2014.

| | |
|---|---|
| **Ralph Thurm** | Founder & MD of A\|HEAD\|ahead, previously head of the Siemens Sustainability Strategy Council, Director Sustainability & Innovation at Deloitte & COO of the GRI |
| **Christopher Cooke** | 5 Deep Integral Ltd – Founders – CultureView |
| **Sheila Cooke** | 5 Deep Integral Ltd – Founders – CultureView |
| **Bill Baue** | The SustainAbility Context Group, Convetit |
| **Paul van Schaik** | Co-Founder of Integral Without Borders and Integral*MENTORS* and Trustee of the ThriveAbility Foundation |
| **Greg Wood** | Sales Director of Boardex at The Street and The Deal, and Trustee of the ThriveAbility Foundation. |
| **Elena Wood** | Co-Founder – Chateau La Tour Apollinaire and Renaissance2, and as my wife, a continual source of support, encouragement & healthy critique. |
| **Scott Noppe-Brandon** | Our trusted colleague, friend and Imagination Index co-founder. |
| **Gyöngyi Bolbas** | As my personal assistant and a researcher for the ThriveAbility team Gyöngyi has been a superb organizer and communicator, getting things done at warp speed! |

## Embedding ThriveAbility Participants

| | |
|---|---|
| Nicholas Beecroft | Psychiatrist, UK Ministry of Defence, Author- Future of Western Civilization |
| Laura Bechthold | MSc Student in Sustainability |
| Graham Boyd | LTS Global Managing Director |
| John Elkington | Founder SustainAbility, Chairman of Volans, "B-Team" Board Member |
| Pauline Engelberts | Global Head of Investment Products at ABN Amro |
| Chris Laszlo | Associate Professor at Case Western Reserve University |
| Ervin Laszlo | Co-Founder - Club of Budapest and Club of Rome |

| Sabine Oberhuber | Co-founder at Turntoo Foundation (circular economy) |
| Tim Odell | Founder - GiveAll2Charity |
| Lars Schipholt | Integrality BV |
| Sebastian Straube | Co-Founder and CEO – BSD Consulting, Germany |
| Tiia Tammaru | Chairman of the Board of Estonian Quality Association |

*And a special word of thanks to two supporters from the very beginning:*

| Tani Jarvinen | Founder and CEO – Lautukeskus Excellence Finland |
| Kari Keskinen | Vice-President - Lautukeskus Excellence Finland |

*And to:*

| Ken Wilber | Integral Philosopher and Founder – Integral Institute |

# The ThriveAbility Core Team

# 83 Thought Leaders and Organisations Engaged during the Consultation Phase

We would like to thank those listed below for their example, conversation time and inputs during the ThriveAbility Consultation Process between October 2014 and April 2015 in Berlin, Perpignan, Amsterdam, London, New York, Boston, Amherst and via Skype and email, which made this book possible.

| Name | Company/Organisation | Title |
|---|---|---|
| Alma, Marjella | eRevalue | CEO & Co-Founder |
| Arts, Muriel | Flow Foundation | Co-Founder and Researcher |
| Baldachin, Jon | Added Value | CIO |
| Baltzell, Hewson | MSCI | Executive Director |
| Banerjee, Jyoti | IIRC | Programme LEAD, Technology Initiative |
| Bartels, Wim | KPMG Netherlands | Global Head of Sustainability Reporting & Assurance |
| Bloom, Lawrence | Intentional Investment Bank | Co-Founder |
| Boerner, Hank | Governance & Accountability Institute | Chairman & CEO |
| Bostwick, Sarah | UN Global Compact | Manager, Reporting |
| Braungart, Michael | Cradle-to-Cradle | Co-Founder |
| Breitman, Randy | | Entrepreneur |
| Bruce, Mike | ThinkStep (PE International) | Sales Manager UK |
| Buck, Bastian | GRI | Director Reporting Standard |
| Ceroni, Marta | Donella Meadows Institute | Executive Director |
| Chang, Susan Arterian | Capital Institute | Director, Content Development & Field Guide to Investing in a Regenerative Economy |
| Chase, Robin | Zipcar, Veniam, Buzzcar | Founder |
| Collins,Katherine | Honeybee Capital | Founder & CEO |
| Confino, Jo | The Guardian | Executive Editor |
| Coppola, Louis | Governance & Accountability Institute | Partner & Executive Vice President |
| Curtis, Susan | Credit 360 | Marketing Manager |
| Dawlabani, Said | Memenomics Group | Founder |
| Dreyer, Susan | Carbon Disclosure Project (CDP) | Director, DACH region |
| Duncker, Sibylle | Otto Group | Senior Manager Social Compliance |
| Dunne, Niall | BT | Chief Sustainability Officer |
| Dyal, Candace | Dyalcompass LLC | Owner |
| Ebert, Thomas | Apple GmbH | Environmental Program Manager |
| Fullerton, John | Capital Institute | Founder & President |
| Fürst, Marion | Danone | Director Public Affairs, Sustainability and Science |
| Gillies, Richard | Kingfisher | Chief Sustainability Officer |

| | | |
|---|---|---|
| Gogerty, Nick | Thoughtful Capital | Partner |
| Goode, Rich | Ernst & Young | Senior Manager, Climate Change and Sustainability Services |
| Gordon-Brander, Alex | Bridgewater Associates | Application Portfolio Manager |
| Hoezen, Didi | KPMG Netherlands | Manager at KPMG Sustainability |
| Howard, Alan | Southern Poverty Law Center | Chair |
| Howard, Steve | Ikea | Chief Sustainability Officer |
| Irwin, Rodney | WBCSD | Managing Director - Financial Capital |
| Jan Joustra, Douwe | IMSA | Associated Partner |
| Kamal, Assem | A.K Consultancy | Free Lance HR & Development |
| Kamsler, Victoria | Katerva | Director |
| Kendall, Geoff | Future Fit Bechmark | Co-Founder& Chief Executive |
| Kumpelmann, Tjeerd | ABN AMRO | Head Business Advisory, Reporting & Stakeholder Management |
| Landry, Chris | Landry Communications | Principal |
| Le Gall, Philippe | Nestlé | Sustainability Executive |
| Leblanc, Brendan | Ernst & Young | Partner - Climate Change and Services |
| Ligteringen, Ernst | GRI | Advisor to the Chief Executive |
| Lindhardt, Jesper | Novo Nordisk A/S | Director TBL Strategy& Performance Management |
| Lissack, Michael | Institute for the Study of Coherence & Emergence | Director |
| Macdonald, Tim | Capital Institute | Senior Fellow |
| MacGregor, Alastair | Trucost | Chief Operating Officer |
| Mattison, Richard | Trucost | CEO |
| McElroy, Mark | Center for Sustainable Organizations | Founder |
| Meehan, Michael | GRI | Chief Executive |
| Mollner, Terry | Calvert, Ben & Jerry's | Chair of StakeHolder Capital |
| Morey, Mark | Institute for Natural Learning | Founder and CEO |
| Mulder, Herman | TruePrice Foundation | Chairman |
| Murphy, Amanda | Towie at Lime Pictures | Brand Manager |
| Park, Andrew | Bloomberg | Sustainability Manager in Bloomberg's Global Sustainability Group |
| Pinkepank, Thorsten | BASF | Director, Corporate Sustainability Relations |
| Porritt, Jonathon | Forum for the future | Founder Director |
| Ravenel, Curtis | Bloomberg | Global Head of Sustainable Business & Finance |
| Robins, Nick | UNEP | Head of UNEP Initiative on Sustainable Finance |
| Rosen, Jeffrey | Solidago Foundation | Chief Financial Officer |
| Rubinstein, Robert | TBLI | CEO & Founder |
| Rzepa, Andrew | Gallup International | Senior Consultant |
| Sillanpaa Maria, | Sustainability Advisory Group | Founding Director |
| Sipkens, Annette | Deloitte Netherlands | Director Sustainable Strategy & Innovation |
| Smith, Sandy | ThinkStep (PE International) | Consultancy Services Director |

| | | |
|---|---|---|
| Stangis, Dave | Campbell Soup | Chief Sustainability Officer |
| Straube, Sebastian | BSD Germany | Director General and Co-Founder |
| Stuart, Emma | Autodesk | Head of Sustainability Solutions |
| Tantram, Dominic | Terrafiniti | Partner - Corporate Sustainability |
| Tantram, Joss | Terrafiniti | Partner, Environmental Sustainability |
| Thamotheram, Raj | Raj Thamotheram Associates | Independent Strategic Adviser, Investment |
| Thomas, Martin | Call4Change | Owner |
| Tideman, Sander | Flow Foundation | Founder & Director |
| Tulay, Mark | GISR | Chief Operating Officer |
| van Arkel, Geanne | Interface | Sustainable Business Development |
| van de Wijs, Peter Paul | GlobeScan | Senior Communications Advisor |
| Van den Berg, Franc | EY Netherland | Partner at Sustainability |
| van Keken, Ton | Interface | Director |
| Waygood, Steve | Aviva Investors | Chief Responsible Investment Officer |
| White, Allen | Tellus Institute, GISR, GRI Co-Founder | Vice President & Senior Fellow |
| Williams, Stuart | Intentional Investment Bank | Co-Founder |

# About the Author

Dr Robin Lincoln Wood has been making a positive difference for four decades as a leader in businesses, banks, insurers, business schools, consulting firms, social and environmental movements in 35 countries on 4 continents. Through his passion for transformation Robin has helped hundreds of the world's largest organizations catalyze beneficial change.

His lifelong passion for environmental and social justice included leading campaigns for Nelson Mandela's release and making Sandton cleaner, greener and more serene. Robin has been involved in sustainability since he worked with the World Bank to develop the first sustainable energy strategy for the first Rio conference. He also helped create the modern Internet and E-Business in Silicon Valley and Europe from 1995-2001.

Robin has been advising business and political leaders at all levels since then, as an integrally informed practitioner, social entrepreneur and integral leader. He has also been a celebrity speaker for over two decades at large conferences around the world.

Since creating the Renaissance2 Foundation in 2008 at La Tour Apollinaire, his green Chateau in France, Robin has now founded the ThriveAbility Foundation in London to help leaders make more ThriveAble decisions through the ThriveAbility Index.

Robin has authored several books including the award winning "Managing Complexity", "The Great Shift" and "The Trouble with Paradise". More details about his life and career can be found at his website: www.rlw.zone. He was awarded a doctorate from London Business School for his development of the strategic alignment diagnostic tool, based on research with 30 of the world's major corporations to understand the link between strategic alignment and sustainable strategic success.

In writing this book Robin enjoyed support and input from his colleagues in the ThriveAbility Foundation including Ralph Thurm, former COO of the GRI and Head of Sustainability for Deloitte, Paul van Schaik, co-founder of integralMENTORS and International Sustainable Development veteran, and Bill Baue, co-founder of Sustainability Context Group and Blended Stakeholder Engagement, Convetit online engagement platform and Context Reporting dashboard.

# Endnotes

1  "When you realize it's a dream you can afford to play. The same thing happens when you realize that ordinary life is a dream, just a movie, just a play. You don't become more cautious, more timid, more reserved. You start jumping up and down and doing flips, precisely because it's all a dream, it's all pure Emptiness. You don't feel less, you feel more - because you can afford to. You are no longer afraid of dying, and therefore you are not afraid of living. You become radical and wild, intense and vivid, shocking and silly. You let it all come pouring through, because it's all your dream. Life then assumes its true intensity, its vivid luminosity, its radical effervescence." - Ken Wilber

2  http://en.wikiquote.org/wiki/Incorrect_predictions

3  Sources for ThriveAbility Leaders - Activists/Advisors
   http://biomimicry.net/about/our-people/founders/
   http://biomimicry.org/janine-benyus/
   http://www.braungart.com/en/content/vision
   http://makewealthhistory.org/2011/01/17/cradle-to-cradle-by-michael-braungart-and-william-mcdonough/
   http://www.sustainability.com/team/john-elkington
   http://volans.com/people/team/john-elkington/
   https://en.wikipedia.org/wiki/John_Elkington
   http://www.algore.com/about.html
   http://www.biography.com/people/al-gore-9316028#bush-v-gore
   http://www.paulhawken.com/paulhawken_frameset.html
   http://www.theguardian.com/sustainable-business/2014/oct/22/first-look-environmental-entrepreneur-paul-hawkens-long-awaited-new-book
   https://en.wikipedia.org/wiki/Ban_Ki-moon
   http://www.un.org/sg/biography.shtml
   https://en.wikipedia.org/wiki/James_Lovelock
   http://www.dailymail.co.uk/news/article-2134092/Gaia-scientist-James-Lovelock-I-alarmist-climate-change.html
   http://www.rmi.org/Amory+B.+Lovins
   https://en.wikipedia.org/wiki/Amory_Lovins
   http://usa.ashoka.org/fellow/amory-b-lovins
   http://natcapsolutions.org/team/staff/l-hunter-lovins/
   http://www.thelegacyproject.co.za/hunter-lovins-founder-natural-capatalism-solutions/
   http://www.denverpost.com/ci_23252162/l-hunter-lovins-teaches-virtues-green-business-development
   https://en.wikipedia.org/wiki/Kumi_Naidoo
   http://www.democracynow.org/blog/2014/9/25/part_2_kumi_naidoo_of_greenpeace
   http://www.foet.org/JeremyRifkin.htm
   https://en.wikipedia.org/wiki/Jeremy_Rifkin
   http://www.globalzero.org/our-movement/leaders/mr-jeffrey-skoll
   http://www.skollfoundation.org/staff/jeff-skoll/
   http://www.theguardian.com/sustainable-business/ebay-jeff-skoll-movies-message-sustainability

4  Sources for ThriveAbility Leaders - Entrepreneurs:
   http://www.interfaceinc.com/who/founder.html
   http://www.director.co.uk/magazine/2007/2%20Feb/blood_60_7.html
   http://www.mckinsey.com/insights/sustainability/investing_in_sustainability_an_interview_with_al_gore_and_david_blood
   http://www.triplepundit.com/2013/06/richard-branson-b-team-for-sustainable-business/
   http://www.businessgreen.com/bg/news/2307887/virgin-atlantic-and-lanzatech-prepare-low-carbon-jet-fuel-for-take-off

https://en.wikipedia.org/wiki/Sergey_Brin
https://en.wikipedia.org/wiki/Larry_Page
https://en.wikipedia.org/wiki/Robin_Chase
http://robinchase.org/
http://thecityfix.com/blog/innovating-smart-sustainable-cities-qa-zipcar-founder-robin-chase-carsharing-ryan-schleeter/
Kingfisher 2014_Net_Positive_Report
http://www.greenbiz.com/blog/2014/02/04/natura-cosmetics-sustainability-amazon
http://www.sri-connect.com/index.php?option=com_content&view=article&id=649&Itemid=1192
http://whygreeneconomy.org/information/who-should-value-nature-interview-with-richard-mattison/
https://en.wikipedia.org/wiki/Elon_Musk
http://www.teslamotors.com/about

5   Sources for ThriveAbility Leaders: Intrapreneurs
http://president.wbcsd.org/about-peter-bakker.html
http://www.globalopportunitynetwork.org/peter-bakker-on-the-advisory-board/#.VK5JLiuG_Xo
http://www.zoominfo.com/p/Paul-Tebo/335842
2014-dupont-sustainability-progress-report
http://www.ethicalcorp.com/business-strategy/management-spotlight-mike-barry-marks-spencer
http://www.sustainablebrands.com/user/mike-barry/bio
http://www.theguardian.com/sustainable-business/marks-and-spencer-mike-barry
http://www.businessandleadership.com/appointments/795-niall-dunne-bt-group/
http://letstalk.globalservices.bt.com/en/2012/01/chief-sustainability-officer-niall-dunne-green-business-behaviours/
http://www.wired.co.uk/news/archive/2014-10/06/multinationals-and-non-profits-launch-collectively
http://www.edie.net/library/view_article.asp?id=6341
http://www.thecrownestate.co.uk/who-we-are/our-people/management/
http://www.triplepundit.com/2013/12/sustainability-crown-estate/
http://www.thecrowd.me/john-lelliott
http://www.forbes.com/sites/terrywaghorn/2013/04/19/steve-howard-ikea-style-sustainability/
http://www.theguardian.com/activate/hannah-jones
http://www.greenbiz.com/blog/2012/02/06/how-she-leads-hannah-jones-nike
http://rebuild21.org/portfolio-item/santiago-gowland/
http://www.forbes.com/profile/gail-kelly/
http://www.theguardian.com/sustainable-business/
embedding-sustainability-drives-profitability-unilever-polman
https://www.environmental-finance.com/content/news/robins-to-leave-hsbc-to-spearhead-unep-inquiry.html
http://www.sustainablefinancialmarkets.net/participants/nick-robins/
http://www.theguardian.com/environment/2012/oct/01/50-months-nick-robins
http://www.unep.org/inquiry/About/Secretariat/NickRobins/tabid/132068/Default.aspx
https://events.au.autodesk.com/connect/speakerDetail.
ww?PERSON_ID=1FBD7FC248E953E168EBD4B911D2F74F
http://www.economistinsights.com/infrastructure-cities/opinion/rethinking-urban-technology
http://www.sustainablebrands.com/user/dave-stangis/bio
http://www.greenbiz.com/blog/2014/04/17/dave-stangis-VP-sustainability-campbell-soup
http://business.un.org/en/documents/10242
http://www.sustainablebrands.com/users/kathrin-winkler#
http://www.greenbiz.com/blog/2011/07/11/how-she-leads-kathrin-winkler-emc-corporation
http://www.aviva.com/corporate-responsibility/responsible-investment/
case-study-milestone-un-sustainable-stock-exchanges/
http://ga-institute.com/Sustainability-Update/tag/steve-waygood/
http://www.sri-connect.com/index.
php?option=com_comprofiler&task=userProfile&Itemid=4&user=1001286
https://en.wikipedia.org/wiki/Jochen_Zeitz
http://www.fastcompany.com/57905/catalyst

http://www.sustainablebrands.com/user/koann-vikoren-skrzyniarz/bio
http://www.forbes.com/sites/work-in-progress/2012/11/26/
creating-brands-for-the-future-one-womans-quest-for-sustainable-brands/
http://www.huffingtonpost.com/laura-dunn/women-in-business-qa-with_b_5357176.html
http://www.sustainablebrands.com/user/gil-philip-friend/bio
http://www.cityofpaloalto.org/civica/press/display.asp?layout=1&Entry=996
http://www.waynevisser.com/biography
https://en.wikipedia.org/wiki/Wayne_Visser
http://www.waynevisser.com/writing/quotable-quotes
http://www.andrewwinston.com/contact/
http://www.theguardian.com/sustainable-business/blog/
american-businesses-redefine-corporate-leadership
https://www.apple.com/pr/bios/lisa-jackson.html
http://www.wsj.com/articles/lisa-jackson-on-apples-green-initiatives-1427770864
http://www.thedp.com/article/2014/11/lisa-jackson-apple-speaker-event

6   For example, here is one example of how academics are beginning to make this link: http://www.slate.com/blogs/future_tense/2015/03/03/designing_for_happiness_the_ultimate_sustainability_solution.html
"Research is now connecting the dots between sustainability and happiness and the results are promising. In a **recent study** published in the journal *Environment, Development and Sustainability*, researchers found that cities with strong sustainable development practices and policies self-report higher levels of happiness. In fact, sustainable practices, such as community gardens, green spaces, green homes, and sustainable transportation, have all been shown to increase happiness. Sustainable design can also enhance and strengthen social networks—and the importance of that can't be overstated. In Charles Montgomery's ***Happy City***, he writes, "The most important psychological effect of the city is the way in which it moderates our relationships with other people." More, he states, "[C]onnected people sleep better at night. They are more able to tackle adversity. They live longer. They consistently report being happier."

Let's intentionally design and redesign our systems for happiness. We can start with the place we spend most of our time—the neighborhood. Communities (and anything that can be designed) should be designed to offer the greatest opportunity for people to pursue their own happiness. On the neighborhood level, this would include, but is certainly not limited to, the following:

- clean water
- access to affordable and healthy foods
- economic opportunity
- green spaces and access to nature
- equitable, clean transportation
- clean, reliable energy sources
- social gathering and interaction spaces
- equal education opportunities
- minimal to zero waste
- global happiness governance and support
- culturally sensitive design"

7   Based on the work of the neurologist Paul MacLean.

CPSIA information can be obtained at www.ICGtesting.com
Printed in the USA
BVOW09s1939180715

409302BV00002B/3/P